# SOCIAL SUPPORT STRATEGIES

Sage Studies in Community Mental Health 7

# SAGE STUDIES IN COMMUNITY MENTAL HEALTH

Series Editor: **Richard H. Price**
*Community Psychology Program,*
*University of Michigan*

SAGE STUDIES IN COMMUNITY MENTAL HEALTH is a book series consisting of both single-authored and co-authored monographs and concisely edited collections of original articles which deal with issues and themes of current concern in the community mental health and related fields. Drawing from research in a variety of disciplines, the series seeks to link the work of the scholar and practitioner in this field, as well as advance the state of current knowledge in community mental health.

*Volumes in this series:*

1. Gary VandenBos (Editor): *PSYCHOTHERAPY: Practice, Research, Policy*
2. Cary Cherniss: *STAFF BURNOUT: Job Stress in the Human Services*
3. Richard F. Ketterer: *CONSULTATION AND EDUCATION IN MENTAL HEALTH: Problems and Prospects*
4. Benjamin H. Gottlieb (Editor): *SOCIAL NETWORKS AND SOCIAL SUPPORT*
5. Morton O. Wagenfeld, Paul V. Lemkau, and Blair Justice (Editors): *PUBLIC MENTAL HEALTH: Perspectives and Prospects*
6. Terry F. Buss, F. Stevens Redburn, with Joseph Waldron: *MASS UN-EMPLOYMENT: Plant Closings and Community Mental Health*
7. Benjamin H. Gottlieb: *SOCIAL SUPPORT STRATEGIES: Guidelines for Mental Health Practice*

*Additional Volumes in Preparation*

# Social Support Strategies

## Guidelines for Mental Health Practice

# Benjamin H. Gottlieb

**Volume 7, Sage Studies in Community Mental Health**

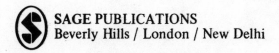

**SAGE PUBLICATIONS**
Beverly Hills / London / New Delhi

*For information address:*

SAGE Publications, Inc.
275 South Beverly Drive
Beverly Hills, California 90212

SAGE Publications India Pvt. Ltd.
C-236 Defence Colony
New Delhi 110 024, India

SAGE Publications Ltd
28 Banner Street
London EC1Y 8QE, England

Printed in the United States of America

**Library of Congress Cataloging in Publication Data**

Main entry under title:

Gottlieb, Benjamin H.
   Social support strategies.

   (Sage studies in community mental health ; 7)
   Includes bibliographical references.
   1. Mental health—Social aspects. 2. Helping behavior.
3. Social systems—Therapeutic use. I. Title. II. Series.
[DNLM: 1. Mental disorders—Rehabilitation.
2. Social environment. W1 SA126M v. 7 / WM 29 G686s]
RA790.G63  1983        362.2'0425        83-6653
ISBN 0-8039-2031-8
ISBN 0-8039-2032-6 (pbk.)

FIRST PRINTING

*In memory of my mother,*
*Eva Stahl Gottlieb*

# Contents

# Series Editor's Preface

The literature on social support is now large and rapidly expanding. In an earlier volume of Sage Studies in Community Mental Health, *Social Networks and Social Support,* Gottlieb and his colleagues surveyed the research literature on social support and examined promising new directions for research. Now, in this new volume, Gottlieb summarizes the literature on social support so that practitioners can take advantage of both the burgeoning research literature and its implications for effective practice.

This is a book full of practical ideas and examples. It ranges broadly over a number of different fields of application, including the role of social support in preventive programs, in medical practice, in the world of work, in delivering care to the elderly, and, finally, in addressing the question of the role of human service professionals in mobilizing social support.

This volume is notable because it suggests new programmatic ideas that professionals may implement and because it allows us to draw out the implications of research for institutional practice. Alterations in organizational structure and institutional practice can, as Gottlieb points out, transform a previously unsupportive milieu into one in which supportive norms and practices become prominent.

In this volume, Gottlieb does not avoid the still unresolved issues of definition and measurement in the field of social support. Nor does he produce a simplistic cookbook for the administration of social support programming. Instead, ideas and insights from the research literature, in the hands of a skilled writer and thinker, are transformed into a wide range of practical ideas that will enhance the work of those of us involved in the human service enterprise. While this volume was designed with a practitioner audience in mind, it has much to recommend to researchers since, in a number of cases, provocative research hypotheses emerge from the description of various efforts to enhance social support.

I believe this is a book that anticipates a new era in the human services in which the lines of demarcation between the natural helping community and the professional community will become blurred. It is a time when we will rediscover the strength of community ties to help cope with problems of life transitions and chronic illness, and when we will learn to create new relationships between institutional and community sources of social support.

*— Richard H. Price*

# Acknowledgments

The impetus for this book was originally provided by my colleague and series editor, Rick Price, who encouraged me to translate the empirical research and conceptual formulations on the topic of social support into knowledge that could be used by mental health practitioners engaged in treatment and preventive activities. I hope that this volume to some extent repays his confidence in me and his trust that the ideas would enrich professional practice. I am also indebted to three friendly critics who made helpful comments on earlier drafts. Sheldon Cohen and Tony D'Augelli offered cogent advice about particular chapters, while Ken Heller graciously agreed to review the entire manuscript. Ken's lucid analysis of its strengths and weaknesses resulted in revisions that significantly improved my ideas and prose.

I am bound to fall short of recording the full extent of the practical help and personal affirmation that my wife, Lois Gottlieb, gave me. It is my singular fortune to have married a woman who is an intellectual companion, a patient and tolerant supporter, and a sterling editor to boot.

I am also indebted to the Social Sciences and Humanities Research Council of Canada for awarding me a Reorientation Grant. This grant provided generous support for a period of leave, enabling me to familiarize myself with the gerontological literature that deals with the concepts of social networks and social support.

I also wish to acknowledge the assistance of certain key personnel in the University of Guelph's Psychology Department. My appreciation is due to Wilma Hollywood, who expedited arrangements for the final preparation of the manuscript, and Donna Mokren, an exceptionally patient and proficient typist. My thanks also go to Karen

Gillespie, who proofread several versions of the manuscript and ensured that the final list of references was in order.

Finally, the permission of the following two journals to reprint tables is gratefully acknowledged: *Canadian Journal of Behavioural Science* and *The Journal of Primary Prevention*.

*– Benjamin H. Gottlieb*

# Part I

# SUPPORT NETWORKS AND MENTAL HEALTH
## Theory and Research

# Chapter 1

# *EARLY THEORETICAL FORMULATIONS*

In the crowded maternity unit of the Social Security Hospital in Guatemala City, Guatemala, routine care for women in labor consists of infrequent vaginal examinations, fetal heart monitoring, and assistance during delivery. Given an average of 60 deliveries every 24 hours, and the small physical size of the unit, the hospital does not allow family members or friends to attend the labor and delivery of expectant mothers. However, the hospital administration gave special permission to a group of medical researchers to mount an experimental study involving the random assignment of a *doula* or supportive companion to accompany half of the women admitted for their first delivery (Sosa, Kennell, Klaus, Robertson, & Urrutia, 1980). The doula, an untrained laywoman previously unknown to the expectant mothers, was in constant attendance from the point of admission until delivery, providing support in the forms of physical contact, dialogue, and simple companionship. A comparison group of expectant mothers had contact only with the medical staff who followed normal routines.

This companionate care produced dramatic effects on both the medical outcomes of labor and delivery and on the quality of the mother-infant interactions observed postdelivery. Of the 103 women admitted for their first pregnancies and assigned to the routine care offered in the unit 83 experienced serious complications in labor or delivery. In contrast, only 13 of the 33 women assigned to a doula experienced any complications. Furthermore, the presence of the doula mysteriously speeded delivery time; an average of 8.7 hours elapsed from the point of admission to delivery among the experimental group, compared to more than double that period (19.3 hours) among those receiving routine care. The apparent salutary effects of the companionate care also extended to certain maternal behaviors deemed to foster attachment beteen mother and infant, and predictive of later positive maternal and child development. During the first hour after birth, mothers in the experimental group were observed to stay awake longer than those in the routine care condition, to stroke their infants more, to talk to them more, and to smile at them more. Moreover, the difference between the two groups' average length of labor was not associated with these differences in maternal behaviors.

A second intervention also illustrates the role of supportive peer ties in cushioning the impact of stressful life events. Moreover, it offers another perspective on the phenomenon of social support and its significance for mental health practice. Roskin (1982) identified a sample of 45 adults, each of whom had recently experienced two or more stressful life changes for which they had not received professional treatment. Specifically, the majority of these changes involved the death of a family member or close friend, illness in the family, or personal illness or accidents. Recognizing that these events could trigger adverse emotional reactions, thus increasing the sample's vulnerability to psychopathology, Roskin (1982, p. 334) invited these people to participate in a series of six seminars "concentrating on mutual aid among members and fostering warm, supportive, nonconfrontive participant interactions." Each session was guided by a social worker who made short presentations about aspects of the stress management process and encouraged members to ventilate their feelings and to extend support to one another.

By dividing the sample into two groups and staging the interventions during two consecutive six-week periods, it was possible to compare the health status of the two groups before and after intervention as well as to make control comparisons. The latter were performed by assessing health changes among the members of the second group while the first received the intervention. The results showed that the intervention had a significant impact on the emotional health of the participants. Their pooled scores on five health dimensions were significantly improved following the intervention, registering a reduction in somatic complaints, obsessive-compulsive and depressive symptomatology, anxiety, and interpersonal (over)sensitivity. While the last dimension was the only one showing significant improvement in the control analysis, there was a marked trend toward a reduction in stress for the intervention group on the other four dimensions. The support group sessions also resulted in the development of new friendships and increased social activity. Roskin (1982) notes that some members contacted each other outside the group meetings and many expressed a desire to hold additional group sessions after the last one that had been arranged for them.

I have selected the third in this introductory set of studies not only because it reflects yet another way of conceptualizing the nature of social support, but also because it deals with a ubiquitous life stressor that can have pronounced adverse emotional effects: the experience of job loss. In her longitudinal study, Gore (1978) set out to assess whether men who differed in their level of social support would show evidence of better or worse health following the loss of their jobs due to a plant closing. Four indexes of health status were examined over a period extending from before the actual shutdown to a point two years later, including measures of depression, self-blame, reported illness symptoms, and serum cholesterol levels. The magnitude of stress that the men experienced was reflected not only by the stage of their job change, but also by counting the number of weeks they had been unemployed, and by gathering data from them about their subjective sense of economic deprivation. Social support was assessed via a composite measure of the terminees' perceptions of how supportive or unsupportive their wives, friends, and relatives were, how frequently they engaged in activities with these people outside their homes, and the extent to which they felt they had sufficient opportunities for the sort of socializing conducive to problem-centered discussions.

Gore (1978) found that perceived support did moderate some negative health consequences of job loss. Among the subgroup of men who were not promptly reemployed following termination, those with low levels of support had significantly higher levels of cholesterol than they did prior to job loss, while the supported group's cholesterol levels remained stable over this period. The same pattern was reflected in the number of illness symptoms reported by the groups; symptoms did not fluctuate over time among the highly supported terminees, but were significantly more frequent among members of the unsupported group following loss of their jobs. Support also moderated feelings of economic deprivation, a critical finding, given the fact that these feelings of economic deprivation lead to symptoms of depression. Thus, among the unsupported men, perceived economic deprivation was highly correlated ($r = .58$, $p < .05$) with depression.

These three examples are just a small sampling of a large and rapidly expanding literature that is attempting to unravel the nature and health-protective effects of social support. Spanning the fields of medicine, social work, and community mental health, these studies only begin to illuminate the diverse ways investigators have defined social support. Other conceptualizations of the construct have been offered by anthropologists, sociologists, psychologists, and social psychiatrists who have shown interest in both the clinical and preventive impact of naturally occurring social resources in people's lives.

This volume traces the history and current status of these efforts to identify the core dimensions of social support and addresses the role of social support in the coping process. In addition, it aims to inform the planning of clinical and preventive interventions that mobilize social support and discusses how existing programs bolster or undermine the fund of support available in the community. Indeed, two of the three studies I have already described strongly suggest a reexamination of current institutional policies and programs because they inadvertently supplant or disregard critical sources of support. Maternity wards may be easier to manage when family members and friends are denied entry, but this policy cannot be justified in terms of the health and morale of the expectant mothers. However reluctant employers may be to terminate workers, they can cushion the impact of job loss by encouraging their employee assistance personnel to establish support groups, such as job-finding clubs (Azrin, Flores, & Kaplan, 1975), or to work with union officials to create special family counseling programs.

## CONTRASTS AMONG MEANINGS AND MEASUREMENTS OF SOCIAL SUPPORT

The three studies I have outlined provide early glimpses into the various ways social support can be defined and measured. I wish to highlight some of these differences in a preliminary way so as to sensitize the reader to the protean nature of social support and to provide a first perspective on this subject. Moreover, the definitional issues raised in these studies reappear in bolder outlines in the keystone papers that launched much of the present work on social support.

The first noteworthy contrast among the three studies I have presented concerns the sources of support they examine. Sosa et al. (1980) introduced expectant mothers to a stranger, Roskin (1982) prompted affiliation among a small group of strangers who had in common a recent stressful life event, and Gore (1978) was essentially concerned with the support expressed in the words and deeds of close family members and friends. Thus the expectant mothers had contact with only a single source of support, while the group participants and the unemployed men received support from multiple sources. Second, the substance of the support extended by these sources differs markedly. The doula offered companionship, dialogue, and physical contact with the expectant mothers, while those who had experienced life changes exchanged ideas about coping strategies, expressed empathic sentiments, and offered each other new friendships. The job terminees interacted with family members and friends in the natural environment, where support consisted of socializing and the affirmation communicated by the caring and affection they offered. Thus we can tentatively infer that the common denominator underlying the social support described in these three studies consists of an expression of reliable alliance with the respondents and a genuine concern for their well-being.

A third and related distinction among these studies centers on whether they mark social support by objective or subjective measures. Gore's (1978) study is unique in relying on the respondents' reports of the perceived adequacy of the support expressed by family members and friends. In contrast, neither the expectant mothers nor those who had undergone life changes were asked to provide qualitative evaluations of the support rendered by the key figures with whom they weathered their stressful ordeals. Instead, sheer exposure to companionate care and the process of mutual aid were taken as indicators of the mothers' and group members' respective access to social support. Fourth, the studies differ in the length of time the respondents were exposed to social support, reflecting differences in the period of adaptation to the life stressors they examine. Companionate care continued only as long as it took until delivery, usually less than 24 hours, while the group participants' and the job terminees' contacts with supportive peers lasted several weeks. Finally, although all three studies aim to assess the preventive impact of social support — its role in buffering the respondents from the adverse effects of chronic and acute life stressors — they differ a great deal in the dependent variables they have adopted. These outcome measures range from such sturdy indicators of good health as complication-free labor and delivery and low cholesterol levels to measures of adaptive functioning such as low self-blame among the job terminees and decreased depressive symptomatology among the support group members.

To summarize, the studies I have reviewed epitomize much of the current controversy about the nature and effects of social support. Disagreement arises about whether social support is predicated upon contact with intimate primary group members or with any allies who express concern and caring. It is not clear whether access to a single source of support is enough to attenuate stress or whether multiple sources are required. Ideas about the supportive provisions of social ties also abound, ranging from simple companionship to the expression of active forms of aid and problem solving. Another unresolved issue revolves around the desirability of measuring social support via phenomenological as opposed to more objective measures that are less susceptible to attributional biases. In addition, there is scant evidence about optimal levels of exposure to socially supportive interactions with others. Above all, the process whereby social support accomplishes its preventive health functions has not been adequately documented; is it indirectly linked to health outcomes via its ameliorative influences on the way people appraise and cope with life stressors, or does it exert an independent and direct effect on health? These and other issues concerning the nature and sources of social support and its significance for mental health practice have been addressed in three major theoretical statements that are reviewed below. Collectively, they lend greater precision to the conceptualization of the social support construct, although they do not resolve present points of controversy.

## THREE EARLY INTERPRETATIONS OF SOCIAL SUPPORT

John Cassel and Sidney Cobb are two epidemiologists whose formulations regarding the nature and health-protective effects of social support have spurred much of the present work on this topic. Both were essentially concerned with understanding why some people were able to withstand stressful life experiences so well, while others seemed less able to mobilize those resources necessary for healthy adaptation and developed symptoms of illness or maladjustment. As epidemiologists, both authors were more interested in differences in the ecological niches of the two groups as these affected their access to protective resources than in the characteristics of the individuals themselves. That is, Cassel and Cobb attended to environmental or situational resources for resisting stress, not to dispositional differences affecting health outcomes.

Cassel (1974) and Cobb (1976) each undertook reviews of the empirical literature concerning the psychosocial modifiers of stress and marshaled a great many studies that converged on the following point: persons (and animals) who experienced high levels of stress either in the company of "significant others" or with the knowledge that they had access to supportive social ties did not develop the adverse health consequences experienced by those who were relatively isolated or who felt unsupported. This conclusion, which applies equally well to the three studies described at the outset of this chapter, prompted both authors to encourage new initiatives directed toward the mobilization of social support in the community. For example, Cobb (1976, p. 312) concludes his review by announcing:

> There appears to be enough evidence on the importance of social support to warrant action, although, of course, all the details as to the circumstances under which it is effective are not yet worked out. . . . we should start now to teach all our patients, both well and sick, how to give and receive social support.

Similarly, Cassel (1974, p. 479) exhorts his readers to "attempt to improve and strengthen the social supports rather than reduce the exposure to the stressors." While it is uncertain whether practitioners and program planners in the mental health field have heard their calls to action, Chapters 3 and 4 of this volume describe actual and potential preventive programs that are consistent with their reveilles. Moreover, these interventions have generally attempted to mobilize and develop social support based on what Cassel and Cobb had to say about its very substance and its sources.

The psychosocial processes that Cassel (1974, p. 478) designates as health protective inhere in "the strength of the social supports provided by the primary groups of most importance to the individual." Further, Cassel maintains that social support consists of feedback conveyed in signs and signals from primary group members that correct deviations from course at the behavioral, cognitive, and emotional levels. In addition, Cassel proposes that this kind of social support only moderates stress when it is expressed by primary group members *who are present* during the course of the stressful episode. He writes: "These studies would suggest that at both the human and animal levels, the presence of another particular animal of the same species may, under certain circumstances, protect the individual from a variety of stressful stimuli." (p. 479). Unfortunately, because these definitional statements are so global in nature, they leave much guesswork to practitioners and program planners about how to optimize primary group feedback on behalf of their clients.

Cobb's (1976) definition of the construct provides more details than Cassel's about the nature of the feedback that lies at the heart of social support, yet it, too, offers few leads for practitioners. Cobb (1976, p. 300) views social support as *information* "leading the subject to believe that he is cared for and loved . . . that he is esteemed and valued . . . (and) that he belongs to a network of communication and mutual obligation." While these aspects of social support were probably conveyed to Gore's (1978) job terminees, they do not seem to capture the companionate doulas in Sosa et al.'s (1980) experimental study. Cobb's (1976) definition fails to account for forms of support that are "action oriented" or those that involve the rendering of tangible goods and services; furthermore, due to its exclusive emphasis on support as information, it ignores physical touching or the simple presence of companions. The unique facet of Cobb's (1976) definition is its conspicuous accentuation of the cognitive or phenomenological basis of social support. Hence any information from the social environment that conditions the subject's *perceptions* that he or she is the recipient of positive affect, affirmation, or aid signifies the expression of social support. This highly subjective orientation to the construct, sidestepping as it does any consideration of how people are induced to perceive or believe that they are supported, is of little practical value. In short, Cobb's formulation emphasizes that support is in the mind of the beholder, while Cassel's account stresses the feedback expressed in actual primary group transactions. The nature of this feedback, the contexts in which it arises, and its specific implications for the design of preventive interventions figured centrally in Gerald Caplan's (1974) challenging paper, "Support Systems."

Caplan's interest in community support systems was a natural extension of ideas he had developed much earlier in his work with community gatekeepers in particular, and in the more general context of his ideas about community mental health practice. He had long recognized that citizens frequently approached people in certain key occupations for help in dealing with emotional difficulties and that these gatekeepers represented prime targets for mental health consultation. Family physicians, public health nurses, teachers, members of the clergy, and law enforcement personnel were often the first to notice or hear about the adjustment strivings of citizens and so they were naturally involved in the secondary preventive activities of early case finding and early intervention. They also tended to be "on the spot" when crises occurred, sometimes intervening directly as best they could, sometimes providing referral advice. Hence Cassel's (1974) ideas about the stress-moderating power of primary group feedback were easily accommodated within Caplan's framework of social psychiatry. He had only to enlarge his view of the field of health-protective social forces that are active in everyday community life.

Caplan (1974, p. 19) defines support systems as "continuing social aggregates (namely, continuing interactions with another individual, a network, a group, or an organization) that provide individuals with opportunities for feedback about themselves and for validations about others, which may offset deficiencies in these communications within the larger community context." The hallmark of these social aggregates is their members' keen, highly personalized regard for one another, and their readiness to monitor continuously, to reward periodically, and to reprimand one another as the need arises. They perform the social comparison functions normally associated with reference groups, and, in times of crisis, they offer three kinds of supportive provisions:

> (a) the significant others help the individual mobilize his psychological resources and master his emotional burdens; (b) they share his tasks; and (c) they provide him with extra supplies of money, materials, tools, skills, and cognitive guidance to improve his handling of his situation [Caplan, 1974, p. 20].

Such forms of support are expressed, according to Caplan (1974), in a variety of contexts ranging from institutionally based systems to spontaneous support systems in the open community. He discusses the importance of mutual-help groups, neighborhood-based helping networks, civic and fraternal organizations, and community gatekeepers in the affective life of citizens. Equally important, he outlines roles for community mental health professionals that would stimulate the formation and development of these supportive social aggregates in society, stating that professionals must learn to appreciate the fortifying potential of the natural person-to-person supports in the population, and to find ways of working with them through some form of partnership that fosters and strengthens nonprofessional groups" (Caplan, 1974, p. 20).

The sort of alliances that Caplan believes could be formed by professionals interested in mobilizing social support involve both direct organizing activities and the buttressing activities typically practiced in consulting relationships. Examples of the former include efforts to bring together people facing a common life transition or shared life difficulty, and to assist them in forming mutual-help groups capable of continuing independently. Another example consists of linking neighbors with similar needs and complementary resources so that together they can provide whatever human services they collectively require, and, in the process, gain a sense of common alliance and security. Caplan also spotlights new forms of consultation to community gatekeepers. The professional's new role would be to identify and link existing human resources, rather than to educate gatekeepers about mental health screening and treatment practices. Finally, Caplan exhorts community mental health agents to identify prevailing indigenous patterns of lay support in rural and ethnic communities, and to find ways of shoring up these helping patterns without casting them in the professional's mold.

Caplan's pioneering ideas about the sources and functions of social support in the life of ordinary citizens greatly amplify both Cassel's and Cobb's central theses. Indeed, Caplan goes far beyond notions of simple feedback or personal affirmation in his disquisition on this subject. He may even go too far by suggesting that social support is ubiquitous in the community, by extolling only the health-enhancing functions of people's primary group ties, and by leaving the false impression that support systems are recognizable entities, containing resources waiting to be tapped. Whether his ideas simply amplify Cassel and Cobb's messages or distort them and whether or not he reifies social support matter only theoretically; Caplan's chief legacy has been both to lend greater shape and meaning to our understanding of the forms of support that people give and receive, and to outline a variety of meaningful initiatives directed toward creating a greater fund of social support in the community.

## ON THE RELATIONSHIP BETWEEN
## SOCIAL SUPPORT AND PROFESSIONAL HELP

I have described the conceptual breadth of the social support construct and pointed to its potential significance for mental health practice. In addition to the research issues requiring attention, there are also practical issues that professionals must consider in their work with informal helping networks. Practitioners will be called upon to initiate relationships with a variety of lay helping systems and to accommodate themselves to informal caregiving arrangements. In the relationships they cultivate, they will have to be sensitive to the fundamental differences between social support and professional help. These differences merit fuller discussion because numerous problems have surrounded past efforts to collaborate with nonprofessionals in the human services area.

Since its inception in the early 1960s, the community mental health field has strived to incorporate ordinary citizens in its clinical and preventive activities. As I have already noted, Caplan regarded community gatekeepers primarily as key resources in crises intervention activities and secondarily as referral agents. He felt that programs of mental health consultation could increase the scope and efficacy of these caregivers' help-giving activities, while administrative consultation promised to reform institutional policies and redesign programs. However, Caplan's approach to providing prompt treatment for troubled people without resort to costly specialists represented only one avenue toward involving informal caregivers in the mental health sphere. In addition, volunteers with minimal training in mental health were manning the phones at crisis intervention centers, college students were offering "companionship therapy" (Goodman, 1972) to mental hospital patients, high school students were serving as mental health aides, well-educated housewives were offering psychotherapy, and nonprofessionals were staffing halfway houses and extending milieu therapy in many different treatment settings (Cowen, Gardner, & Zax, 1967).

New service patterns, heavily reliant on nonprofessionals, were instituted in poor and minority group catchment areas, some involving community organizing, some oriented to the resolution of concrete, everyday problems in living, and some largely concerned with expediting a link between needy citizens and agency resources (Riessman, Cohen, & Pearl, 1974). Citizens were also involved in program planning and in the development of priorities for community mental health services in local catchment areas. They conducted needs assessment surveys, sat on the executive boards of the centers, and helped to create career ladders for subprofessionals. In short, nonprofessionals were deployed in almost every aspect of community mental health services, their involvement stimulating the development of novel human resource selection, training, and supervision practices. Further, evaluative research has testified to their efficacy as helpers (Karlsruher, 1974; Durlack, 1979) and to the cost savings incurred when they can be substituted for professional personnel.

Despite the widespread involvement and apparent effectiveness of nonprofessionals in community mental health work, fundamental conflicts and dissatisfactions have existed in their relationships with professionals and the entire professional helping enterprise. These tensions can be analyzed at a theoretical level in terms of the basic discontinuities between bureaucratic modes of functioning and primary group modes (Litwak & Meyer, 1966), and in terms of more practical problems such as barriers to communication and differences in beliefs between professionals and lay helpers about the nature of helping. On the former score, it has been suggested that when nonprofessionals are closely tied to professionals, they are formally trained or subtly socialized into the professional mold, they begin to respond to a reward system designed by and for professionals, and, gradually, they become more socially distant from the host community from which they were recruited. Lusky and Ingman (1979, p. 118) have recorded this transformation process among the nonprofessional staff of the Fellowship, a club for alcoholics:

> an increasing tendency for core staff to see themselves as professional counselors and educators who provide "services" to "clients" rather than as "fellow travelers" or even informal leaders. In part, the tendency may stem from a well intentioned desire to fulfill responsibilities associated with their new administrative titles. Obviously staff members enjoy the superordinate status, prestige and income associated with their new roles.

Although this process of gradual assimilation into the professional culture is mitigated somewhat when nonprofessionals are not required to be in close contact with their employers, the process only unfolds more slowly because professional supervision persists and professional criteria for judging health and illness, appropriate "treatment," and ethical practice are still operative. Litwak and

Meyer (1966) have argued that, because of differences in their structures, bureaucracies and primary groups perform different and complementary functions. Too close a relationship will result in one,
usually the bureaucracy, overpowering the other. Indeed, the power
differential between professionals and nonprofessionals is the single
most important source of tension in their relationship.

Practically, professionals and nonprofessionals are at odds about
helping on many grounds. They often differ in their interpretations of
the causes (personality versus environmental) of human distress, in
their beliefs about how active the agent of change ought to be, in their
stance toward the authority of expert versus experiential knowledge,
and in their expectations for client change. Indeed, most points of
disagreement between them are reflections of the special assets that
set the nonprofessional apart from the professional in the first place
and that underscore the former's unique contribution to community
mental health. Thus, nonprofessionals have been criticized for being
overinvolved with clients, for "objectifying" client problems, for
naively trying to "change the system," and for feeling personally
culpable when their unproved methods fail to effect rapid changes in
people, policies, and institutions.

The hallmarks of nonprofessional helping, prior to its casting in
the professional mold, are isometric to those of social support. Indeed, nonprofessionals were often recruited for community mental
health work from among the pool of talented, resourceful indigenous
helpers and opinion leaders of the community. That is, nonprofessionals often occupied central roles in the natural helping networks
that existed in local catchment areas. It follows that their removal
from these networks depleted the human resources of the community.
Prior to their contact with the formal service delivery system, nonprofessionals were part of the fabric of informal helping in the natural
environment. Their contribution to health and human welfare differed
from that of professionals by virtue of: (a) its natural accessibility; (b)
its congruence with local norms about when and how support ought to
be expressed; (c) its rootedness in long-standing peer relationships;
(d) its variability, ranging from the provision of tangible goods and
services to simple companionship; and (e) its freedom from financial
and psychological (stigmatizing) costs incurred when professional
resources are used.

Since these attributes lie at the heart of social support and distinguish it from professional modes of helping, concerted efforts must be

made to preserve and fortify them. In our zeal to capitalize on the native strengths of nonprofessionals, we must not harness them to the professional helping enterprise in a way that undercuts their work in the community or subjugates them to our control. Professionals must adopt a new perspective on the community's informal system of care, recognizing that *mutuality of helping* is the cornerstone of social support. Once lay helpers are removed from the web of mutually supportive relationships they maintain with their families, their friends, and their neighbors, and once they are brought under the influence of the professional helping culture, power imbalances become more salient, mutual help is submerged, and support takes the form of interaction with a specialist whose job it is to lend resources to those who are impoverished. At worst, the sense of interdependence and reliable alliance that is the bedrock of social support is supplanted by the unilateral exercise of power characteristic of superordinate-subordinate relationships.

To sum up, social support is an expression of the ongoing interdependence between people; mutuality is its cornerstone. Subordinating lay help to professional control and performance standards threatens this sense of mutuality. The helping functions that spring from people's interactions with primary group members — the companionship of a doula, the empathy expressed in support group members' interactions, and the affirmation of the job terminees' family and friends — lend coherence and well-being to people's lives. The challenge to mental health practitioners is to discover ways of fostering primary group attachments among citizens, reinforcing those that already exist, and developing a better understanding of ways to intensify the supportive processes that contribute to health protection.

## SOME TERMINOLOGICAL DISTINCTIONS

Despite the absence of conceptual unity among various definitions of social support and the consequent lack of agreement about its operationalization, it is still useful to provide a tentative working definition of the construct that distinguishes it from related terms such as "support systems," "natural helping networks," and "personal networks." *Social support consists of verbal and/or nonverbal information or advice, tangible aid, or action that is proffered by social intimates or inferred by their presence and has beneficial emotional or behavioral effects on the recipient.* Collectively, the people who routinely provide social support have been referred to as members of an individual's "support system." However, I wish to emphasize the fact that there is no such *thing* as a support system; rather, individuals are embedded in a social network composed of close associates who are important in the individual's affective life and who generate both support and stress at different times and in response to different life demands. Social support arises from interaction in this social field; people's transactions with significant others produce both supportive and conflictual effects.

The term "support system" has also come to signify the combined deployment of professional and informal resources on behalf of the mentally ill in the community. Chapter 4 of this volume addresses the ways agency and voluntary resources have been blended in psychosocial treatment programs that provide continuous and coordinated care or aftercare to psychiatric patients. Thus this volume deals with social support's bearing on two fields of mental health practice: the community mental health field, where social support can be marshaled to maintain and promote the adjustment and morale of people exposed to developmental or situational stressors, and the field of clinical treatment and rehabilitation.

Finally, "natural helping networks" is a term introduced by Collins and Pancoast (1976) in the context of their research on neighborhood-based forms of informal support. They have examined a variety of arrangements for the delivery of human services in locales, focusing especially on the role of certain central figures or "natural neighbors" in organizing these services. Thus they have restricted their attention to those network members who, because of their residential proximity, can conveniently exchange needed services, goods, and emotional support, and, in the process, also strengthen neighborhood attachment and cohesion. Thus natural helping networks have been explored as avenues for delivering certain health and social welfare services with minimal reliance on professionals.

## OVERVIEW OF THE VOLUME

Chapter 2 reviews contemporary studies investigating the role of social support in the coping process. The chapter begins by examining the direct and indirect ways that social support may affect health, assessing its place in a broader epidemiological context. In addition, the chapter provides a detailed discussion of methods of measuring social support, concluding with a multidimensional formulation of the construct.

Chapters 3 and 4 outline directions for mental health practice that involve the mobilization and strengthening of social support. Chapter 3 discusses preventive interventions on behalf of persons undergoing life transitions and stressful events that entail social readjustments, and outlines strategies of strengthening the informal sources of support existing in the natural environment. Special attention is paid to the characteristics of helping networks in ethnic communities. Chapter 4 deals with the relevance of social support to the design of psychosocial rehabilitation programs and reviews several clinical strategies that directly involve the patient's social network. The chapter also touches on the sort of diagnostic assessment that is called for when the patient's network is drawn into the treatment process, and concludes by reviewing new approaches to the prevention of patient relapse that involve modifications of the family's affective influences.

The final section of the volume includes two chapters that consider the impact of social networks and social support on specific populations and settings. Chapter 5 deals with ways that social support can be brought to bear on the psychosocial problems faced by men recovering from an acute heart ailment and by women who have developed breast cancer. The value and design of supportive interventions in these areas of medical practice are discussed. The chapter also reviews recent work on social support in the workplace, examining how coworkers, supervisors, and the organizational structure can moderate work-related stressors.

The concluding chapter presents a broader social-ecological framework for analyzing the influence of social networks on the help-seeking process. It highlights the tensions and the benefits resulting from collaboration between professional mental health practitioners and laypeople, and it touches on certain societal trends that are bound to increase the need for support-mobilizing interventions in the future.

Chapter 2

# *THE NATURE OF SOCIAL SUPPORT AND ITS HEALTH IMPACT*

My aim in this chapter is first to familiarize mental health practitioners with a theoretical model that integrates information about life stressors, physical and mental health, and a set of variables that intervene between the two. I will use this model to explain the several potential pathways whereby social support may maintain and promote people's health and morale. Next I will review selected studies that have uncovered evidence in support of these several pathways, highlighting differences among these studies' measures of social support. The chapter concludes with suggestions for research that might shed more light on environmental and dispositional variables affecting people's access to informal social resources in the community. While I also touch on implications of present research for the design of clinical and preventive interventions, Chapters 3 and 4 more fully address these topics.

## EXAMINING THE ROLE OF SOCIAL SUPPORT IN THE LIFE STRESS-HEALTH RELATIONSHIP: A RESEARCH FRAMEWORK

Present inquiries into the nature and health protective effects of social support are best understood within the context of a broad theoretical framework that implicates life stress in the onset of psychological and somatic disorders. The origins of this framework date back to the work of Hinkle and Wolff (1957, 1958), two medical ecologists who attempted to unravel the causal links among cultural, geographic, and interpersonal changes in people's lives and their vulnerability to physical and emotional illness. A decade later, Holmes and Rahe (1967), drawing upon a list of stressful events culled from the life charts of more than 5000 medical patients, advanced the proposition that disease onset closely followed a clustering of these life events. Dohrenwend and Dohrenwend (1974) have described much of this early work in their book, *Stressful Life Events*. More recently, they have updated our understanding of the complex interplay among stressful life events, personality variables, social resources, and illness (Dohrenwend & Dohrenwend, 1981).

Figure 2.1 outlines the four basic elements of the theoretical framework that explains the causal sequence leading to stress-induced illness and the factors modifying the sequence. The model begins with (individual or group) exposure to life stressors, proceeds to the reactions to those stressors, and culminates with the health consequences stemming from these reactions. For example, Gore's (1978) study of job terminees was framed around the proposition that job loss represents a stressor incurring emotional and behavioral reactions capable of generating symptoms of depression. More generally, the accumulation of life stressors triggers changes in the established pattern of social adjustment, these changes in turn having emotional and behavioral sequelae that lead, either directly or through some largely unknown neurochemical process, to a weakened state and greater vulnerability to illness or disordered functioning.

The fourth component of the model consists of those variables that produce individual variations in the sequence leading from stressor to reactions and from reactions to illness. These variables have been termed "mediators," "moderators," or "conditioning variables" and include dispositional and environmental factors that intervene among the three primary links in the model. Empirically, they have been introduced in the etiological model because most studies have found that life events are only moderately (but significantly) correlated with subsequent illness episodes (Rabkin & Struening, 1976), thus suggesting that other factors may interact with life stressors and their emotional effects, adding power to the prediction of health outcomes. As noted in Chapter 1, social support represents a critical, situational resource that may exert a health-protective effect. In addition, dispositional (personality, perceptual, cognitive, and behavioral) mediators are capable of attenuating the links among life stressors, reactions, and health consequences. In what follows, I briefly discuss the kinds of moderating influences associated with these dispositional variables and elaborate on both the main effects and moderating power of social support in the life stress-health nexus.

## Dispositional Modifiers

Both stable personality factors and situationally specific organismic reactions seem to play a part in conditioning people's responses to life stressors. The former include such well-known personality traits as self-esteem, locus of control, habitual modes of defense, and a constellation of traits subsumed by the "Type A" label (Jenkins, 1976). Generally, these personality variables serve protective functions by shaping people's interpretations of stressful life events in ways that minimize their threatening aspects, thus circumventing the initial process whereby life stressors are converted into feelings of distress (see Figure 2.1). Situationally specific organismic responses to stressors have been intensively studied by Lazarus and his colleagues (Lazarus, 1974; Lazarus & Launier, 1978), who have identified certain cognitive processes and behavioral responses minimizing emotional arousal while aiding adaptation. They distinguish between primary and secondary appraisal processes, the former evaluating the significance of a stressor for personal well-being and the latter evaluating potential coping resources. They have also enumerated a range of coping strategies that are activated following exposure to a stressor and that are directed toward the regulation of its emotional concomitants and the resolution of the demands it imposes (Lazarus, 1981). Since very recent work by Kanner, Coyne, Schaefer, and Lazarus (1981) reveals that everyday nuisances such as losing things and getting stuck in traffic jams (hassles) predict psychological symptoms better than life events, they are also represented as stressors in Figure 2.1. To the extent that these hassles are not confounded with preexisting psychopathology, their distressful effects may also be moderated by cognitive and coping factors. Finally, an individual's past experience in dealing with a given stressor also ought to constitute an advantage when the same or a similar stressor is introduced again. Habituation thus represents another source of individual difference moderating the emotional disequilibrium attending exposure to stressors (Dohrenwend & Dohrenwend, 1978).

## Situational Modifiers

Before turning to an examination of the role of social support in moderating the response to stressors and in improving the coping process that leads from emotional distress to health outcomes, two other situational factors or circumstances that are likely to soften the impact of exposure to stressful life events merit brief comment: anticipation of the stressor and control over its onset (Dohrenwend & Dohrenwend, 1978). When people know in advance that they will be exposed to a stressor, for example, when workers are forewarned of an imminent layoff or preschoolers are told they will soon enter kindergarten, they are likely to experience much less shock or trauma when faced with the actual event. This is only natural, since a process of psychological preparation, which Janis (1965) calls "the work of worrying," takes place among those alerted to the coming stressor. Second, when people actually have control, or feel that they do, over the onset and extinction of stressors, they experience less enervation, thus attenuating the stressor's adverse effects. For example, the chronic stress associated with the work of air traffic controllers may be mitigated by allowing them to take breaks at will rather than forcing them to work according to a schedule that precludes their control over chronic work stress. In sum, consideration of the joint effects of these circumstances that condition the impact of events leads to the conclusion that personal vulnerability to ill health is lowered when stressful events are anticipated and their onset controlled by the individual. Conversely, susceptibility increases in the face of unanticipated and uncontrollable stressors.

## THE EFFECTS OF SOCIAL SUPPORT ON HEALTH

At present, it is possible to identify four junctures in the process leading from exposure to stressors to health outcomes at which social support may exert a salutary influence. Two of these junctures occur in the process leading from stressor to distress and from distress to health outcome and pertain to the much heralded "stress-buffering" effects of social support. In fact, much of the literature has failed to distinguish between these two types of stress-moderating effects of social support, and this may be due to the empirical difficulty of disentangling people's reactions to stressors from the health-related effects of those reactions. Indeed, the vast majority of studies examining the buffering role of social support have concentrated on its power in ameliorating distressful reactions to life stressors.

The other two junctures at which social support may be influential pertain to its direct effect on health and thus to its primary preventive functions. First, social support may shield people from exposure to certain types of stressors; second, it may enhance health and morale in general, thus serving a health-promotive function. In what follows I first elaborate on each of these four preventive functions of social support, citing examples of empirical studies that testify to each function. Later, I give separate attention to some noteworthy differences among the measures currently used to operationalize the social support construct.

*The buffering functions of social support.* Several studies claiming that social support can condition or buffer people's responses to stressors and moderate between distress and illness have found a statistical interaction between stress and support or between a health status measure and support. In other words, as Cassel (1974) and Cobb (1976) have pointed out, under conditions of high life change or chronic exposure to stressors, social support buffers the individual from potential adverse effects on mood and functioning, and facilitates coping and adaptation, reducing the likelihood of illness. By inference, social support does not vitiate stress under conditions of low exposure to stressors.

Three empirical strategies have typically been used to confirm social support's buffering role. The first, adopting an analysis of variance procedure, divides people into high- and low-stressed groups and then examines the health or adjustment status of those high and low in social support. Evidence confirming social support's buffering effect is the presence of a significant interaction between stress and support. The second procedure involves a regression equation that adopts a health-related criterion variable and enters one or more stress × support interaction terms as predictors, after adding the independent effects of stress and support. Here too the interaction term should account for a significant proportion of the criterion measure's variance if a buffering effect exists. The third and statistically weakest procedure compares the zero-order correlations between (high) stress and health measures among those with high and low access to social support. Here, the stress-buffering effect is suggested by a lower, significantly different correlation coefficient between stress and health among the supported compared to the unsupported group. The programmatic implications arising from evidence of the buffering effect are straightforward: *High-stressed groups lacking support in the community are at greatest risk of maladjustment and/or illness and represent prime candidates for support-mobilization strategies.*

Two examples among a host of recent studies (see Table 2.1) expose the buffering effects of social support. The first is Medalie and Goldbourt's (1976) epidemiological research on angina pectoris and the second is Barrera's (1981) study of adolescent mothers and their adjustment to parenthood. The former study examined the role of social support in moderating the relationship between distress and health consequences (arrow B2 in Figure 2.1), while the latter revealed that support buffered the effects of a life stressor on symptoms of distress (arrow B1 in Figure 2.1). Medalie and Goldbourt (1976) found that men who experienced high levels of anxiety and who perceived their wives as unloving and unsupportive were about twice as likely to develop angina pectoris as men who experienced anxiety but who reported that their wives were very loving and supportive. Under low anxiety conditions, high spousal support had no significant effect on the incidence of this disorder. This study echoes Gore's (1978) research, cited at the outset of this volume, both in terms of its reliance on subjective measures of support adequacy and its adoption of physiological measures of health. Similar stress-buffering effects of support have also been reported in a widely cited study by Nuckolls, Cassel, and Kaplan (1972), who found that women who had experienced high levels of life change and who had high "psychosocial assets" developed far fewer complications in labor and delivery than those women with low psychosocial assets. These findings, in turn, are entirely consonant with Sosa et al.'s (1980) research on the beneficial effects of the companionate care extended by the doulas in the maternity unit.

Barrera's (1981) study is particularly germane to my explanation of the two types of stress-buffering effects of social support. On the one hand, he found a significant statistical interaction between two of his support measures (network size and unconflicted network size) and

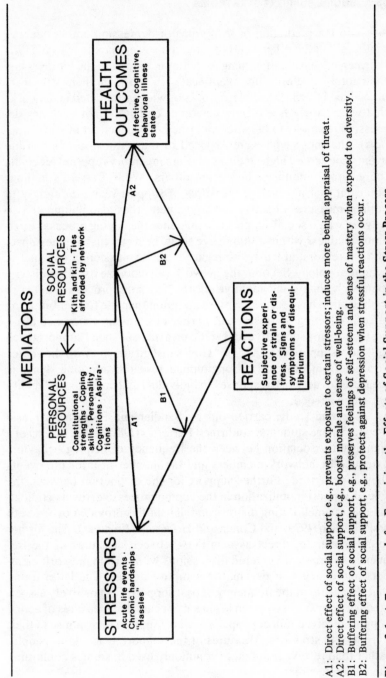

A1: Direct effect of social support, e.g., prevents exposure to certain stressors; induces more benign appraisal of threat.
A2: Direct effect of social support, e.g., boosts morale and sense of well-being.
B1: Buffering effect of social support, e.g., preserves feelings of self-esteem and sense of mastery when exposed to adversity.
B2: Buffering effect of social support, e.g., protects against depression when stressful reactions occur.

Figure 2.1 A Framework for Examining the Effects of Social Support in the Stress Process

stress in the prediction of symptoms of depression among teenage mothers. On the other hand, he found a strong, positive association between a measure of helping activities extended to the mothers and their total score on a life event scale. In short, mothers who were embedded in sizable social networks or who participated in networks that were largely free of interpersonal conflict did not evidence depressive reactions to life stressors (the buffering effect of social support), and those who were exposed to the greatest number of life events and scored highest on a symptom inventory reported receiving the greatest amount of help from others. While Barrera's findings point out that alternative measures of support relate differently to various measures of stress and adjustment, they also illuminate two ways in which social support can influence the coping process. First, embeddedness within a supportive social field can cushion the impact of life stressors, at least with regard to the expression of psychiatric symptomatology. Second, the network can mobilize itself to bolster a member's coping and adaptive efforts. The latter process of network mobilization has received far less attention than the former buffering effect, reflecting the historical, perhaps expedient preference of investigators for subjective and static measures of social support (such as "How supportive is X?" or "How satisfied are you with the advice you get from others?"). Longitudinal research adopting dynamic measures of network responses to individual and collective adversity are much needed.

A second study, carried out by Sandler and Barrera (in press) among college students, confirmed Barrera's (1981) earlier finding of a significant association between the frequency of helping behaviors extended by network members and the number of prior life events they experienced. Further support for the distinction between the role of support mobilization in the coping process versus its etiological role in ameliorating distress and ill health is provided by Carveth and Gottlieb (1979) and Cohen and Hoberman (in press). The former found moderate, direct associations between measures of the frequency of problem-centered discussions with certain network members and concurrent psychiatric symptomatology. The latter found that a measure of the frequency of past support was positively associated with physical symptoms. Thus it appears that measures of actual support received reflect people's need for support in response to their exposure to stressors. Measures of the support available to people, rather than received, are more commonly used in studies confirming the buffering effect.

Additional studies that confirm the stress-buffering role of social support include Burke and Weir's (1977) work on the effect of perceived spousal support on psychophysiological symptomatology; Eaton's (1978) investigation of the protective effect associated with being married as opposed to being single; LaRocco, House, and French's (1980) research documenting a significant interaction effect between social support and job stress on mental health; and Wilcox's (1981b) study of community residents. Studies partially confirming the stress-buffering hypothesis — those that have demonstrated both direct and moderating effects of social support on symptomatology — include Lowenthal and Haven's (1968) inquiry into the effect of elderly persons' access to a confidant in moderating the stress associated with major transitions in later life; Lin, Simeone, Ensel, and Kuo's (1979) report attesting to the ameliorative effects of social integration on the expression of symptomatology among a sample of Oriental persons; and Sandler and Lakey's (1982) study that found a significant stress-buffering effect of support on symptoms of depression and anxiety among college students who had high levels of internal control.

Details about the samples, measures, and findings of these and other studies that tested the stress-buffering effects of social support have been summarized by Mitchell, Billings, and Moos (1983). Table 2.1 shows that buffering effects have been found in a great many studies, but the types and sources of support that were examined and the measures of functioning differed so widely that we cannot as yet generate a coherent theory about the conditions under which social support moderates stress. Nor can we identify precisely the change processes underlying social support's health-protective impact. Peer feedback, expressed either covertly through the process of social comparison or overtly through discussion, can moderate the initial appraisal of the contextual threat posed by a stressor, preventing excessive levels of emotional and physiological arousal (Epley, 1974). The reassurance and affirmation of supportive comparisons may prevent damage to the party's sense of self-esteem and efficacy. They may buttress the individual's active coping efforts by extending a variety of supportive provisions such as cognitive guidance and tangible aid. In addition, they may offset feelings of self-recrimination by normalizing the individual's experience or by dispelling pejorative self-attributions about the causes of the problem. Finally, they encourage the venting of fears and assist the individual to reestablish a meaningful social identity in a network of relationships.

(text continues on page 46)

**TABLE 2.1  Cross-Sectional and Longitudinal Studies Examining Buffering Effects of Social Support**

*I. Cross-Sectional Studies Examining Buffering Effect of Social Support*

| Study | Sample | Stress Measure(s) | Support Measure(s) | Functioning Measure(s) | Results for Buffering Effect(s) |
|---|---|---|---|---|---|
| Andrews, Tennant, Hewson, & Vaillant (1978) | Community residents (N = 863) | Life change events | Social support composite (e.g., perception of crisis support, neighborhood interaction, community participation) | Psychological health | None found |
| Barrera (1981) | Pregnant adolescents (N = 81) | Negative life change events | −Total network size<br>−Conflicted network size<br>−Unconflicted network size<br>−Support satisfaction<br>−Support need score<br>−Receipt of specific helping behaviors | −Total symptoms<br>−Depression<br>−Anxiety<br>−Somatization | The effect of stress on depression is buffered by:<br>−total network size;<br>−unconflicted network size. |
| Henderson, Byrne, Duncan-Jones, Scott, & Adcock (1980) | Community residents (N = 756) | Life change events | −Availability of close affectional ties<br>−Adequacy of close affectional ties<br>−Availability of social integration (i.e., more diffuse ties)<br>−Adequacy of social integration | −Depression<br>−Neurotic symptoms | −For men, the effect of stress on depression and psychiatric symptoms is buffered by social integration.<br>−For women, the effect of stress on depression and psychiatric symptoms is buffered by close ties. |

| Study | Sample | Stress measure | Social support measure | Outcome | Findings |
|---|---|---|---|---|---|
| LaRocco, House, & French (1980) | Occupationally stratified random sample of men from 23 occupations (N = 636) | Perceived job stress:<br>—Work-load quantity<br>—Role conflict<br>—Job ambiguity<br>—Underutilization of skills<br>—Participation<br>Job-related strain:<br>—Job dissatisfaction<br>—Work-load dissatisfaction<br>—Boredom | —Supervisor support<br>—Coworker support<br>—Support from wife, family, and friends | —Depression<br>—Anxiety<br>—Somatic complaints<br>—Irritation | —The effect of job stress on health is buffered by social support.<br>—The effect of job strain on health, particularly depression, is buffered by social support.<br>—Coworker support seemed to buffer more strongly than supervisor or home support. |
| Lin, Simeone, Ensel, & Kuo (1979) | Community residents (N = 170) | Life change events | Social support composite (e.g., feelings about neighborhood; close friends in area; satisfaction with job) | Psychiatric symptoms | —Some evidence for the buffering effect was provided by comparison of high/low support and high/low stress subgroups.<br>—The interaction term in the regression analysis was not significant. |
| Linn & McGranahan (1980) | Community residents (N = 1423) | —Presence of health problems<br>—Separation/divorce<br>—Unemployment | Frequency of talking with close friends | —Life satisfaction<br>—Happiness | —The effect of health problems on life satisfaction and happiness is buffered by talking with friends.<br>—The effect of unemployment on happiness is buffered by talking with friends. |

*(continued)*

**TABLE 2.1** Continued

| Study | Sample | Stress Measure(s) | Support Measure(s) | Functioning Measure(s) | Results for Buffering Effect(s) |
|---|---|---|---|---|---|
| Sandler (1980) | Inner-city grade school children (N = 71) | Life change events<br>—Total event score<br>—Undesirable event score | —Presence of an older sibling<br>—One- vs. two-parent family<br>—Ethnic congruence with neighborhood | Parental ratings of<br>—Inhibition<br>—Aggression | —The effect of total event and undesirable event scores on aggression is buffering by the presence of an older sibling.<br>—The effect of total event scores on inhibition is buffered by the presence of an older sibling. |
| Sandler & Barrera (in press) | College students (N = 45; 71) | Undesirable life change events<br>—Past year<br>—Past month | —Network size<br>—Network utilized<br>—Satisfaction with support<br>—Receipt of specific helping behaviors | —Total symptoms<br>—Depression<br>—Anxiety<br>—Somatization | —For total symptoms, stress is buffered by network size and network satisfaction.<br>—For anxiety, stress is buffered by the receipt of specific helping behaviors.<br>—For somatization, stress is buffered by network size, utilization of network, network satisfaction, and receipt of specific helping behaviors. |

| | | | | |
|---|---|---|---|---|
| Sandler & Lakey (1982) | College students high (N = 52) or low (N = 41) on locus of control | Life change events | −Depression<br>−Anxiety | −The effect of stress on anxiety and depression is buffered by support for internals, but *not* for externals. |
| Wilcox (1981) | Community residents (N = 320) | Life change events | −Psychological distress<br>−Anxiety | −The effect of stress on psychological distress and tension is buffered by both support indices. |
| Receipt of specific helping behaviors | | | −Number of supporters<br>−Social support composite (e.g., items reflecting the presence of supportive behaviors) | |

*II. Longitudinal Studies Examining the Buffering Effect of Social Support*

| | | | | |
|---|---|---|---|---|
| Eaton (1978) | Community residents (N = 720) | Life change events | Psychiatric symptoms | The effect of stress is buffered by:<br>−marital status;<br>−not living alone. |

Receipt of specific helping behaviors column (Eaton):
−Marital status
−Belonging to clubs
−Belonging to church
−Having visits from friends
−Having visits from relatives
−Going out for a visit with others often
−Having a very close friend
−Living alone

*(continued)*

**TABLE 2.1 Continued**

| Study | Sample | Stress Measure(s) | Support Measure(s) | Functioning Measure(s) | Results for Buffering Effect(s) |
|---|---|---|---|---|---|
| Henderson (1981) | Community residents (N = 177) who displayed no psychological distress at Time 1 | Life change events | −Availability of close affectional ties<br>−Adequacy of close affectional ties<br>−Availability of social integration<br>−Adequacy of social integration<br>−Attachment persons with whom the respondent has been having rows | Neurotic symptoms | −The relationship between the perceived adequacy of ties and symptoms was much stronger under conditions of high adversity. |
| Pearlin, Lieberman, Menaghan, & Mullan (1981) | Community residents (N = 620) | Job loss (i.e., presence or absence of job disruption) | Social support composite (e.g., having someone you can count on for understanding and advice) | −Depression<br>−Mastery<br>−Self-esteem | −The effect of job disruption on mastery and self-esteem, but not depression, was buffered by social support. |
| Schaefer, Coyne, & Lazarus (1981) | Community residents (N = 100) | Life change events | −Network size<br>−Tangible support<br>−Emotional support<br>−Informational support | −Depression<br>−Positive morale<br>−Negative morale<br>−Physical health | None found |

| Study | Sample | Stressor | Social support measure | Outcome measure | Results |
|---|---|---|---|---|---|
| Turner (1981) | New mothers (N = 293) | Life change events | Social support measure (i.e., vignettes used to assess the degree to which one sees oneself as cared for, valued and belonging to a network of mutual obligation) | Summary psychological well-being measure | – No significant interaction effects were found in the regression analyses.<br>– When the sample was trichotomized into low, high, and medium stress groups, the correlation between support and well-being was significantly higher in the high stress group.<br>– Results also varied as a function of social class. |
| Warheit (1979) | Community residents (N = 517) | Life change events involving loss | – Spouse present<br>– Close relative nearby<br>– Friends to talk about problems with<br>– Close friends nearby to help | Depression | None found |
| Williams, Ware, & Donald (1981) | Community residents (N = 2234) | – Negative life change events<br>– Physical limitations | Social support composite (e.g., number of close friends/relatives; telephone contacts; etc.) | Mental health index | None found |

*The direct effects of social support.* Several studies have revealed that social support has a positive influence on people's health regardless of their levels of stress. That is, social support may play a role in insulating people from exposure to stressors and in fostering good health and morale. Moss (1973, p. 240) succinctly summarizes this viewpoint as follows: "Social support of an individual as a whole person, with the approval being unconditional and not dependent on performance, is a general well-being factor having a positive influence on health in general." It follows that people who are socially isolated or who have little access to social support are at greater risk of ill health and are likely to experience a greater number of environmental stressors than those who are socially integrated or who have access to social support. Furthermore, the absence of social support, in and of itself, implies a stressor of considerable import in people's lives. When people experience the loss of supportive social ties for which they cannot readily compensate through other social ties, they are at greater risk of adverse health consequences.

Data supporting these inferences come from a much cited epidemiological study by Berkman and Syme (1979) and from Bloom, Asher, and White's (1978) review of the literature pertaining to the health consequences of marital disruption. In a longitudinal study of the age-adjusted mortality rates of a large sample of Californians, Berkman and Syme discovered that people with the lowest levels of social contact at the time the study commenced had mortality rates from 2 to 4.5 times greater after 9 years than those with many social contacts. The "social network index," composed of information about the respondents' marital status, their extent of contact with close friends and relatives, and their participation in both formal and informal group associations, continued to predict mortality even when a variety of statistical controls for the respondents' health behaviors and initial health states were applied. Thus social isolation or impoverished social participation seems to be a generalized risk factor. In Michigan, House, Robbins, and Metzner (1982) replicated Berkman and Syme's work, finding that mortality rates of men reporting a high level of social relationships and activities were significantly lower than those with low levels 9 to 12 years earlier. Based on the evidence surveyed by Bloom, Asher, and White (1978), marital disruption specifically constitutes a significant stressor that increases the risk of subsequent physical and emotional disorders. Married people have lower mortality rates for a variety of medical conditions than do the unmarried (Syme, 1974), and they are relatively underrepresented among those admitted to psychiatric inpatient and outpatient facilities. While a number of competing hypotheses have been advanced to account for this strong pattern of associations, Bloom, Asher, and White's (1978, p. 886) conclude: "First, illness (physical or emotional) can precede and can help precipitate marital disruption. Second, marital disruption can precipitate physical and psychiatric difficulties in some persons who might otherwise not have developed such problems." The second conclusion underscores the fact that social ties — in this instance the profound marital bond — provide certain conditions and/or resources that enhance well-being and counteract stress.

Several studies have documented a direct relationship between the presence of supportive social ties, or the perception of such, and stress-free functioning. LaRocco and Jones (1978) examined the relationships between various types of work stressors and support from supervisors and coworkers as they affected the expression of distress in the forms of job dissatisfaction, poor self-esteem, and intentions to leave the job. Their sample consisted of young men who had served in the navy for approximately five years. They found no evidence of the stress-buffering role of social support; instead, they discovered a direct correlation between "leader facilitation and support" and job satisfaction (r = .29, p < .01) and between "work-group cooperation" and job satisfaction (r = .22, p < .01). LaRocco and Jones (1978, p. 633) conclude that "support, whether from one's leader or peers, did not appear to be an effective means of removing the negative influences of stress produced by conflict and ambiguity." That is, regardless of the levels of stress experienced by these navy personnel, support was associated with positive job and self attitudes. Indeed, it would appear that social support appears to be associated with positive mental health in numerous human milieux. Kiritz and Moos (1974, p. 109) reviewed much of the evidence linking dimensions of the perceived social environment to the physiological responses of the occupants and concluded that "the social stimuli associated with the relationship dimensions of *support, cohesion* and *affiliation* generally have positive effects — enhancing normal development and reducing recovery time from illness, for example."

These findings are consistent with several other recent reports of a direct relationship between support and adjustment, including Holahan and Moos's (1981) longitudinal study of depressive and psychosomatic symptomatology in relation to life stress and both family and workplace support; Henderson, Byrne, Duncan-Jones, Adcock, Scott, and Steele's (1978) preliminary report on the link between a paucity of confiding social relationships and the expression of neurotic symptomatology; Andrews, Tennant, Hewson, and Vaillant's (1978) work; and Schaefer, Coyne, and Lazarus's (1981) investigation. Considered together, these findings suggest that social support ought to be conceived as an inoculant against stress, not just as a resource that is mobilized for resisting stress-induced illness.

Very little research has explored the second pathway directly linking social support to health, namely, the way social support precludes exposure to certain types of life stressors. People who are enveloped in a network of close relationships may receive guidance that allows them to anticipate imminent stressors and alter aspects of the environment or of their own behavior so as to circumvent exposure to adversity. For example, coworkers may intensify their support of an associate who is soon to be evaluated for a promotion, parents may guide their adolescent children about the proper means of birth control, and the close friends of a couple who are about to have their first child may proffer their own parenting advice and skills in a way that grades the stress to which the couple will later be exposed. Gore (1981, p. 203) states that these ongoing support activities serve a "preventive support function" that "may determine vulnerability to the occurrence of those stress events that are not totally fortuitous happenings." Eckenrode and Gore (1981) have also recently pointed out the conditions that limit the ability of network members to extend support to any one of their number. Principally, they maintain that support will be weakened when the network itself is undergoing a great deal of adjustment resulting from exposure to chronic or acute stressors. For example, network mobilization in response to one member's loss of a job is likely to be sharply curtailed when network members collectively experience employment difficulties. Similarly, one vacancy in a network due to that occupant's hospitalization may radiate throughout the network, depleting it of critical supportive provisions. In short, the health status and morale of network members is tied to collective well-being and collective exposure or insulation from environmental stressors.

## Summary

The conceptual formulations that have been advanced regarding the various ways in which social support can enter into the coping process and how it can influence health and morale have received mixed empirical support. While Table 2.1 leaves the impression that social support does cushion the impact of stressful life events, it also reveals wide discrepancies among the approaches that researchers have taken to measure the support construct itself, and it calls attention to the diverse health and behavioral measures that have been adopted. In the face of the methodological inconsistencies that surround the burgeoning research on social support, conclusions about its influence in the coping process must remain tentative.

As Mitchell et al. (1983) point out, future research progress in the area will depend on the ability of investigators to make finer distinctions among the types of stressors and the types of stressful reactions that are moderated by different sources and kinds of support. For example, certain types of later-life transitions involving social losses may be buffered by the presence of a confidant, but events precipitating medically related debilitations among the elderly may not be moderated by access to this source of support (Lowenthal & Haven, 1968). In addition to identifying the circumstances under which different sources and forms of support mitigate stress, researchers will need to attend more closely to questions surrounding the way support accomplishes its health-protective effects. Does it buttress the individual's behavioral strivings to adjust by rendering certain provisions? Does it reduce his or her level of emotional arousal regarding the stressful experience by inducing less threatening cognitions? Or does it preserve the individual's sense of confidence, esteem, and control in the situation by providing emotionally sustaining feedback and offering ego-protective attributions? Each of these possibilities reflects a different conception of the mechanisms underlying social support's effects on health.

## ON THE MEASUREMENT OF SOCIAL SUPPORT

Research reviewed in the previous section reveals that a legion of social support measures have been used to operationalize the construct, making it virtually impossible to draw firm conclusions about the actual effects of social support in the life stress process. Measures of social support range from indicators of people's participation in voluntary organizations to their receipt of specific types of aid from specific associates. Moreover, researchers have taken different perspectives on the phenomenon, some relying on the subjective perceptions of support recipients and some basing their measures on more external markers known to be associated with access to support, such as participation in a social network characterized by particular structural properties. With each new study a new definition of support surfaces.

In order to bring some organization to this heterogeneous set of definitions, I have classified current measurement strategies into three types, each taking a different level of analysis. The first approach is the most macroscopic and treats social support as a byproduct of people's participation in various social aggregates. From this perspective, social integration is tantamount to social support. Implicitly, it is assumed that people gain a "psychological sense of community" (Sarason, 1974) from such communal activities as church attendance and block club participation, and that these forms of affiliation are valid indicators of people's embeddedness in a reliable network of supporters. Other indirect or proxy measures of social support that also fall within the social integration approach include the amount of contact people have with close friends and family members, their attachment to their neighborhoods, and the extent to which they experience a sense of shared history and common values. Accordingly, alienation and social isolation characterize those lacking in social support.

At the opposite extreme, social support is predicated upon the existence of one or more dyadic relationships characterized by intimacy, stability, spontaneity, and mutuality. These "deep" relationships invite the disclosure of emotions, offer companionship, and, by the fact of their existence, communicate to the parties that they are valued in and of themselves. This approach thus emphasizes the quality of social relationships, rather than their quantity or diversity, and it probes the adequacy of the psychosocial supplies exchanged in these relationships. Henderson and his colleagues (Henderson, Duncan-Jones, Byrne, & Scott, 1980) have developed an interview schedule carefully exploring the six "provisions" of social relationships that were originally proposed by Weiss (1974). The following quotation summarizes their understanding of attachment, the provision they investigate in greatest detail in their interview:

> We have in mind that attribute of relationships which is characterized by affection and which gives the recipient a subjective sense of closeness. It is also pleasant and highly valued, commonly above all else. In adults, the attachment is usually reciprocated, at least in enduring relationships. Self-revelation and emotional intimacy are

more likely within such relationships than in more diffuse ones. . . .
In the absence of the other person, the individual feels affectively
uncomfortable and restless; he is likely to seek reunion with the
other [Henderson et al., 1980, p. 3].

By emphasizing "a subjective sense of closeness," this approach
relies extensively on the respondent's perception of the adequacy of
his or her primary social ties, a perception that may be colored by a
host of stable personality factors, temporary affective states, and the
reactive effects ("demands") arising from the inquiry itself. Henderson et al. (1980) have examined these influences in the course of
assessing the validity and reliability of the ISSI (Interview Schedule
for Social Interaction). They achieve satisfactory levels of test-retest
reliability, but also find a moderate correlation between respondents'
reports of the adequacy of their social ties and a measure of trait
neuroticism (correlations averaging $-.30$). In addition, they show
that response styles such as the need for approval and social desirability also influence their respondents' reports. Finally, they caution researchers about drawing conclusions from studies that relate
the ISSI to psychological disturbances at any single point in time
(cross-sectional designs), noting that these correlations may simply
reflect the effect of present disorders or predisposing personality
abnormalities on perceptions of social relationships.

The two approaches I have described differ in the emphasis they
place on aspects of the social field from which support arises. The first
approach regards support as a resource arising from people's participation and integration in society; the second views it as an expression
of the affective intensity of particular intimate relationships. While
the former approach has tended to concentrate on quantitative issues
and the latter on qualitative issues, neither viewpoint has considered
the actual extension of help in social interaction, and neither has
inquired into the structure of the social field and its influence on
people's access to support. Both of these topics deserve attention
because they inform our understanding of the process of network
mobilization. The study of helping behaviors gives us an appreciation
of the content of support, while the study of network structure tells us
how the social environment may be patterned or organized as a
flexible *system* for maintaining health and responding to crises.

The actual helping transactions that occur naturally can be organized into such broad classes as emotional support, tangible aid and

services, cognitive guidance, and companionship, or they can be disaggregated into a series of discrete categories of help. I conducted an interview study of the specific types of informal aid that were received by a sample of low-income mothers who were facing a variety of life difficulties (Gottlieb, 1978). These forms of aid were identified through a content-analysis procedure using four judges who read these women's descriptions of the help they received from family members, friends, neighbors, and informal community caregivers, and then independently generated 26 categories that comprehensively summarized their descriptions. The final classification scheme, reprinted in Table 2.2, illuminates several unique aspects of social support.

First, within the class of "emotionally sustaining behaviors," categories A10-A12 vividly express Cassel's (1974) ideas about the simple presence of others as a stress buffer, while the preceding categories shed light on the sorts of information that lead people to believe that they are "cared for and loved . . . esteemed and valued" (Cobb, 1976). Second, the eleven categories subsumed by the label "problem-solving behaviors" together reflect virtually every aspect of Caplan's (1974) original definition of the functions of support systems in the community (see Chapter 1). Category B9, "models/provides testimony of own experience" is particularly interesting because it closely resembles the modal type of help expressed by members of mutual-help groups, while category B11, "distracts from problem focus," reveals that people view as helpful opportunities to avoid thinking about their difficulties temporarily. The two categories under the heading "indirect personal influence" betray the fact that the scheme does not deal purely with actual helping behaviors. Respondents frequently mentioned both categories, and they were incorporated in the scheme because they suggest that support is, in part, also founded on a sense of security that certain people and certain resources *would be forthcoming* should they be needed. Moreover, these categories illuminate much that is entailed in the psychological sense of community people gain from their close relationships, and they seem to amplify Cobb's (1976, p. 300) third proposition about the sort of messages that signal the presence of social support: "information leading the subject to believe that he belongs to a network of communication and mutual obligation." The final category of helping behavior, assigned to a class of its own (D1), reflects the variety of advocacy-oriented actions that laypersons can perform for one another but that professionals generally eschew.

Recently, Barrera, Sandler, and Ramsay (1981) have used these and other categories of helping behaviors to develop a survey instrument called the Inventory of Socially Supportive Behaviors (ISSB). Respondents are asked to rate the frequency with which forty behaviorally specific types of aid were extended to them during a fixed time interval and the sum of these ratings may be used to predict adjustment. The authors report that the inventory achieved high internal consistency coefficients and adequate test-retest reliability. When administered to a sample of adolescent mothers, the ISSB was positively correlated with both a measure of psychiatric symptomatology and the total number of life events experienced by the respondents (Barrera, 1981), suggesting that it is a potentially useful measure of the network's mobilization of support. The same pattern of direct associations between the ISSB and both symptoms and life events has been reported by Sandler and Barrera (in press) in the context of a study of college students. Regrettably, both studies that have used the ISSB to document behavioral forms of support were not prospective inquiries and therefore do not conclusively show that the direct associations between the ISSB and measures of both environmental stress and subjective distress reflect the process of network mobilization.

My initial classification scheme of informal helping behaviors and its elaboration by Barrera et al. (1981) can be adapted for the purpose of studying ongoing transactions in mutual-aid groups and in other settings where peer helping is deliberately planned. It probes the supportive exchanges arising from the social field, not its structure. Network analysis represents a relatively new tool for assessing the structural bases for coping and adaptation, a tool that differs from other approaches to measuring social support in its emphasis on the links between personal health and morphological features of the primary social systems that people inhabit.

In applying network analysis to the study of social support, researchers typically begin by restricting their attention to an individual's personal network, and then focus on how its composition, the character of its internal links, and its overall structural configuration affect its potential as a support system. The focal party's personal network generally consists of those family members, close friends, work associates and neighbors deemed most important in the individual's affective life and with whom there is regular and frequent contact. About ten people are usually nominated as members of this personal community (Hammer, Makiesky-Barrow, & Gutwirth,

**TABLE 2.2    A Classification Scheme of Informal Helping Behaviors**

| Category | Definition | Example |
|---|---|---|
| **A. EMOTIONALLY SUSTAINING BEHAVIORS** | | |
| A1  Talking (unfocused) | Airing or ventilation of general concerns without reference to problem specifics | "she'll talk things over with me" |
| A2  Provides reassurance | Expresses confidence in R as a person, in some aspect of R's *past* or *present* behavior, or with regard to the future course of events | "he seems to have faith in me" |
| A3  Provides encouragement | Stimulates or motivates R to engage in some *future* behavior | "she pushed me a lot of times when I was saying, 'oh, to heck with it'" |
| A4  Listens | Listening only, without reference to dialogue | "he listens to me when I talk to him about things" |
| A5  Reflects understanding | Signals understanding of the facts of R's problem or of R's feelings | "she would know what I was saying" |
| A6  Reflects respect | Expresses respect or esteem for R | "some people look down on you; well, she doesn't" |
| A7  Reflects concern | Expresses concern about the importance or severity of the problem's impact on R or for the problem itself | "just by telling me how worried or afraid she is" (for me) |
| A8  Reflects trust | Reflects assurance of the confidentiality of shared information | "she's someone I trust and I knew that it was confidential" |
| A9  Reflects intimacy | Provides or reflects interpersonal intimacy | "he's just close to me" |
| A10  Provides companionship | Offers simple companionship or access to new companions | "I've always got her and I really don't feel alone" |
| A11  Provides accompaniment in stressful situation | Accompanies R in a stressful situation | "she took the time to be there with me so I didn't have to face it alone" |

| | | |
|---|---|---|
| A12 Provides extended period of care | Maintains a supportive relationship to R over what R considers an extended period of time | "she was with me the whole way" |

## B. PROBLEM-SOLVING BEHAVIORS

| | | |
|---|---|---|
| B1 Talking (focused) | Airing or ventilation of specific problem details | "I'm able to tell him what's bugging me and we discuss it" |
| B2 Provides clarification | Discussion of problem details which aims to promote new understanding or new perspective | "making me more aware of what I was actually saying other than just having the words come out" |
| B3 Provides suggestions | Provides suggestions or advice about the means of problem solving | "he offered suggestions of what I could do" |
| B4 Provides directive | Commands, orders, or directs S about the means of problem solving | "all Rose told me was to be more assertive" |
| B5 Provides information about source of stress | Definition same as category name | "she keeps me in touch with what my child's doing" |
| B6 Provides referral | Refers R to alternative helping resource(s) | "financially, he put me on to a car mechanic who gave me a tune-up for less than I would pay in a garage" |
| B7 Monitors directive | Attempts to ensure that R complies with problem-solving directive | "making sure that I follow through with their orders" |
| B8 Buffers S from source of stress | Engages in behavior which prevents contact between R and stressor | "he doesn't offer it (alcohol) to me anymore" |
| B9 Models/provides testimony of own experience | Models behaviors or provides oral testimony related to the helper's own experience in a similar situation | "just even watching her and how confident she seems has taught me something" |

*(continued)*

**TABLE 2.2** Continued

| Category | Definition | Example |
|---|---|---|
| B10 Provides material aid and/or direct service | Lends or gives tangibles (e.g., food, clothing, money) or provides service (e.g., babysitting, transportation) to R | "he brought his truck and moved me so I wouldn't have to rent a truck" |
| B11 Distracts from problem focus | Temporarily diverts R's attention through initiating activity (verbal or action-oriented) unrelated to the problem | "or he'll say, 'Let's go for a drive' . . . some little thing to get my mind off it" |
| C. INDIRECT PERSONAL INFLUENCE | | |
| C1 Reflects unconditional access | Helper conveys an unconditional availability to R (without reference to problem-solving actions) | "she's there when I need her" |
| C2 Reflects readiness to act | Helper conveys to R readiness to engage in future problem-solving behavior | "he'll do all he can do" |
| D. ENVIRONMENTAL ACTION | | |
| D1 Intervenes in the environment to reduce source of stress | Intervenes in the environment to remove or diminish the source(s) of stress | "she helped by talking to the owners and convincing them to wait for the money a while" |

NOTE: Copyright (1978) Canadian Psychological Association. Reprinted by permission.

1978), although demographic, family life cycle, and psychiatric status variables produce variations in this number. The size of people's personal networks, then, will depend a great deal on the breadth of their participation in community life. Elderly retired persons are likely to participate in fewer social settings than middle-aged employed persons; and those elderly who live in institutional settings are likely to have diminished networks relative to those living in the open community. The link between social participation and access to support is sharply drawn by Stack (1974) in her book about adaptive behavior in a Black ghetto. Here she records one of her respondents' sentiments about how to get support:

> I don't believe in putting myself on nobody but I know I need help every day. You can't get help just by sitting at home, laying around, house-nasty and everything. You got to get up and go out and meet people, because the very day you go out, that first person you meet may be the person that can help you get the things you want [p. 32].

The character of the focal individual's links to network members can be described along several dimensions, including duration, intensity (affective), the number of "exchange contents" typically comprised (Barnes, 1972), and symmetry or degree of equitable exchange. In addition, the structure of the overall network can be analyzed in terms of homogeneity, geographic dispersion, size, and density. Useful reviews of these features of network analysis and their bearing on issues of support access have been written by Mueller (1980), Pilisuk and Froland (1978), and Wellman (1981).

A network-analytic view of social support thus can combine and interweave structural and functional variables within the immediate social system that exert an impact on personal adjustment. For example, Hirsch (1980) has shown that one aspect of a network's density represents a structural resource aiding adaptation to certain life transitions and that, on a subjective level, it is associated with greater satisfaction with different types of support. Specifically, Hirsch found that young widows and women returning to university studies who had fewer connections between their family members and friends dealt with their respective transitions more easily and experienced more satisfaction with certain types of support. Apparently, the friends who were not tied closely to people in the domestic sphere helped both groups of women to enter a nondomestic world. Wilcox (1981) reports similar beneficial effects of low network density in his examination of the adjustment of fifty women who had recently separated from their husbands. Those women making a poorer adjustment had significantly denser postdivorce networks than those who adjusted well, a finding that Wilcox (1981) explains in terms of the greater proportion of kin ties in their networks. That is, a greater number of kin entails greater density, and since kin generally have been found to have more difficulty accepting the divorce of family members, their overrepresentation in the postdivorce network is likely to undermine adjustment.

Both Wilcox's (1981) and Hirsch's (1980) studies attest to the superiority of loose-knit networks in fostering adjustment to major life transitions, but they must be considered alongside other studies (for example, Stack, 1974) that document the strengths associated with more solidary social structures. Clearly, universally applicable assertions about the "adaptive quotient" of social networks are not warranted. Instead, certain structural configurations will be best suited for certain persons undergoing certain life stressors and transitions while other structural patterns will provide the best conditions during periods of relative stability. Network analysis is only beginning to unravel how patterns of social connections generate or deplete resources for resisting stress. Further, little knowledge has accumulated about how people deliberately attempt to establish a personal community, or about how they maintain it and reshape it over time. Moreover, since networks as whole units are themselves affected by environmental conditions — since they do not stand still in the face of challenge and adversity — we must constantly shift our post of observation from the individual to the ecological milieu in which he or she is embedded, seeking to identify the circumstances that optimize personal and collective well-being.

## DIRECTIONS FOR FUTURE RESEARCH

Methodological shortcomings and conceptual divergencies beset several aspects of research on the nature and effects of social support. By enumerating these difficulties, I hope to stimulate the development of new research strategies that might enlarge and correct present knowledge. In addition, I address the need for research concerning the personal and environmental conditions favoring access to social support in the community.

First, researchers will have to attend more closely to the interplay between dispositional variables and interpersonal factors (the two sets of mediators in Figure 2.1) in the process leading from life stressors to health outcomes. Both stable personality attributes and personal coping responses are likely to affect and be influenced by the social context. Greater knowledge of their joint effects will improve prediction of the outcomes of exposure to stressors and will further our understanding of the interactional nature of the coping process. Current research suggests that locus of control beliefs relate to the receipt and impact of social support (Sandler & Lakey, 1982), that certain temporarily adaptive modes of defense, such as denial, may be disrupted by primary group members (Meyerowitz, 1980), and that a constellation of personality traits subsumed by the Type A construct may also affect people's responses to the immediate social milieu, conditioning their ultimate efficacy. On the last point, since the Type A individual is prone to respond to frustration with hostility (Friedman & Rosenman, 1974), supportive responses from others are unlikely to occur or will be rejected. Finally, social comparison processes are bound to influence an individual's appraisal of the threat or challenge associated with an imminent or actual stressor. People in the immediate social environment thus condition both personal coping responses and prior judgments about the significance of stressful demands for personal well-being.

Second, researchers need a better understanding of the process of network mobilization in response to daily needs and exceptional crises. How do personal networks rally around distressed members? There is a good deal of knowledge about the kinds of informal helping behaviors that members typically extend, but only sparse information about how the pattern of social response differs from one occasion to the next and whether, over time, the structural configuration of the whole network changes. Knowledge gained from the study of *episodes* of social support must be counterbalanced by an appreciation of ongoing network *transactions*. Hammer (1963) pointed out some years ago that an individual's position in a social network determined the network's speed of response to signs of emotional disturbance. She found that central figures — persons whose structural positions in social networks involved activities important to the maintenance of the whole network — were hospitalized faster than were persons who occupied more peripheral positions. No doubt other unknown features defining an individual's structural position in a network affect the speed and nature of the network's response. Further, do stressful life events entailing temporary or permanent social losses from a network, such as job termination, hospitalization, death, divorce, geographic moves, and migration, have reverberating effects throughout the network and entail a deterioration of support, or does the network somehow compensate for these vacancies and replenish its resources over time? These and other issues concerning the mobilization process can be best addressed through the application of naturalistic methods of research such as those used by Stack (1974).

Numerous methodological weaknesses vitiate the evidence of social support's health-protective effects. Most studies give scant attention to the psychometric properties of their support measures. Further, the adoption of phenomenological measures of support requires the particularly difficult separation of judgments about the adequacy of support from the effects of personality, response styles, norms prescribing socially desirable attitudes toward kith and kin, and present morale and psychiatric status. As Brown (1974) has shown, the latter confound often besets cross-sectional studies; people are prone to justify their present state of health or illness in terms of the prior quantity or adequacy of support from their networks. This retrospective bias or defensive attribution can be minimized in prospective research designs, although the other enumerated confounds threaten the validity of subjective measures of social support. For example, in a recently completed study of over 200 low-income mothers, Carveth and I found correlations averaging .23 between a measure of the adequacy of support from intimate companions and 3 dispositional variables: 2 personality measures (I-E and self-esteem) and a measure of the respondents' confidence in their social skills (Gottlieb & Carveth, 1981). Thus it is likely that this phenomenological measure of social support is colored by one or more attributes of the respondents. Dohrenwend and Dohrenwend (1981, p. 18) similarly note the potential confound between social skills and subjective measures of social support: "Social support measures that confound environmental supports with personal competence will probably be more strongly related to health indicators than social support measures thus not confounded. For etiological investigations, the former are poor measures, however, since they do not provide an accurate assessment of the strength of the effect of social support as an element in the life-stress process." Finally, since subjective measures of social support are predicated on the assumption that individuals differ in their requirements for support, group or population-centered interventions cannot be planned. Instead, interventions would have to be planned on a case-by-case basis and directed toward conditioning people's perceptions that they have adequate support.

Despite the methodological problems accompanying subjective measures of social support, my intention is not to dismiss the etiological significance of people's feelings about their social resources. In fact, my own classification scheme of helping behaviors highlights the value that people attach to a sense of milieu reliability. However, the subjective perception of being sustained by a personal community is only one dimension of social support. Other dimensions I have reviewed pertain to the helping resources that are actually extended in interaction, the structural properties of the social system in which people are embedded, and the characteristics of people's links to others. In short, *social support is properly conceived of as a multidimensional construct and should be measured accordingly.* These dimensions are likely to be associated with one another, and their empirical relations will be of interest. For example, they may inform our understanding of the phenomenological correlates of different network configurations among different populations. Ultimately, a multidimensional approach promises to disclose how different aspects of social support are causally related to adjustment and health.

A final issue that merits closer attention in future research touches on the fundamental distinction between support and stress It is important to distinguish between the psychological distress produced by the loss of social support and the distress experienced by persons who lack or have access to very little social support. That is, distress and ill health produced by *stressors involving social losses* must be disentangled from the adverse results that are due to *levels of ongoing support that are insufficient to buffer stress*. Studies that fail to consider whether low levels of support result from exposure to particular life events or are independent of such exposure cannot empirically assess the stress-buffering hypothesis. Therefore, researchers ought to separate life events into two categories: those involving "exits" from the social network and those that do not deplete the network.

Finally, virtually no attention has been given to the origins of the skills underlying the expression and receipt of social support. The argument that support measures are confounded with personal competence (Dohrenwend & Dohrenwend, 1981; Heller, 1979) is certainly reasonable, but it leaves unanswered questions about the aspects of personal competence that are of greatest importance. Social-psychological research on the formation and maintenance of close interpersonal ties may be germane here (for example, Bercheid & Walster, 1978) and research on the topic of self-disclosure is of special relevance, because it suggests that intimate relationships are threatened when the partners fail to match each other's levels and speed of disclosure (Duck, 1980). Thus mutuality of social exchange and symmetrical helping may prove to be important underpinnings of socially supportive ties.

In addition, research in the field of developmental psychology may shed light on the genesis of empathic skills, another area of social competence that bears on the expression of social support. If emotional helping first arises from the ability to take the perspectives of others, to "feel with" them, and to communicate these shared feelings (Shantz, 1975), then it may be possible to teach children these skills in the hope that they will endure. Childhood social relationships are also bound to have an impact on the development of social skills. Cochrane and Brassard (1979) have discussed the myriad contributions to infant and child development that are mediated through parental social networks, and Lewis and Feiring (1979) report that the personal networks of three-year-old children contain an average of six frequent peer contacts apart from those adult contacts arising from their parents' social orbits. Furthermore, Kauffman, Grunebaum, Cohler, and Gamer (1979) have found that, among children of psychotic mothers, the presence of a close chum and extensive contact with an adult outside the family are associated with high social competence. Considered together, these studies point to the promise of research on the childhood antecedents of social competence and later-life access to social support.

## STRESSFUL ASPECTS OF SOCIAL NETWORKS

The social network should not be viewed exclusively as a support system that is unconditionally helpful to its members and always empathic. While close associates can often be counted on to provide help in emergencies and to offer a psychological sense of community, they also generate conflict and impose demands. Researchers must therefore guard against a romantic view of social support and adopt measures that examine the overall balance of sustaining and discordant influences stemming from social interactions.

There are numerous instances when the primary groups in which people participate exert harmful influences and therefore cannot be brought into support-mobilizing interventions. Notably, there are families whose members victimize one another physically or psychologically and whose extended networks condone this behavior. Indeed, when family members suffer physical abuse at the hands of a parent, child, or spouse, they usually suffer double adversity, because they are too embarrassed or fearful to seek the support of other close associates (Browne, 1982). Moreover, their abusers enforce their isolation from potential sources of support (Hilberman & Munson, 1977-78). And even when they do disclose their plight to their intimates, the latter's responses are likely to be ambivalent, at best, due to the widely held belief that such matters are outside their proper sphere of influence. That is, out of respect for the privacy of the family, especially in socially unacceptable matters, the network fails to serve social welfare. In situations such as this, even greater damage could be done if attempts were made to mobilize the victim's network. If child abuse is transmitted from one generation to another, or if it is maintained through interaction with a network that condones this manner of child rearing, then grievous harm would result from interventions that mobilize the network. Here, the professional must either change the norms and behaviors of the entire network that sustains the pattern of abuse or attempt to remove the victim from its influence. More generally, before we proceed to the task of marshaling informal resources or fostering greater reliance on them, we must assure ourselves of their prosocial character. If the network is not equipped to respond to certain problems, or if it is likely to exacerbate them, we may need to intervene directly in the network, substitute a new network, or circumvent it.

Even when network members intend to offer support they may do so in ways that augment the stress experienced by the intended beneficiary, reminding us that the latter's viewpoint must be taken into consideration in the measurement of social support. The recipient of aid may experience reactance when a well-intentioned family member is perceived as interfering or too controlling. When several parties in the network recommend a single course of action, the helpee may resent the constraint they have placed on his or her freedom of choice. Moreover, unpleasant feelings of indebtedness and dependency may arise from repeated receipt of help, adding to the burdens of the helpee.

Under certain conditions, the network may fail to mobilize support or may do so inappropriately. For example, in a recent study of

100 breast cancer patients, Peters-Golden (1982) found that only half of the women felt that the support they received adequately met their needs. They reported that once others learned about their illness, they "misunderstood," "avoided," or "feared" the patients. Their interaction with network members was strained by the latter's false cheerfulness and inauthentic sentiments. In short, the majority of the patients found that support failed to materialize at all or was expressed in ways that met the helpers' emotional needs rather than those of the patients. These findings suggest, more generally, that support may not be forthcoming when the helper feels threatened by the helpee's plight, sensing his or her vulnerability to it. Dunkel-Schetter and Wortman (1981) suggest that the elderly often fail to receive support because their suffering also gives rise not only to feelings of vulnerability in potential helpers, but also to feelings of helplessness.

To summarize, measurement of the social network's influence on the coping process must take into consideration the balance of support and stress incurred by the network's responses. Nonmaterialization of support or inappropriate expression of aid may stem from the negative affect aroused by the helpee's plight or life circumstances. Helpers, after all, are not obliged to render aid when it entails a personal threat, nor do they possess natural wisdom about the most beneficial ways of helping. Sometimes their intervention will disrupt the helpee's psychological coping style, constrain problem-solving efforts, or exacerbate feelings of emotional isolation and dependency. Study of the social network's impact on matters of health and well-being can be improved by simultaneously examining its supportive provisions and deficiencies.

# Part II

# MOBILIZING SOCIAL SUPPORT IN PRACTICE

Chapter 3

# PREVENTIVE INTERVENTIONS

This chapter reviews several current and potential strategies for marshaling informal sources of support to improve coping and to enhance morale and health. Generally, these are preventive approaches, some having a primary preventive objective and some occurring at the secondary preventive level, when early intervention can minimize the adverse effects of exposure to life stressors and abrupt transitions. These interventions fall into two categories. The first involves the development of "event-centered support groups" that can be convened on behalf of specific groups of people known to be at risk due to their common exposure to certain life events and transitions requiring extensive social readjustment. Adding to the armamentarium of secondary preventive interventions, these groups supplement people's adjustment strivings by mobilizing similar peers who offer mutual support and cognitive guidance, and express confidence in their members' ability to master emotional and situational difficulties. The second type of preventive intervention involves the restructuring of existing social networks or the optimization of their helping capabilities so that they reach more people and more adequately fulfill people's requirements for support. This type of intervention is a mass-oriented, health-promotion strategy. Its beneficiaries are not assumed to be at risk of ill health, and its aims are to extend and fortify the supportive dimension of community life. In addition, this chapter touches on the activities that professionals can undertake to preserve existing supportive attachments among citizens, and concludes with a discussion of some unique characteristics of the informal sources of support existing in ethnic/minority group communities.

## EVENT-CENTERED SUPPORT GROUPS

### Basic Characteristics

In January 1982, during the height of a blizzard, an Air Florida jet liner departed from Washington, D.C.'s close-in National Airport. Thirty seconds later it struck the inbound lanes of the 14th Street Bridge and then toppled over into the icy Potomac River. The crash swept 4 motorists to their deaths and resulted in 74 casualties among those who were aboard. Within the space of a few days an area radio station announced that a local community mental health center was offering "support groups" for the family members of the crash's victims. Moreover, the announcement also invited the participation of bystanders on the bridge, air traffic controllers who had been on duty that afternoon, and rescue workers.

This dramatic example is only one of numerous instances in which people in similar stressful predicaments can be assembled in order to ventilate their fears, gain an understanding of the significance of an adverse event for their personal well-being, and compare notes about how to come to terms with a new set of circumstances and resume their lives. Other occasions that call for the formation of support groups composed of similar peers include bereavement, even when it does not follow such tragic, accidental death; marital separation; retirement; unemployment; job and school transitions that entail entry to a new environment; major geographic relocations; and even more auspicious occasions that nevertheless challenge people's adaptive capabilities, such as the birth of a first child or the marriage of the last child remaining at home. Each of these events involves an important change in the parties' primary social relationships, whether this change is triggered by an addition to, a disruption of, or a departure from their social field. In Antonovsky's (1979, p. 125) terms, each of these events disturbs the parties' "sense of coherence" — "a perception of one's environments, inner and outer, as predictable and comprehensible." Furthermore, these events exert a powerful, disequilibrating impact not only because of the removal of one or more anchoring relationships, but also because these losses radiate throughout the primary social field. That is, many of these events have ripple effects on the parties' social networks, shifting their ongoing social patterns in unexpected ways, and sometimes depleting the resources they can secure from their remaining close associates.

The social sequelae of marital separation illustrate these second-order network effects. When the marital bond is severed, so too are many of the relationships the partners enjoyed with other couples who now withdraw, either because they feel threatened by the specter of separation in their own marriage, or because they feel they must now determine their allegiance to one or the other party and are unable to do so. In short, a network perspective lends a broader contextual understanding of the social resources that underpin mental health and those that are depleted when environmental events rend the social fabric.

Although secondary prevention in the form of crisis services has figured prominently in community mental health practice, thanks to the pioneering work of Lindemann (1944) and Caplan (1964), the support group format offers several advantages over individual crisis intervention. First, the approach is more cost-effective since many clients receive service simultaneously. Second, support groups need not be led by a highly trained professional. Typically, the group leader suggests topics for discussion, facilitates interaction, and only occasionally provides expert guidance. (Chapter 5 describes the circumstances requiring certain technical knowledge and skills of the support group leader.) Leaders can be selected from a pool of veterans of past groups, they can be informal caregivers in the community, or they can be recruited from the ranks of agency volunteers and non-professional staff. Third, the group offers unique supportive provisions because of its composition and processes. The very fact that people make contact with peers who are experiencing similar emotional upheavals in response to similar environmental events is reassuring. It signifies to them that they have not been "singled out" due to some extraordinary personal failing but that many people in different stages and walks of life have experienced the stressful event and its attendant emotional reactions. Through the process of social comparison, people see and hear about the many changes wrought by the event, and they can compare notes about strategies of coping that have proved more and less effective. Equally, participants learn that there are various means of coming to terms with the event's personal consequences, and the group's collective experience teaches participants about how much change in their feelings they can expect over given periods of time. They also learn about how they can best deal with other people's reactions to their plight. Further, when the groups are composed of persons at various stages in the process of adapting to the same difficulty, they bear witness to the healing effects of time and sustained adjustment efforts. Besides its normalizing, supportive, and modeling functions, the group experience also provides a "psychological sense of community" (Sarason, 1974) that cannot be obtained from traditional, individual crisis intervention. The group experience counteracts feelings of loneliness and uniqueness that compound the stress of life events by offering the company of peers who "feel with" one another.

Involvement in support groups also accomplishes broader social purposes. A chief virtue is that such groups do not transfer the responsibility for effecting change to a professional or an institution. The power of the support group rests in the collective hands of the participants who have the experiential knowledge, not the expert technology, upon which to ground their helping exchanges (Borkman, 1976). In fact, when initiating support groups, professionals can be most effective by encouraging the empowering elements of the group process. They can do this by applauding concrete changes of participants resulting from the group's suggestions, by reinforcing members' sense of personal efficacy, by encouraging them to sponsor new group members, and by suggesting ways of publicizing their groups' work in the community and among other health service providers. In some cases, group members may also become involved in advocacy efforts to bring about changes in institutional policies and programs affecting the development and course of their difficulties. Thus forcibly retired employees of a corporation who have formed their own support groups can become involved in planning more effective preretirement programs. Parents who have first met while visiting their premature infants in the hospital nursery can approach the hospital administration, describe the sense of relief they gained from their informal exchanges, and petition for changes in hospital procedures that might give greater heed to the parents' needs for contact with one another and their infants at this stressful time.

A second social purpose that can be served through participation in support groups is the gradual assimilation of group members in one another's ongoing social networks and/or the inculcation of support group norms in these networks. On the latter score, a long-term outcome of participation in support groups may be to increase the frequency of mutual-aid activities in people's everyday lives. That is, the group experience may orient people toward taking more active roles in other spheres of their lives and toward forming other sorts of helping alliances with similar peers in their neighborhoods and work-places. It may prompt people to make greater use of the helping resources that currently exist in their networks and to enter new settings where they are likely to find people who share their interests and needs. On a social-psychological level, participation in support groups may bring about an increase in self-esteem, may condition stronger beliefs in the use of other self-care health practices, and may give members a greater sense of personal control over their emotional well-being. Furthermore, as I have noted, the integration of group members within one another's ongoing social networks increases the group's impact, its support extending to activities and decisions out-side the group. For example, a widow whose support group suggests that she enroll in an evening class at the local college is more likely to act on this idea if a group member accompanies her to registration or joins the class, too, than if such support is not available. Similarly, in the presence of a comember of her support group, an unmarried teenage mother might be strengthened in her determination not to leave her baby sleeping at home to go to a party. These sorts of generalizing effects of support groups give them their greatest advan-tage over the encapsulated helping context that characterizes profes-sional crisis intervention.

## Professionally Initiated Support Groups

I would briefly like to present three examples of preventive inter-ventions involving the establishment of support groups among the widowed, new parents, and the parents of premature infants. I have selected these examples primarily because they offer a general model of support group intervention during life transitions and because they spotlight the role that the professional can assume in creating the groups and monitoring their progress. In addition, rigorous methods have been used to evaluate the effects of these interventions on the participants' mental health and social functioning. These interven-tions are also of heuristic value since they point to several unresolved issues about the nature of the support generated in the groups and the personal characteristics of those who benefit from participation. A secondary reason for selecting these programs is that they reflect diverse settings and auspices under which community mental health workers can initiate support groups.

## SUPPORT FOR THE BEREAVED

During the past decade, programs for the bereaved have been developed by community mental health centers, religious institutions, and family service agencies, and frequently they have used the support group format. This is partly because they have been influenced by Phyllis Silverman's (1976) well-publicized Widow-to-Widow program, and partly because they have recognized that the bereaved not only need temporary outside assistance in coping with acute emotional reactions to loss, but also need to develop new peer ties that can provide continuing support in the community.

The following action-research program was implemented by a team of public health nurses and social psychiatrists working in the social and community psychiatry section of a large mental health treatment and research institute (Vachon, Lyall, Rogers, Freedman-Letofsky, & Freeman, 1980). The team established collaborative relationships with 7 area hospitals, each hospital agreeing to send letters introducing the project to women whose husbands had died there one month earlier. By following up the letters with phone calls inviting their participation in the project, the program planners were able to enlist 162 widows, achieving an 88 percent consent rate. The final sample was composed of middle-class housewives who were widowed at a relatively young age ($\overline{X} = 52$ years), more than half of whom continued to live with someone else following their spouse's deaths. For the most part their spouse's deaths were not sudden or unexpected; their final illnesses lasted for about 6 months.

Because the authors were interested in understanding changes over time in postbereavement adaptation and the effects of support group involvement on the process of adjustment, all the participants were interviewed initially, and about two-thirds were interviewed again 6, 12, and 24 months following their spouses' death. Although some respondents were lost to follow-up and 7 of the 68 women who were randomly selected to enter the support groups refused to join, sufficient numbers were available for a meaningful statistical comparison between the experimental and control groups. The former initially received intervention on a one-to-one basis from a widow who had successfully resolved her own bereavement and who had participated in a seminar that touched on aspects of supportive counseling, community resources serving the recently widowed, and general problems of bereavement; later, they participated in small support groups. The one-to-one contacts consisted of "practical help in locating community resources, supportive telephone calls, and face-to-face interviews" (Vachon et al., 1980, p. 1382). Regrettably, the authors provide no details about the frequency or content of the support group sessions, and therefore their analyses of the program's effects ignore differences in levels of exposure to individual and group support. Similarly, they did not closely monitor the frequency and nature of the control group's access to supportive contacts in the community, nor did they conceive of the interviews themselves as instances of supportive intervention.

The Goldberg General Health Questionnaire (Goldberg, 1972) was used to monitor postbereavement adjustment and cutoff scores were developed to designate those experiencing low distress and those highly distressed. In addition, a questionnaire designed to tap extraneous factors potentially influencing the women's adaptation included information about other sources of social support in their lives, other past and current stressors to which they were exposed, and additional demographic and psychological variables.

The effects of the intervention on the course of postbereavement adjustment were analyzed in terms of their successive impact in hastening the widows' psychological and interpersonal adaptation. By analyzing the questionnaire items that most strongly distinguished the treatment and control groups at 6, 12, and 24 months, the authors discovered that those who received individual and small group support first achieved a greater measure of emotional integration and subsequently achieved a higher level of social integration. That is, at 6 months they showed a pattern of more rapid movement than the control group toward emotional equilibrium (less depressive symptomatology and preoccupation with the past), and at 12 months they achieved a greater degree of social reintegration (making new friends and engaging in new activities). Furthermore, by 24 months this accelerated pattern of adaptation cumulatively resulted in lower symptom scores on the General Health Questionnaire. In short, the authors conclude that those who were the beneficiaries of the supportive intervention moved more quickly along a "pathway of adaptation" following bereavement. The additional support they received spurred the adaptive process, thus achieving its intended secondary preventive objective.

As an aside, it is noteworthy that the women who were most distressed at the outset of the study benefited most from the intervention and that those women among this group who initially had a relatively large number of "people to count on" (for support) in their own social networks were at the greatest health advantage by 24 months. Conversely, those highly distressed women who did not have many natural sources of support and who were assigned to the control group fared worst at the time of final follow-up. These findings echo the results of studies reviewed in Chapter 2 that confirm the stress-moderating effects of social support.

## SUPPORT FOR THE TRANSITION TO PARENTHOOD

A second illustration of the use of support groups to foster a smoother life transition is drawn from an action-research study I undertook in collaboration with a colleague (McGuire & Gottlieb, 1979) and two family physicians. The idea of creating these groups evolved from discussions about the need of new parents for some form of psychoeducational support that would build their confidence in their parenting skills, increase their knowledge of normal infant development, and allow them to assume their parenting role with less anxiety. The physicians' secondary objective was to reduce the frequency with which these young couples called on them for help with infant-related problems that reflected the parents' lack of experience with infant behavior, rather than a serious medical need. The physicians felt that parent education would stem the tide of calls and visits they received from new parents who presented problems of a self-limiting nature or problems that could be addressed through appropriate self-care methods. My colleague and I took this opportunity to explore the usefulness of support groups in moderating the parents' anxieties and in providing them with both expert and experience-based standards for their own and their infants' behavior. In addition, we used this occasion to assess whether involvement in support groups would stimulate the parents to turn to *members of their own social networks* for parenting support. That is, the long-run preventive objective of the support groups was to encourage the participants to increase their use of appropriate informal helping resources in the natural environment, while, in the short run, the group experience might moderate the anxieties surrounding the couples' transition to parenthood. Since the physicians accepted these health and social objectives and were willing to participate in an experimental design requiring them to convene support groups among randomly selected new parent couples in their practice, we proceeded to develop suitable measures to document the program's effects.

A 10-page questionnaire was mailed to the homes of the 24 couples who participated in the study. It contained measures tapping 9 aspects of the couples' use of and satisfaction with the ongoing support available to them as parents. At posttest time, we instructed the parents who had been assigned to the support groups not to include any of the group members when providing this information because we were interested in the extent to which their group experience caused them to make more use of their natural social networks. Our health status measures delved into both negative and positive emotions. Ten items probed feelings of strain in different domains of parenting, and three items tapped global, subjective feelings of well-being. We also included a validated measure of physical health that had proved useful in past survey research, and nine social comparison questions asking how certain the parents were about where they personally stood, relative to other parents, on different emotional and behavioral aspects of infant rearing. The sum of these items was used as an index of the program's success in providing a broader, more accurate perspective on parenting standards.

The support groups were convened by each of the two physicians and their respective wives and met six times biweekly in the physicians' own homes. The physicians did not assume group leadership roles, nor did they lecture to the groups or analyze their process. Instead, they told the participants that the group's purpose was to encourage the sharing of experiences concerning parenting and that, accordingly, their own needs and interests should dictate the topics of discussion. Short readings on various parenting and infant development issues were provided to both the group participants and the twelve control couples. Although the couples had been randomly assigned to the support group and comparison conditions, several initial differences in their pretest scores were found, thus requiring their statistical control through the use of covariance analysis. In community studies it is virtually impossible to achieve random assignment without substitution because people may not wish to join a support group or cannot work it into their schedule.

The results of the intervention were mixed. On the one hand, there were no significant differences between the groups on the social comparison and health measures. Couples in the support groups were no more confident than those who had only received educational materials about their relative standing as parents, and they were no better off in terms of their levels of stress and their sense of well-being. More accurately, if they were any better off we would not have known it since, at pretest, the entire sample did not show much anxiety. Therefore, there was very little room for improvement on the measures we used, a point I will return to later in my summary of the difficulties involved in evaluating the effects of support group interventions in the general population. The changes that did occur among the support group couples involved the intervention's social consequences. Five weeks after the last group session, group members discussed child-rearing matters with people in their own social networks more frequently than did control couples, and participants in one of the groups also enlarged the range of network members with whom they discussed general child-rearing matters. Beyond these statistically significant differences between the treatment and comparison groups, there was a marked trend among the former toward increasing the number of people with whom they could comfortably discuss specific parenting concerns. In light of these findings we speculated that the group members

> . . . became aware of a greater number of child-rearing matters as a result of the group discussions and were prompted to seek out support for their own networks as a result of the value they attached to the support they had received in the group sessions. In short, it is likely that their group experience in the use of informal social support generalized to the natural networks in which they participated [McGuire & Gottlieb, 1979, p. 115].

### SUPPORT FOR THE PARENTS OF PREMATURE INFANTS

An excellent illustration of the development of support groups as an adjunct to professional treatment is provided by Minde, Shosenberg, Marton, Thompson, Ripley, and Burns (1980), who incorporated such groups as one component of services to the parents of premature infants. The authors, who were affiliated with a premature nursery of a large children's hospital, recognized that the parents of these high-risk infants typically experienced acute feelings of sadness, fear, guilt, and a sense of being left on their own to deal with these feelings. Further, they observed that these feelings, in turn, interfered with both the parents' ability to learn about the medical routines practiced in the nursery and their enjoyment of their infants. Accordingly, they mounted an experimental study to evaluate the impact of support groups on the parents' attitudes toward hospital personnel and practices, their own parenting competence, their frequency of visiting the nursery, and, most important, the actual quality of the interactions between mother and infant in the nursery. The last entailed observational study of twelve infants and ten caretaker behaviors that were deemed important indicators of sound maternal and infant development. The infant observations were conducted twice each week in the nursery continuously over a forty-minute period, while the parent-child interactions were observed during visits in the nursery and in the home at three monthly intervals following discharge. Earlier studies by Minde and his associates had confirmed the validity and reliability of the observational system that was used.

The 16 couples who were randomly assigned to 5 support groups met for a period of 1½ to 2 hours on a weekly basis for 7 to 12 weeks. The groups were also attended by a nurse counselor, who was a member of the hospital staff, and a "veteran mother," who had also had a premature infant in the nursery during the preceding 12 to 15 months and who was chosen because of her personal sensitivity and integrity. Her role was to stimulate discussion about both the emotional and technical demands accompanying the birth and care of a premature infant and to help arrange presentations by resource people and other educational input. The nurse counselor also met frequently on a private basis with individual couples, thus adding another dimension to the support they received.

The results showed that mothers who had attended the support groups averaged 5.2 visits per week to their newborns, in comparison to 2.7 weekly visits for the control mothers. Upon discharge they also expressed more favorable attitudes toward their ability to care for their infants at home, had a greater understanding of their babies' condition, and had engaged in more interaction with other parents. Group differences in infant and maternal behaviors over the course of the intervention are most impressive of all. Mothers who were in the support groups touched their babies more, looked at their faces more frequently, and spoke to them more often than did those who were assigned to the control condition. Each of these increments was observed at different points over a 5-week period after the infant's birth, and although they do not provide conclusive evidence of the supportive intervention's impact, they reflect a positive and gradual

trend among support group members toward greater maternal involvement with their infants. The promise of this intervention format
lies in its potential long-term effects on maternal and child development among this population. Minde et al. (1980, p. 938) comment on
this primary preventive consequence:

> If . . . there exists a "critical period" during which contact between
> the mother and her infant has implications for their later relation-
> ships, such group meetings may indeed be highly relevant for the
> later development of these children. Data from other studies
> suggest that the number of visits alone are predictive of some later
> maternal interactive behavior and that mothers who visit frequently
> have infants who have superior speech development two years later.

## Summary: Some Issues Warranting Greater Attention

Each of the preceding experimental programs systematically
examined the extent to which the social comparison processes of the
support groups moderated the particpants' stress. Each developed a
temporary supportive milieu in which persons similarly exposed to a
life stressor or transition could ventilate their emotions, gain a better
understanding of their new personal situation, and exchange ideas
about means of coping. The interventions were delivered soon after
the stressful event, thus constituting a form of secondary prevention.
They gauged both the psychological and social outcomes of the
support groups over a time span ranging from about four months in the
new parents study to two years in the bereavement study. Finally,
although professionals created each of the support group programs,
they did not assume leadership roles in the groups themselves. At
most, they provided expert information about the nature of the life
event or transition or about services provided by other community
agencies.

The unique features of the programs' designs and objectives are
also noteworthy. In regard to objectives, the project involving new
parents aimed to spread the effect of the group lessons about the
usefulness of informal support to the participants' everyday lives.
Powell (1979) similarly used the support group approach to enhance
parent-child interaction and to strengthen the network ties among a
sample of low-income neighborhood residents. Minde et al. (1980)
looked at whether the tension-alleviating function of their support
groups improved maternal caretaking behaviors. Vachon et al. (1980)

also assessed the widows' social reintegration, not just the number of symptoms or levels of distress they experienced. The programs' designs differed strongly in the sources and extent of exposure to social support. The parents of premature infants and the widows both received individual support (a nurse counselor and a resourceful widow, respectively) in addition to group sessions. Unfortunately, Vachon et al. (1980) do not report the number of individual or group sessions their widows attended. The new parents attended six group meetings and the parents of the premature infants attended seven to twelve sessions.

While these three programs offer a general model for the development of support group interventions, they leave unanswered important questions about the supportive conditions necessary to produce a reduction in levels of distress. What is the optimal intensity and duration of support? What are the group dynamics that facilitate the process of social comparison? Who are the most appropriate candidates for this type of intervention? On the latter score, both Vachon et al. (1980) and Minde et al. (1980) note that their lowest social class participants tended to be the dropouts and the low attenders. Referring to this segment of their sample, Minde et al. (1980, p. 936) report that "parents who showed the highest degree of overt psychological and social pathology (i.e., had a husband in jail, were physically mistreated and showed symptoms of a major psychiatric disorder) had the lowest attendance. In three cases they attended their first group meeting only after they had four to six individual sessions with the group coordinator." Vachon et al. (1980, p. 1381) report that the widows who were lost to follow-up "were of a lower social class, seemed to have more psychological problems and fewer social supports than the women who stayed in the study."

These findings are consonant with other reports on the low service utilization patterns of the poor (McKinlay, 1972) and on the difficulty of involving low-income clients in preventive parent education programs (Birkel & Reppucci, 1981; Chilman, 1973). Numerous hypotheses have been advanced to account for this low pattern of service use, ranging from those that blame the intended service beneficiaries to those that indict the delivery system. Within the context of the support group approaches I have described, the low-income participants may feel that they are disadvantaged in group discussion skills, a hypothesis that reiterates the potential relationship between social competence and access to social support. They may prefer to deny the emotional aspects of the stressful experience or to postpone dealing with these feelings. They may believe that the experience is fateful and turn for help to religious institutions or to people in their own social milieu who share their beliefs. On the other hand, various modifications in the program's design may increase the level of participation. Perhaps the support groups should be composed along more demographically homogeneous lines, or perhaps they should include more structured activities that encourage emotional ventilation and incorporate specific guidelines for coping, much like the Twelve Steps to Sobriety that govern the meetings of Alcoholics Anonymous. In fact, professionals who establish support groups are well advised to read about and, when permitted, to attend the meetings of self-help groups, since they offer a variety of program formats that have broad appeal (Gartner & Reissman, 1977).

A corollary question prompted by these three examples is that of who benefits most and who least from the support group methods of intervention. Vachon et al. (1980) note that their program had the greatest impact on the widows who, at one month following their husbands' deaths, had GHQ scores of five or more, signifying high levels of distress. They also note that those women in this group who had more informal sources of support on whom they could rely had significantly lower GHQ scores at 24 months. Thus, rather than extending support groups to all those persons undergoing stressful life events and transitions, it may be feasible to develop a screening procedure that identifies those who are greatest risk of maladjustment, concentrating on ways of involving them in support groups. Such a screening instrument should incorporate both measures of psychological functioning and measures of available social resources and their adequacy. And when screening shows that certain individuals have an impoverished social field, extra information should be gathered about why this is so. Is the individual so disordered as to have alienated others? Does the individual have poor social skills? Is this person shy, or uninterested in maintaining a network of friends? The answers to these sorts of questions can inform decisions about whether a support group intervention is appropriate immediately, or after a period of one-to-one counseling, or if it should be ruled out altogether. Furthermore, these sorts of questions can also yield knowledge about whether the support group sessions ought to aim specifically at enlarging participants' access to informal sources of support in the natural environment. That is, among those candidates for support groups with meager social resources in the community, special efforts can be made to extend the group's support beyond the formal sessions. Members can be paired on a rotating basis and assigned certain exercises to complete together between meetings, the meetings themselves can be held in members' homes or workplaces, and the group can be encouraged to continue independently after a period of time and even to reach out to new members. In short, decisions should be made not only about whether people's personalities, social skills, and coping styles suit them to support group interventions, but also about whether those who are involved in such groups require temporary or continuing access to their new peer ties. Barrett's (1978) study details the amount of contact that widows initiated with coparticipants of informal support groups fourteen weeks after their formal group meeting. Her data revealed high rates of contact among individual group members and continued group meetings for four of the six groups. She argues that this high level of spontaneous contact contributed to the maintenance of the widows' treatment gains.

One final observation about the candidates for support group intervention bears spotlighting. Virtually all published reports of support groups that focus on life transitions reveal that men are conspicuously absent. (This is not the case when the group members share a medical illness or condition; see Chapter 5.) Aside from invoking sex-role stereotypes to account for this absence, the literature offers no leads. Surely there are life events that men undergo, such as retirement, bereavement, job loss, and job relocation, that might be usefully addressed by the support group method. In fact, the obvious site for the development of such groups is in the workplace, and, if situated in that context and introduced as a routine component of a company's in-house assistance program, they may prove more acceptable. In the meantime, however, there is no information on record regarding the type of format, the kinds of supportive inputs, or the effectiveness of support groups designed primarily for men.

Although my examples illustrate the role that support groups can play in the secondary prevention of psychopathology, they can also be used as a forum for anticipatory guidance, thus shifting their emphasis to primary prevention. Prenatal classes have been organized by public health departments for this purpose. They prepare the mothers for the birth experience by teaching relaxation methods, instructing them in infant care, emphasizing proper dietary regimens during pregnancy, and mobilizing support by encouraging the spouse's attendance and forming discussion groups among the expectant couples. Another illustration from the medical field is the introduction of patient education sessions for those awaiting surgery and other fear-arousing medical procedures. Typically, these sessions are attended by a member of the medical staff and a patient who has already undergone the procedure and can tell new patients what will happen and what they might experience. However, here too there is evidence that some people benefit more and some less from such psychological preparation, and that prior assessment of coping styles such as denial or sensitization should be performed to determine the appropriate candidates for these groups.

Indeed, present knowledge of the relationship between personal coping styles and supportive interactions is sorely limited (Cohen, 1980). Schachter's (1959) work on the role of affiliation in diminishing emotional reactions to threatening situations revealed that, although the majority of people facing imminent stressors express a preference for being with others who are "in the same boat," a significant minority prefer to cope alone. Moreover, Epley's (1974) review of the literature on the effects of the presence of companions in moderating behavioral reactions to actual or imminent aversive stimuli led him to conclude that calming effects are produced under either of two conditions: when imitation of calm companions occurs or when companions interfere with excessive arousal in the face of aversive stimuli. The former conclusion implies that support groups may be more effective in tension reduction if they include people who have already successfully managed a stressful life event or transition. Again, self-help groups are instructive since they are often led by a "veteran sufferer" who serves as a model of successful coping.

Support groups for anticipatory guidance can be offered when there is advance knowledge that people will face life transitions. Messinger, Walker, and Freeman (1978) organized groups for couples contemplating or already involved in remarriages. Some industries and unions have developed brief seminars for employees who face imminent retirement, job relocation, or temporary layoffs. High school guidance workers have developed groups for seniors who are facing the transition to college and full-time employment, and agencies and religious institutions involved in international missions typically hold preparatory workshops to acclimate workers to the culture of their host countries. Other foci for the creation of support groups with an anticipatory coping emphasis include groups for women preparing to resume full-time work or studies after prolonged absences, for children who will soon be part of a reconstituted family, for relatives of patients with terminal illnesses, and for families that take in dependent elderly parents to avoid institutionalizing them.

## NETWORK-CENTERED INTERVENTIONS

A second class of preventive interventions involving the optimization of social support has a broader community focus. It aims to restructure people's networks or to improve their helping processes so as to enlarge their access to social support. These support development activities, having a primary preventive focus, are not aimed at people with impaired ability to cope with specific stressors, nor are they timed to coincide with imminent or actual exposure to stressors. They are predicated on the proposition that social support generally enhances functioning and morale, and, in particular, it increases people's abilities to deal with adversity. Thus only the most general social risk factors govern decisions about where or to whom to extend these support development activities, namely, in settings where people tend to be socially isolated or marginal, and among populations whose social networks are resource deficient or structurally too weak to provide adequate access to support.

Support development activities are grounded in research on people's everyday help-seeking behavior and in studies that have identified the factors underlying a high quality of life. Numerous surveys have shown that people deal with periods of unhappiness and unexpected reversals in their lives by initially talking with family members and friends from work and the neighborhood, and by engaging long-known and trusted community figures such as family doctors, members of the clergy, and other indigenous caregivers (Eddy, Papp, & Glad, 1970; Gurin, Veroff, & Feld, 1960; Ryan, 1969). Furthermore, when people are asked about the aspects of their lives that contribute most to their sense of well-being, or when they describe the conditions that would make for an ideal life, they inevitably rank primary group relations high on the list (Campbell, 1981). Moos's (1974) research on the dimensions that underlie people's perceptions of their work, family, and residential environments has amply documented the fact that the quality of life in these contexts is perceived in large measure as a function of the support and interpersonal cohesion that they offer. Similarly, when Blake, Weigl, and Perloff (1975) asked a large stratified sample of Indiana residents about their orientations to the ideal residential community, they placed proximity to family members and friends among their primary desiderata. Collectively, these empirical studies provide strong grounds for initiatives to embed people in primary group networks that optimize their access to and use of informal supportive resources.

As I have noted, support development activities are best conceived of as primary prevention, their fundamental aim being to strengthen the capacity of social networks to provide ongoing and crisis support in advance of any stressors. The dual means of accomplishing this end are: (a) educating people, usually through focused training procedures, in certain skills that will improve their capacity to resist stress and to adapt flexibly to environmental challenges; and (b) altering aspects of the environment that create stress or that inhibit people's ability to withstand present and future stressors. Thus support development interventions can take the following forms:

- training activities that enhance the support extended by those people in the community who are not mental health professionals but who nevertheless are involved in a great deal of informal counseling and referral work

- training activities that reinforce and enlarge the repertoire of interpersonal helping skills in ongoing social networks

- educational activities that increase people's awareness of structural factors affecting their access to social support and that prompt structural changes to improve their access to supportive resources

- lobbying and organizing activities that aim to prevent events from occurring or policies from taking effect that threaten to destroy or weaken existing informal support systems

- educational and advocacy activities that are specifically aimed at preserving the informal support networks of certain vulnerable populations such as the elderly and the mentally ill

In what follows, I elaborate on each of these types of support development and preservation activities, and I review recent work that illustrates each approach.

## Caregiver-Centered
## Support Development Activities

One set of support development activities is directly based on the recognition that people rely heavily on family members, friends, and community caregivers for ongoing and crisis support. Given this reality, efforts have been made to examine more closely the nature of the help that is extended and then to improve it or at least to buttress these informal help-giving processes and roles. These efforts fall into two categories: interventions to improve the helping functions and the reach of informal community caregivers, and interventions directed toward the same goal but targeted at the existing social networks in a particular geographical area.

Cowen's (1982) recent work with four groups of informal community caregivers is an excellent example of the first category of approaches. He and his colleagues used both interviews and surveys to obtain an in-depth understanding of the informal support and help extended by hairdressers, bartenders, divorce lawyers, and foremen in Rochester, New York. Data were collected about the numbers of clients who talked to these caregivers about their personal problems, the types of problems typically addressed, the strategies used to deal with these problems, and the caregivers' perceptions of their own effectiveness in providing help. Cowen also inquired about the respondents' attitudes toward this aspect of their work roles and about their needs for additional guidance in fulfilling it. His data both confirm earlier survey findings about the magnitude of the "caseloads" of community caregivers and extend our understanding of their helping activities.

First, each group of caregivers reported that in the normal course of their work, a significant proportion of their clientele voiced moderate to serious personal problems. As a group, lawyers were most extensively involved with the psychosocial needs of their clients, a finding that is not surprising given the emotional concomitants of the divorce process. Hairdressers were next, reporting that about one-third of their clients raised personal problems, while bartenders and foremen reported that 16 percent and 17 percent of their clients, respectively, disclosed their problems. On the whole, the kinds of problems they fielded did not differ much from those typically brought to mental health specialists, although each caregiver group heard more about some types of problems than others. For example, divorce lawyers dealt more frequently with marital conflicts and feelings of depression among clients; bartenders heard more about marital, job, and financial difficulties; hairdressers typically fielded problems concerning children, health, marriage, and depressed and anxious feelings; and foremen usually dealt with such job-related problems as tensions among coworkers, job dissatisfaction, and poor job mobility. The groups also differed in the ways they typically responded to their clients' problems. The hairdressers and bartenders relied extensively on responses that expressed sympathy, a "light-hearted" attitude to the difficulty, and interest communicated just by listening, while the divorce attorneys engaged in more active responses, such as asking questions, providing advice, and pointing out the implications of their clients' ideas. All four groups felt that their help was "moderately effective." The hairdressers expressed more interest in receiving mental health consultation than the bartenders and more of them actually participated when such a program was later offered to them. As Cowen hints, hairdressers may be more receptive to improving their help giving because they sense that clients take this into consideration when they choose hairdressers. It may be good for business to learn more about interpersonal helping.

Cowen's group has followed up these assessment activities with two intervention programs to improve the support that hairdressers and divorce attorneys extend to their clients. The first was mounted by Weisenfeld and Weis (1979), consisting of a ten-week group consultation and training program that concentrated on teaching several core helping skills, provided information about other general aspects of interpersonal helping, and addressed specific problems that clients had raised. Pre- and posttests were used to assess changes in the participants' dominant helping strategies compared with those of a control group. The results showed that they markedly increased their use of one recommended helping response — "reflecting feelings" — and decreased the frequency with which they offered specific advice. Doane (1977) implemented a support development program along similar lines among family practice attorneys.

Although Cowen and his colleagues' work with these community caregivers bears some resemblance to consultee-centered consultation, particularly in its emphasis on helping the caregivers to identify ways of responding more effectively to the psychosocial needs of their clients/customers as a group, their approach and their stance toward these caregivers is distinctive. First, they recognize that they have no special expertise in determining the kinds of help that should be extended to these caregivers' clients. They realize that they must balance their zeal to upgrade the helping strategies of the caregivers with an appreciation both of the latter's natural instincts about how best to help and with their clients' or customers' expectations about the kind of help these caregivers provide. Cowen (1982, p. 16) signals his recognition that professionals may be unduly skeptical of the helping activities performed by lay caregivers when he states: "Just *talking* about helping techniques that laypersons use is 'fightin' words' for many mental health professionals. That's seen as *their* private turf, where they alone, have: a) special knowledge and wisdom, and b) the right to judge the appropriateness of the words and deeds of anyone who has the temerity to put on interpersonal helping vestments. In that sphere, professionals are trigger-quick to identify foul-ups by aliens."

Second, Cowen's group scrupulously avoided teaching these caregivers about such technical matters as the nature of mental illness, the early warning signs of disorders, diagnostic procedures and nomenclatures, and specialized techniques of therapeutic intervention. In fact, their stance eschews all forms of education that risk lowering the caregivers' tolerance of departures from "normal" functioning or that might condition the caregivers' view of themselves as apprentice psychiatrists. Instead, they have tried first to gain a better appreciation of the actual helping behaviors used by the caregivers and, second, to supplement these practices with generic helping skills that are at the core of most human relations training programs. Third, they have attempted to establish a coordinate, equal-status relationship with the caregivers. They are not supervisors, overseeing the caregivers' progress in effecting client change, nor do they attempt to establish a referral relationship between the caregivers and the formal network of community services. Their purpose is to shore up and optimize the help-giving activities of these caregivers and thereby to buttress this sector of the community's informal helping resources.

## The Physician's Role in Fielding Psychosocial Problems

There are, of course, other opportunities for reinforcing and extending the help-giving activities of informal caregivers. Physicians in general practices are prime candidates since they, too, are approached early in people's help-seeking efforts. Furthermore, they are confronted with an inordinately large share of psychosocial problems presented by their patients in terms of "nervous conditions," psychosomatic disorders, and drug-related difficulties. The family physician is often the first resort for people who do not know or fully understand what mental health professionals do or for people who, knowing these things, wish to avoid the stigma that surrounds the mental health delivery system. In addition, because many third-party payment plans still reimburse only the services of medical practitioners, and because access to psychiatrists often requires prior screening and referral by the family physician, the general practitioner is in a position to perform critical early intervention functions and has a good deal of control over the pipeline that leads to specialized public and private psychiatric services. Unfortunately, scant information exists about the kinds of psychological help that general practitioners extend to their patients, the kinds of psychological problems they are willing and able to address, and the effects of their helping and referral practices. Moreover, we know very little about their attitudes toward this aspect of their work or their willingness to examine it more closely and develop their skills in handling the psychosocial dimension of their patients' lives.

What evidence there is regarding the physician's attentiveness to patients' psychosocial problems suggests that they are not responsive. For example, Harrison (1979) examined the extent to which six residents in a Family Medicine Practice program probed for psychosocial problems in an initial diagnostic interview with patients. Before their examinations, the patients completed a life events inventory. Their interviews with the physicians were then videotaped and coded to determine whether the physicians probed for their psychosocial problems or led their patients to disclose them. Harrison found that none of the physicians detected his or her patients' financial worries even though 75 percent had indicated experiencing this type of problem, that only 9 percent of the physicians probed for the marital problems that 52 percent of the patients were experiencing, and that the physicians probed for "nervousness" in only 18 percent of the interviews, whereas 66 percent of the patients had indicated experiencing such feelings. These findings led Harrison (1979, p. 83) to conclude: "Despite individual differences, physicians are much more likely to collect factual information than they are to explore the feelings and meanings patients have about problems." Perhaps urban practitioners who are surrounded by an abundance of psychiatric services have stronger referral relationships with mental health specialists than those in rural communities, and therefore would be less motivated to participate in programs that develop their help-giving skills. Indeed, they may feel pressure from their specialist colleagues to stay within their own sphere of functioning. Yet, from the patients' point of view, it is not so much the type of problem that dictates their preference for the counsel offered by their family physician, but their trust in an individual whom they already know and respect and who knows them and their families. Thus it is not surprising that so many patients who are referred to mental health specialists by their family physicians do not act on the referral but resort to other informal helping resources in the community.

Medical training and guild politics are likely to complicate educational programs that alert physicians to the psychosocial aspects of medical care and encourage them to consider how they personally can deal more effectively with those emotional problems that do not require expert help. The fact that medical students receive so little instruction in patient counseling skills, coupled with the virtual absence of planned mechanisms for providing them with peer support during their medical training, conditions a disregard for informal help giving. Moreover, medical students who are rewarded for their competitive achievement strivings, their self-sufficiency, and their ability to steel themselves in the face of the stressful demands imposed by professors, patients, and their own sometimes flagging morale are likely to internalize these qualities, and they will dominate their subsequent professional careers. Once in practice, physicians enter high-pressure environments characterized by work overload and have little time to consider how to develop more effective patient-centered human relations skills, much less to develop meaningful workplace supports to sustain their own morale.

Efforts to enlarge and optimize the socioemotional dimension of medical care are unlikely to succeed until fundamental changes are made in the content and process of the training of medical students, in the nature of the relationship between the psychiatric specialists and their nonpsychiatric colleagues, and in the very organization and economics of Western medical practice. Mental health practitioners are unlikely to be interested or effective in making any of these changes, although they can add their voices to those of other citizens who advocate a less impersonal and fleeting relationship with their physicians, and a more coherent, personalized approach to their health. However, less ambitious initiatives of an educational nature may be taken by mental health workers. They can develop continuing education seminars and workshops that emphasize self-help and mutual aid approaches to combating stress in physicians' personal and professional lives. Ideally, the workshops should be led by persons who are familiar with the general practitioners' work context and who are able to help them to discriminate between those problems calling for referral to experts and those that they can address directly. The workshops should also teach stress management techniques that general practitioners can apply to their own lives and impart to their patients. Through role playing and other experiential exercises, physicians can also practice interpersonal skills to enhance their family and work relations.

Continuing education programs can also be organized around such themes as "building patient rapport" and "enhancing patient interviewing skills." That is, physicians may be more interested in programs that specifically teach communication skills to improve the affective component of their daily interactions with patients than in programs that develop generic counseling skills divorced from their medical work. The program's content should highlight discrete physician behaviors that constitute good rapport, such as the verbal expression of respect, empathy, and reassurance, and the nonverbal expression of understanding and caring. Video feedback techniques, such as those used by Kagan (1974), can be incorporated into the training workshop, while group discussion can be channeled toward an examination of ways of overcoming personal and professional barriers to closer rapport with patients.

Advertisements for these programs should highlight the empirical evidence linking physician rapport to such critical dependent variables as patient satisfaction, patient turnover, and the instigation of medical malpractice suits (DiMatteo, 1979). In addition, physicians may become more interested in attending to the psychosocial forces in their patients' networks once they learn that these forces have a major impact on their patients' adherence to the medical regimens they prescribe. Primary care physicians are eternally frustrated by patients' inability to control their health practices, for example, when dietary restrictions are ignored, when medication is prematurely terminated, or when exercise routines are not followed. Empirical studies of patient compliance show that about one-third fail to cooperate with doctors' orders (Davis, 1966). By first calling their attention to the role that the patient's social network plays in undermining or reinforcing compliance with their recommendations and then soliciting their ideas about ways of involving the patient's network in the treatment planning process, workshop leaders will give physicians a deeper appreciation of the interplay between the health of patients and the social ecology in which they participate.

Mental health workers can also take the lead in informing physicians about other lay helping resources that are available to their patients. In particular, they should know that there are mutual-help groups for patients with chronic disorders, such as multiple sclerosis, heart disease, arthritis, emphysema, and cancer (see Chapter 5), and for patients suffering from obesity, physical disabilities, sensory disorders, and those recuperating from various types of surgery (Gartner & Riessman, 1977). However, here again the means of informing physicians about these groups is just as important as the content. Physicians are deluged with information about new drugs, new treatments, and new equipment; simply providing them with a directory of self-help groups that serve the medically ill will not prompt them to refer patients. Instead member-representatives of mutual-help groups should follow the drug detailer's example, making the rounds of physicians' offices to provide explicit information about appropriate candidates for their groups, the groups' formats and helping processes, their links to professional advisers, and evidence of their benefits. In addition, since physicians depend a great deal on one another's recommendations before they try innovative practices (Katz & Lazarsfeld, 1955), their receptivity to collaborative relations with self-help groups would be enhanced by letters of recommendation and personal testimonials from respected physicians whose patients have profited from group participation, and who would be willing to discuss their perceptions of the group's work with other physicians. All of the preceding initiatives are intended in part to expand the interpersonal helping skills that physicians proffer to their patients, and in part to enlarge their orientation to the psychosocial dimensions of medical practice.

## Religious Institutions as Sources of Informal Support

Members of the clergy, whether they belong to mainstream religions or to distinct sects and other small factions united by common spiritual beliefs, also serve as emotional healers in the lives of many citizens. Some have received formal training in pastoral counseling, but the majority rely on their own instincts and a personal manner that soothes and sustains people in times of adversity. Moreover, the religious institutions of the community generally emphasize the primacy of family bonds, attempting to create a spirit of fellowship by encouraging people to meld their own lives with those of other members of the congregation. Thus they represent ideal sites from which to launch programs accentuating social support. For example, in Syracuse, New York, one church has established a model of support development for its parishioners that involves periodic meetings among clusters of families interested in exploring family values and dynamics, clarifying their relationship to the broader community, and developing their skills in rendering emotional support and tangible aid to one another and to their peers at work and school, and in their neighborhoods. At first, the groups meet in the church and are guided by their pastor, but later they gather in one another's homes and eventually become a self-sustaining mutual aid network that reaches out to other families, regardless of their religious affiliations. Similarly, in Minnesota, Roberts and Thorsheim's (1982) action-research project involves numerous Lutheran congregations in a small group process directed toward identifying the social conditions that place people at risk of alcoholism and drug abuse, and mobilizing social support to help them avoid and overcome drug dependency. Their project fosters a process of self-education about the nature and effects of supportive relationships, calls attention to the pattern of relationship dissolution that often precedes and is spurred by alcohol abuse, and invites initiatives that teams of church members can take to strengthen the support that can be extended to known and potential alcohol abusers. The church, very actively supporting family life, has established day-care programs for preschoolers, after-school programs that serve the needs of working couples, and a variety of social activities and support groups for specific age cohorts, such as adolescents, the elderly, and teenage mothers.

In rural areas, the church is a particularly critical site for developing support-enhancement activities, not because citizens in rural areas are more religious than urban residents, but because there are fewer formal and informal associations available to them, and because rural populations are generally not oriented toward the use of formal mental health services. Moreover, as Wagenfeld and Wagen-

feld (1981) have pointed out, rural residents do not see their problems
in mental health terms. They are reluctant to approach specialists and
strangers for help with their emotional difficulties, preferring instead
to call upon their kinship ties and their trust in fate and prayer as
sources of relief:

> Such people might reject the notion of mental illness as a category, or
> be suspicious of professionals, or the primacy of extended family
> ties might preclude going to outsiders for help, or there might be a
> preference for naturalistic or folk healing techniques. Even if they
> do get into treatment, their values are incompatible with the goals of
> psychotherapy and so they are likely to derive less benefit from
> treatment and to terminate earlier [Wagenfeld and Wagenfeld, 1981,
> p. 8].

It follows that in rural areas citizens are likely to be more receptive
to preventive initiatives that are syntonic with their "folk" explanations of mental health and illness and that capitalize on their strong
orientation to informal modes of dealing with personal problems. In
fact, these conclusions in part have spurred a number of innovative
support development programs among rural residents that focus on
expanding their informal helping resources and upgrading the quality
of help they extend. In what follows I describe two programs that
have concentrated their efforts on support development activities in
the ongoing networks or rural residents, thus shifting my emphasis
from caregiver-centered approaches to support development to
network-centered strategies. In addition, I present a more general
model of support optimization that is aimed at enhancing people's
awareness and utilization of supportive resources in their personal
networks.

## NETWORK-CENTERED SUPPORT DEVELOPMENT ACTIVITIES

Support development activities that are organized to improve and
enlarge the help-giving functions of community caregivers can have
an impact on those citizens who bring their problems to these helping
agents. But the larger informal helping domain consists of family
members, friends from work and the neighborhood, and acquaint-
ances met through the voluntary associations that people join for

recreation, education, and social action. Peers are the first to hear about the occurrence of adverse life events, either because they are actually present at the time or because a close friend or relative is sought out immediately. Similarly, when there is good news about the birth of a baby, college admission, job promotion, or a remission in illness, family members and friends are the first to be contacted. In short, people's immediate social networks composed of close peers with whom there is regular contact form the context in which matters of personal health and welfare are first appraised and broached. The structure and helping capabilities of this first-order network will therefore condition people's early responses to positive and negative life events. In particular, the social organization of this primary network and the socioemotional provisions it can offer will have a critical early impact on the course and consequences of people's adaptive strivings. In recognition of these facts, a number of primary preventive strategies have been devised to modify both the structure and helping processes of social networks. These strategies place a dual emphasis on educating people about how the structure of their personal community affects their access to diverse social resources and on training people in more proficient helping responses.

## The Support Development Workshop

Todd's (1980; Gottlieb & Todd, 1979) work on the creation of support development workshops offers a general model that can be adapted by community mental health workers for use with numerous citizen groups. Todd (in Gottlieb & Todd, 1979, p. 205) describes the basic elements of the workshop he implemented among freshmen college students as follows:

(1) an introduction to the topic of social support and the concept of social network as a systems view of relationships;

(2) an exercise in which participants represent their own social networks in the form of a map or matrix;

(3) an opportunity to discuss network patterns and social support with a group of peers; and

(4) techniques of retaining much of this information for research purposes.

The first stage of the workshop oriented the students to the many meanings that underlie the social support construct and encouraged them to consider the kinds and frequency of support they received and extended to others — support in the forms of intimate dialogue, companionship, tangible aid and concrete services, advice, and guidance. They used a network mapping procedure to identify the people of most relevance to their affective well-being, the connections among these people (their networks' density), and the extent to which relationships were encapsulated in a single sphere of their life, such as school, work, or their parental home, or integrated across life sectors. Discussion enabled the participants to gain insight into prior situational factors that had exerted an influence on these structural dimensions of their networks, such as the frequency of geographical moves, their involvement in extracurricular activities, and the size of the town and high school from which they came. In addition, by linking their preferences for certain sources and types of support to aspects of their personality, they began to recognize that important interdependencies existed between their habitual coping styles and others' aiding responses, and between their modulation of the intensity of relationships and their access to emotional support. In the following quotation, Todd (in Gottlieb & Todd, 1979, p. 209) describes what some students learned from examining the spatial configuration of their social fields:

> For example, simply looking at the full array of significant others and the closeness of these various relationships was a novel and informative experience to most participants. Mapping usually produced generalizations about the aggregate qualities of these relationships. Angela, for example, saw more clearly that her relationships were extensive, distant, and specialized and that she was lacking in intimate contacts. Other participants saw that they were closer to more people than they had realized, that they needed a great diversity of contacts, that certain people played unique roles in their lives, or that they had been neglecting important relationships.

Angela's analysis of the social field in which she participated led her to plan ways of developing a more integrated core network that would furnish more emotional support while also bringing more members of her network into meaningful relationships with one another. Other participants formulated different ideas about desirable network changes or alterations in their interactions with members of their social fields. Some planned to increase the reciprocity and diversity of helping exchanges in their relationships with roommates, some wished to extricate themselves from a network that was so tightly interconnected that it constrained their actions and choices, and others decided to join campus clubs in order to gain access to a more diverse peer network.

Todd (1980) views these network workshops as especially valuable preventive/developmental interventions when people face life transitions that entail changes in the structure of their social field. He maintains that successful psychosocial adaptation has as much to do with social-structural resources for coping as with personal coping resources and personality attributes. Thus, from his perspective, a comprehensive approach to primary prevention should give people a clearer understanding of the interplay between their social and personal resources so that they can make better use of both. In short, when people recognize that dispositional variables, social structural variables, and social processes are interdependent and exert a joint impact on the experience of social support, they can then optimize their access to social resources.

Support development workshops could be convened among other populations facing transitions to new settings and roles. Among college students, those arriving on a campus from foreign countries will certainly profit from an opportunity to examine ways of launching the process of network formation in a new culture that adheres to particular norms about helping and relationship development. Similarly, transfer students, adult learners, and married students with children will have special needs for developing supportive peer relationships. Beyond the campus, such workshops could be provided to employees who face relocation to branch offices and plants, to workers who have lost their jobs and have decided to move to other cities less adversely affected by downturns in the national economy, and to those who are about to retire or who have sustained work disabilities that necessitate withdrawal from the workplace. The early results of Hirsch's (1980) study of two cohorts of young women who were attempting to establish themselves gradually in activities outside the domestic sphere also remind us that marital dissolution, either through death or separation, is usually accompanied by profound changes in the structure of the parties' social fields. These events may deplete the resources available or, as Hirsch (1980) found, they may call attention to formerly weak relationships or neglected network zones that now represent important points of reference for forming new social identities. Furthermore, the children of divorcing couples will also sustain disruptions in their social networks, in part because they shared their parents' networks, and in part because new social ties are foisted upon them. They too can benefit from opportunities to consider how these changes in their social world have affected both their actual access to support and their psychological sense of support. In fact, their most immediate need will be to come to terms with the effects of their parents' divorce on their feelings and attitudes toward close interpersonal relationships. No doubt, this event challenges their assumptions about loyalty to others, the permanency of affection, and the dispensability of social attachments. At a structural level, divorce and its aftermath are bound to affect the size, interconnectedness, clustering, and geographic dispersion of the parents' and the childrens' social orbits.

## Strengthening Network Helping Processes

A second approach to network-based support development has recently been outlined by D'Augelli, Vallance, Danish, Young, and Gerdes (1981). Their Community Helpers Project, established in two rural areas of central Pennsylvania, was shaped by their recognition that the local inhabitants were not inclined to use formal mental health services to deal with emotional distress, turning instead to their own networks of kin and friendship ties. The project initially sought to establish a working relationship with people who participated actively in community life, not necessarily as members of established organizations and institutions, but as neighborhood helpers, informal caregivers, and ordinary citizens interested in developing their ability to reach out and help others. By identifying these people and enriching their current help-giving skills through a structured training program, the staff created a primary prevention program that was congruent with the help-seeking style of rural residents and capitalized on the area's existing prosocial resources. Once trained, those in the first generation of informal helpers were expected to return to their own social networks and pass on their new knowledge to other citizens. Thus the project hoped to achieve a radiating effect, multiplying the informal helping resources in the two locales. D'Augelli et al. (1981, p. 214-215) describe the ripple effect they anticipated as follows: "The spread of effect can occur on a time dimension as well. That is, since the local trainers are residing in the community, they provide a continuing resource over time. This longitudinal effect of primary prevention has not been studied, but it is certainly essential for a community-wide impact to occur. It seems unlikely that any primary prevention project not woven into the fabric of community life in some lasting way will endure."

The first cohort of trainees was recruited through public notices, announcements over the media, at church and civic meetings, and through the auspices of the project advisory boards that were established in each locale. It consisted of members of the clergy, hairdressers, housewives, merchants, and teachers, in addition to a sizable group of local human service workers, the latter being unintended beneficiaries of the training and therefore bypassed in subsequent recruitment efforts. Through a structured sequence of learning steps, the training sessions concentrated on basic helping, life development, and crisis-resolution skills. This approach relied extensively on behavioral practice of each skill, peer and trainer feedback, and graded progress toward specific performance criteria. The entire training curriculum involved approximately 46 hours, paced at 2-3 hours each week. Following training, pairs of trainees co-led small group training sessions for local citizens, while still maintaining a tie to the staff that originally trained them, sending them audiotaped recordings for feedback about their work in the community. Evaluation of the success of the Community Helpers Project has centered on both the acquisition of helping skills and their actual utilization in interpersonal help-giving transactions. While the former element of the evaluation was assessed by independent raters who judged the trainees' attainment of skill levels, for ethical reasons the latter was based on the self-reported use of these skills.

The Community Helpers Project differs from Todd's support development workshops by virtue of its emphasis on upgrading the helping skills of citizens and its reliance on a structured training format that had proved successful among human service workers (Danish, D'Augelli, & Brock, 1976). Todd's approach is much less directive in nature; it orients people to the significance of social support in their lives and encourages them to plan changes in the structure of their social worlds to better accommodate their preferences for and their access to particular types and sources of support. To this extent, Todd's workshops acknowledge that individuals differ in their supportive requirements, in their definitions of the nature of support, and in their conceptions of the ideal arrangement of their social orbits. D'Augelli et al.'s (1981) approach omits structural influences on people's access to support, choosing instead to teach rural residents how to improve their basic helping and development skills. They are able to identify specific goals for their participants *as a group,* measure the progress toward these goals, and determine how many rural residents are eventually touched by the helping activities of several generations of trainees.

Todd's and D'Augelli et al.'s approaches could be combined in future support development initiatives, and the intervention model itself could be translated into a series of structured learning modules that could then be disseminated to voluntary organizations, religious institutions, schools, and social agencies. A curriculum framed by a title such as "Building Support Networks" might prove especially attractive to a variety of organizations that are currently seeking efficient and acceptable means of smoothing people's passage through such transitions as geographic moves, retirement, job changes, and other life events involving social disruptions.

## Activities Intended to Preserve Existing Support Networks

Marc Fried (1963) has written a poignant account of the adverse effects of urban relocation on residents forced to leave a neighborhood to which they had been strongly attached. He describes various expressions of grief produced by the displacement, attributing them to the loss of spatial and social continuity in the residents' lives. His interviews with displaced citizens revealed that "another component, of equal importance, is the dependence of the sense of group identity on stable, social networks. Dislocation necessarily led to the fragmentation of this group identity which was based, to such a large extent, on the external availability and overt contact with familiar groups of people" (p. 169). The old neighborhood's longest residents were most strongly affected when they were uprooted because their own identities and sense of coherence were so highly dependent on their spatial and social integration. Perhaps if their new residential environment had been architecturally similar to their old one, or if their former associates had been transplanted to the new neighborhood as well, rather than being dispersed among numerous housing sites, the stress of relocation might have been appreciably mitigated. Mental health workers can forward such ideas during the planning stage of residential relocation.

Mental health professionals can take other steps to preserve viable support systems. First, they can advocate more extensive assessment of the social impact of urban planning enterprises and, in particular, their impact on the existing social networks in the locale. In Toronto, Canada, residents halted construction of a freeway linking the suburbs and the downtown core at the cost of displacing neighborhood residents and bisecting whole neighborhoods. Thus a second strategy is to work directly with neighborhood groups themselves, helping them to formulate a social impact statement and present their collective views to city planners. Third, where housing or neighborhood redevelopment plans threaten to displace long-standing low-income residents, various initiatives can be taken to arrange financing on behalf of the residents. For example, realtors and developers are now offering moderate-income home buyers a "partnership mortgage" whereby they are paired with small-scale investors who, seeking tax relief and long-term capital appreciation, provide the down payment on the new home and pay a portion of the monthly carrying charge. These "equity sharing" arrangements have proved especially attractive to low-income renters facing conversion of their apartments to condominiums. It is a convenient financial arrangement that allows them to stay put while still giving them, the owner-occupants, the right to sell their unit at any time or to buy out the investor's capital interest when finance rates decline. A second approach involves organizing a cooperative association of residents who are threatened by eviction and pooling the members' existing capital, using it to secure commercial loans to purchase the property. For example, in an area just east of downtown Atlanta known as Cabbagetown, residents whose rents were tripled by their landlord took action on the basis of their mutual interests by forming the Fulton Village Cooperative, Inc. They then applied for grants from the city, and received loans from a consortium of banks, a local church, and the National Trust for Historic Preservation, using these funds to purchase and rehabilitate their homes while keeping rents low.

A third approach that has been successfully implemented among senior citizens in Boston and Seattle has been to facilitate a variety of shared housing arrangements. The City of Seattle has developed a program to sustain the community life of the elderly that matches prospective homesharers along several financial and personal criteria, offering them pre- and postplacement counseling and practical assistance in setting up a joint living arrangement. The benefits of this program go beyond financial considerations. Shared housing mitigates feelings of loneliness, offers sources of interpersonal support, counteracts the elderly's fears for their personal safety, and offers those with disabilities a "live-in" partner who can help them to cope with tasks of daily living and thus obviate or delay institutionalization. In the Back Bay area of Boston, group housing arrangements have been developed using a combination of Title II funds obtained from the Area Agency on Aging and loans from local foundations and a church. Here, about a dozen elderly citizens live in a communal environment, pooling their social security benefits, sharing the labor associated with maintenance of the residence, and jointly deciding about changes in the home's occupants and day-to-day operations.

These are only some of the strategies that can be taken either to prevent forced relocation of neighborhood residents and the attendant loss of valued social ties or to safeguard their relocation to housing arrangements that offer viable new sources of informal support or continued close access to their former associates. To implement these strategies, mental health workers will need to foster a combination of self-help and community organization skills among their constituencies, and they will have to work with both local governments and the private sector, whose foremost interests are the economic viability and the legalities (such as zoning ordinances, public health regulations, and fire and safety measures) of the proposed plans.

While geographic relocation, through migration, job changes, or housing changes, is a specific event that calls for efforts to preserve ongoing support, there are other occasions for buttressing informal care. For example, the self-help field has spawned a unique type of group that is composed of the family members, relatives, and close friends of those with serious emotional, addictive, and chronic physical disabilities. Gartner and Riessman (1977, p. 52) state that the purposes of these "living with" groups are "to inform the relative of the nature of the problem faced by his or her family member and to aid the relative both in coping with the problem and providing understanding and support to the afflicted person." As examples, they cite such groups as Al-Anon and Al-Ateen, which serve the needs of the alcoholic's family members; Pilot Parents, a group that serves the caregivers of Down's Syndrome children; Gam-Anon, for the family members of habitual gamblers; and various groups that have been organized to support the informal care extended by the close associates of those with chronic physical ailments. In general, where it is possible to identify people who voluntarily assume the caretaking burdens associated with the illness or dependency of a loved one, mental health practitioners can institute mutual-help groups on their behalf. Moreover, the caregivers not only need information about the nature of the affliction borne by the party, but also can benefit from the group's practical help and concrete services. They need assistance in obtaining disability benefits and prosthetic devices, they can take turns providing respite care during weekends and vacations, and they can obtain discounted group rates for various services and equipment.

Other occasions for sustaining the informal help-giving activities of citizens are less easily identified since they arise from unique interdependencies that exist in the ordinary fabric of community life. For example, recent research, reviewed in Chapter 6, has shown that the institutionalized elderly differ from those who reside in the open community by virtue of their access to informal caregivers (Smyer, 1980) and that teenaged single mothers who are better or worse able to manage their child-rearing responsibilities and who make more or less personal progress academically and economically following childbirth also differ in the supportiveness of their social milieux (Furstenberg & Crawford, 1978; Presser, 1980). In these situations, efforts can be made to identify the factors that threaten the viability of these spontaneous and fragile supportive arrangements, because they will persist only as long as the costs of helping are not overwhelming. When a friendly neighbor can no longer provide day care for an infant while the mother attends school because an illness in the helper's own family requires her attention, or when a pharmacy can no longer provide free delivery of medication to a homebound elderly person, the loss of these resources may engender a crisis in the lives of both these beneficiaries of support. There are limits on the resources of voluntary helpers. The most altruistic of good samaritans are vulnerable to critical events in their own lives that temporarily or permanently call them away from their prosocial activities.

Professionals can therefore play a more active role in first identifying groups and individuals in the community whose well-being is predicated upon voluntary care, and subsequently they can consult with the caregivers, trying to pinpoint events and problems that may interfere with their ability to render ongoing support. Consultation of this sort may result in innovative program strategies such as the development of short-term, agency-staffed relief services at times when the caregivers must temporarily withdraw their aid, or in the formation of a broader neighborhood-based network of helpers that augments the available pool of support. Moreover, based on their review of several model projects that demonstrated various ways of mobilizing support networks on behalf of the elderly, Dichter, Alfaro, and Holmes (1981) conclude that the people who are most critical as sources of support can even assume case management functions in partnership with agency staff. One of their guidelines to agencies regarding this aspect of care for the elderly states:

> The potential of many families as primary care providers with greatest familiarity and contact with their elders, places them in a position to work closely with professionals as case managers in their own right. . . . A detailed knowledge of the numbers, structure, and activities of the informal support network is crucial to knowing and involving it in a constructive partnership helping the elderly person. The elderly person may not be able to adequately describe this network; informal caregivers may have to be interviewed for this purpose. If informal supports exist, a partnership can begin at the intake and assessment phase and continue and develop through all other phases of the agency's work with the elderly person and his/her informal support network [p. III-12-III-13].

## Natural Support Systems in Ethnic/Minority Contexts

Members of minority and ethnic groups in North America, especially in communities where large numbers of recent immigrants reside, are likely to rely extensively on informal sources of support that are congruent with their cultural and religious values. Their definitions of mental illness and health may diverge from those espoused by representatives of the formal service delivery system and from those of the majority community. Their beliefs about the occasions that call for outside assistance also will affect their patterns and levels of use of mental health and medical services, and when they do use these services, their expectations about the kind of help they will receive may not coincide with what is offered to them, resulting in low attendance or premature dropout. Because minority group members are likely to participate in social networks that do not interlock closely with the networks of the majority culture, they are also likely to become involved in a protracted process of lay referral to indigenous helpers rather than immediately availing themselves of the professionally dominated human service network (Freidson, 1960; Gottlieb, 1976). To the extent that their difficulties are effectively addressed within the confines of this informal network of diagnosis, referral, and help, they will avoid the costs associated with the use of formal services. However, if their problems cannot be managed within the informal domain, indeed, if they fester and intensify due to repeated, unsuccessful referrals to lay helpers, these individuals may arrive at the doors of professionals in a deteriorated state. Therefore, mental health workers who wish to develop a stronger integration of lay and professional helping must find means of forming a working partnership with this parallel system of referral and aid.

Mendoza (1981) has outlined one promising approach to collaboration with natural helpers who serve the needs of elderly Latino residents in San Diego County. Through the use of field survey techniques and reputational methods, she identified approximately forty individuals who collectively formed a natural helping network that she called the *"Servidor* System":

> The key actors in the natural system were seen as the *servidores communicativos*. These individuals were described as being readily distinguishable from other helpers within service delivery systems by the extent of their activities. The study identified 23 Mexicanos who were actively engaged as *servidores*. Two other levels of *servidores* were also identified: *la vecina,* the neighbor, and *el servidor de agencia,* the agency link person (p. 23).

Mendoza discovered that these lay caregivers tended to specialize in the type of help they extended to the elderly and that these specializations roughly corresponded to agency career track specialties, including communitywide planning and organizing activities, casework activities, and neighborhood social development activities. For example, the last category of helpers — the *servidoras de los vecinos* – performed a variety of supportive functions within a delimited neighborhood, serving as home helpers, child-care workers, and intermediaries between local residents and the staff of social service agencies. They offered diverse types of assistance to the elderly in particular, including such personal services as running errands, cleaning house, picking up the mail, interpreting forms and writing letters, cooking meals, visiting those who were temporarily hospitalized, and simply offering their companionship. Mendoza notes that although some of these neighborhood helpers had specialized roles as healers, having been trained in herbal remedies, none of them had knowledge of or direct ties to a human service agency. She therefore recommends that agencies develop closer links to these individuals within the context of a model of mutual consultation. The servidoras could provide the agencies with needs-assessment data and with direct training in the modes of help that are preferred by elderly Hispanics, while the agency could, in turn, develop new, more responsive programs of service delivery that supply the informal continuum of care the elderly need to sustain their community life. Readers interested in gaining a more complete overview of the character and service implications of various types of informal helping arrangements among Hispanics are advised to consult Valle and Vega's (1980) excellent volume, *Hispanic Natural Support Systems.*

Garrison (1981) has recently described how community mental health center programming in Newark, New Jersey, is being reorganized to accommodate diverse cultures in the local catchment area. Modeled after the University of Miami's Health Ecology Project, which spearheaded new service approaches among local Bahamian, black-American, Puerto Rican, Cuban, and Haitian populations, the work has entailed: (a) detailed ethnographic study of ethnic zones in the Newark area; (b) analysis of service use patterns in relation to the location of services and the culture of the users; and (c) intensive study of the practices of folk healers and their health beliefs. These folk healers include "rootworkers" and "spiritual advisers" among black residents, spiritualists and *santeros* among the Hispanics, *unbandistas,* a spirit medium healing cult among the Portuguese, charismatic faith healers, and ubiquitous reader advisers. The latter findings have been translated into a training program for the staff of the mental health center, emphasizing cultural information of most relevance to an understanding of mental health care among these ethnic groups. In addition, a "Healer-Liaison Program" has been created to explore ways of improving relations between the formal and indigenous systems of care, and a new cadre of agency staff called "culture specialists" have been designated to act as brokers, interpreting to professional practitioners the cultural dimension of their patient's illnesses, family patterns, and health beliefs and practices. Similar work has been carried out in New York City by Ruiz and Langrod (1976), whose efforts have resulted in a training film for non-Hispanic community mental health staff and the instigation of more productive referral relationships between local spiritualist temples and mental health practitioners.

## SUMMARY

Mental health professionals can engage in a variety of activities to optimize the quality and sufficiency of support that people receive from informal caregivers in the community and from their primary social contacts. Through the creation of support groups and by optimizing the support expressed within ongoing social networks, they can weave people into a social fabric that is more responsive to their needs for emotional nurture, attachment, guidance, and personal affirmation. Support development interventions can be of special benefit to those who are undergoing transitions that alter the structure of their immediate social surroundings. In addition to these proactive roles, mental health practitioners can play an important reactive role in safeguarding the support networks that currently sustain the well-being of citizens. They can intercede by preventing the occurrence of certain life events that threaten to diminish people's access to supportive social ties and they can shore up existing systems of informal care. Their work in the community will require sensitivity to culturally diverse forms of social support and a collaborative working relationship with indigenous helpers.

# Chapter 4

# CLINICAL PRACTICE

Preceding chapters have emphasized the role of social support in maintaining and enhancing mental health. The health-protective effect of social support is demonstrated either when exposure to stressors does not result in the loss of emotional equilibrium or when illness does not follow on the heels of high levels of stress. In addition, I have outlined some approaches to the promotion of mental health that involve either weaving more isolated people into a meaningful web of social relationships or optimizing the quality of the helping resources that flow through existing social networks. In short, thus far this volume has addressed a range of primary and secondary preventive interventions, the latter organized around offsetting human vulnerability following exposure to life events and transitions.

This chapter shifts attention to the social milieu of those who have entered the formal treatment system, bringing to bear information about the characteristics of the patient's primary group, before, during, and following clinical treatment, that influence the tertiary preventive goals of speeding recovery and sustaining long-term stability. Specifically, I consider three topics: First, I describe the types and sources of information that clinicians can call upon in order to assess the social resources and liabilities in their patients' social worlds. That is, I specify the social network assessment procedures that can be undertaken to complement the diagnostic portrait obtained from purely person-centered assessment techniques. Second, I discuss characteristics of the social networks and social interactions in which patients participate. Here, I focus on varied social milieux ranging from the family context to highly structured community-based treatment and rehabilitation programs. Third, I present recent research on the quality of familial interactions affecting relapse and length of community tenure following hospitalization for mental illness. A common theme unifies these topics: the interplay between the patient's therapeutic progress and the enveloping social context.

## ASSESSMENT OF PATIENTS' SOCIAL-STRUCTURAL AND INTERPERSONAL RESOURCES

Typically, the assessment activities that are performed upon intake tend to concentrate on person-centered variables and to pay scant attention to the patient's broader social milieu. The sociodemographic data that are collected are usually confined to the composition of the patient's household, the general quality of his or her domestic relationships, and the family's role in precipitating or maintaining current difficulties. The assessment thus consists largely of an inquiry into the psychological life of the patient and into his or her perceptions of close interpersonal relationships. No systematic, comprehensive investigation is made of the social resources and supportive transactions that actually occur in the patient's life space. Such a partial assessment of the social ecology is likely to produce equally limited options for treatment interventions, concealing social resources that can be mobilized on the patient's behalf. Froland, Brodsky, Olson, and Stewart (1979, p. 92) underscore this viewpoint in discussing the results of their study relating the adjustment of patients to characteristics of their social networks:

> An assessment procedure that identifies the range of available support resources and the emphasis given to various sources of support would provide better understanding of how the client's social network may be enlisted to improve his or her social and personal functioning. Such information would allow the client's network to be considered in identifying appropriate alternatives to institutionalization, understanding the need for continuing care, designing suitable transitional living arrangements, and many other aspects involved in mental health treatment.

Furthermore, since outpatients continue to interact with members of their social networks in their family, neighborhood, and work roles, their commerce with this entire system of influences is likely to affect their treatment progress in both direct and indirect ways, and therefore should be monitored.

The lay system's influence stems in part from its attitudes toward the patient's involvement with professional treatment agents, and in part from its reactions to the interpretations and recommendations offered by the professional. For example, family members and friends may interpret the patient's attendance at an agency as a sign that they have failed to provide the requisite quality or quantity of support, or they may view it as a sign of the patient's commitment to change. The former perception may result in decreased helping from the social network, while the latter may lead to an intensification of the support it renders. Similarly, once the patient has been in treatment for a period, network members may react with hostility or with approval to what they learn about the professional's interpretation of the patient's difficulty, and their reactions will, in turn, condition their willingness to support the treatment measures recommended by the professional. Thus professionals play to an audience of which they are only partially aware, but which either constrains or reinforces the therapeutic enterprise. Hammer (1982, p. 201) forcefully states this position in her discussion of the interface between professional treatment of psychiatric patients and the lay network's involvement with the patient:

> Whether deliberately or not, any treatment program necessarily involves some manipulation of the patient's social network, and it may be as well to do so consciously, and to monitor the consequences. What might be worth emphasizing at this time is that those who are responsible to the patients and the communities should make themselves much more aware of the probable impacts of any treatment on the social contacts of the patient, keep track of them, and contribute to increasing our knowledge of the relevant processes.

It follows that deliberate efforts ought to be made to assess more comprehensively the clinically relevant forces in the patient's primary social network. Such an assessment would include three elements: (1) determining the membership of the patient's primary social network; (2) gauging the balance of support to stress in the ongoing transactions with each of these network members; and (3) monitoring of network members' attitudes and behavioral responses to the treatment process itself.

These three types of information could be gathered during the initial interview, periodically repeated in order to document change over the course of treatment, and applied again at termination and upon follow-up.

## Composition of the Primary Social Network

The patient's primary social network consists of those persons who are perceived as most significant to his or her affective life and with whom there is regular, face-to-face contact. Procedures for eliciting the names of those people entail either drawing up an inventory of important contacts in various life sectors or examining the patient's important role relationships. Using the former approach, contacts can be categorized according to the life spheres of family relations, including nuclear family and extended kin contacts, workplace contacts, neighborhood contacts, and contacts that predominantly arise from involvement in voluntary organizations, such as religious institutions, civic groups, and social clubs. The latter approach inquires into close relationships with role partners, yielding extra information about people with whom relationships are more intimate because they are multistranded or multidimensional as opposed to those less intense, unidimensional relationships. For example, a relationship with a workmate who is also nominated as a personal confidant offers greater intimacy than a coworker who does not assume a dual-role partnership.

A number of studies have shown that this immediate or effective social network is of modest size. Calling on their own data and cross-cultural studies, Hammer, Makiesky-Barrow, and Gutwirth (1978) state that the immediate networks of community samples average 6-10 intimates. Data from a recent study of the primary social networks of a sample of 235 low-income mothers in an urban Canadian setting are consistent with this finding, revealing an average of 9.1 social intimates (Gottlieb & Carveth, 1981). In contrast, preliminary evidence suggests that the primary social networks of disturbed or diagnosed populations are smaller in size (Pattison, de Francisco, Wood, Frazier, & Crowder, 1975; Sokolovsky, Cohen, Berger, & Geiger, 1978); however, these findings await confirmation of the accuracy of patient's reports about their networks. Specifically, the testimony of disturbed samples may be confounded by their present psychiatric state; their present affect and their attendance at professional services may cause them to underestimate the number of people they deem social intimates and to minimize the quality and frequency of support rendered by their primary social network. Thus, to determine the accuracy of patient reports on the composition of their close social field, two sources of supplementary information ought to be obtained.

First, the patient can be requested to nominate a close associate who is knowledgeable about the patient's actual current involvement with social intimates and can therefore offer a judgment not only about the accuracy of the patient's report, but also about any marked changes in his or her pattern of involvement in the recent past. Such an approach has been taken by Henderson, Duncan-Jones, Byrne, and Scott (1980). After administering their Interview Schedule for Social Interaction to a community sample, they asked a random half of their respondents to nominate someone they felt was knowledgeable about their social relationships, and then asked for permission to contact this person to obtain his or her views. A total of 114 informants then completed the same schedule as the respondent, answering questions about the availability and perceived adequacy of the latter's close social involvements. They found that the respondents' and the informants' scores on the four major subscales of the schedule were significantly correlated, ranging from .26 to 59. Moreover, the authors noted that very few respondents were unable or unwilling to nominate someone who knew about the quantity and quality of their social interactions. Since the Interview Schedule for Social Interactions probes much more deeply into aspects of the respondents' relationships than the assessment I have proposed, it is likely that the patient will be even more accurate in simply reporting the composition of his or her primary social network.

Second, by asking both patients and informants to provide information about whether the present composition of the primary social network differs from its composition in the recent past, knowledge is gained about various aspects of the interplay between the patient's distress and his or her network's stability. For example, a patient who reports that his close friend who was also his boss at work was transferred to another branch office three months earlier, and replaced by a more controlling and demanding supervisor, is pointing to a new vacancy in his intimate network that signifies a major loss of a confiding relationship. This information may help to inform both the professional's and the patient's understanding of the recent course of the latter's distress, and it can be used as a basis for considering how another workplace relationship can be developed to compensate for this loss. Similarly, a patient who reports that her primary social field has gained two new members — her spouse's elderly mother, who has moved into the house, and the next-door neighbor, who began dropping in regularly after her marital separation — is providing clinically pertinent information about the altered social ecology that formed the context for her present depression. In this instance, an additional focus for treatment might involve finding ways of unburdening the patient from the demands of these individuals and directing her attention to other members of her primary network who are capable of engaging in less draining, more equitable social interactions. Furthermore, by conducting this assessment of the primary network's composition, the clinician can keep informed about the reciprocal influence between events occurring in the patient's social ecology and the process of therapeutic intervention. Clinical case descriptions and clinical planning can only be enriched through more deliberate efforts to monitor how the changing social surrounding is affected by and affects the individual's adaptive strivings.

## The Balance of Support to Stress in the Primary Social Network

Characterizing the quality of interaction in the primary social network requires an examination of each member's influence on the coping efforts of the patient. As noted in Chapter 2, primary social relationships are sources of both help and strain at different times, and therefore both functions need to be assessed simultaneously. Moreover, this qualitative aspect of the assessment relies to a much greater extent on the patient's subjective experience in ongoing social transactions, and therefore should be supplemented by the opinions of third parties.

One appropriately brief approach to this qualitative task is to inquire about the frequency with which each network member has engaged in five different types of supportive interactions with the patient over a specified period of time. These supportive interactions include the provision of emotional support, usually intimate dialogue that encourages the airing of stressful feelings and provides feedback (for example, empathy, comparison of affective reactions) regarding these feelings; cognitive guidance, typically consisting of advice about problem-solving strategies; socializing and companionship;

environmental action, subsuming efforts to change aspects of the situation so as to reduce its demands; and the provision of material aid and concrete services. These classes of supportive interactions capture many of the discrete types of helping behaviors that appear in Table 2.2 in Chapter 2.

After reporting on the frequency with which their primary network members have extended these types of helping resources, the patient can provide two other global judgments about each member: (a) Does he or she desire more of each type of supportive provision? (b) Is his or her overall relationship with each network member more taxing, burdensome, or conflictual in nature than it is supportive? The latter judgment not only acknowledges the plain fact that primary network members' demands may far outweigh their supportive functions, but it also calls attention to a more subtle aspect of primary group support, namely, that the poor quality of help network members extend or the great psychological cost their help incurs for the helpee compounds the latter's difficulties. On the former score, research discussed later in this chapter reveals that the pattern of a family's emotional involvement with a mentally ill member can precipitate a recurrence of symptomatology, even when this pattern expresses the family's helpful intentions. On the latter score, when members of the social network collectively cast the focal individual in the exclusive role of helpee and intensify their aid, they may lower the individual's feelings of self-esteem and personal control, and heighten the sense of being constrained by outside social pressures. When the primary network does not afford the individual freedom to choose a course of action and to reciprocate the help it extends, it substitutes psychological dependency for the interdependence and equitable social exchange that underpin satisfying peer relationships.

## Monitoring the Lay System's Responses to Professional Treatment

Recognizing that transactions between patients and practitioners regarding the definition of the present disorder and the appropriate treatment strategy are highly subject to the lay system's scrutiny, clinicians can periodically assess the primary network's responses to these transactions. The purpose of this assessment is to monitor the congruence of the therapeutic enterprise to the norms, expectations, and behavioral standards of the patient's primary social network.

When accord about these matters is lacking, there is a greater risk of the patient prematurely dropping out of treatment or failing to adhere to recommended treatment strategies.

Clinicians can initially elicit information about network interpretations of the patient's disorder and treatment expectations by asking the following sorts of questions:

- What do these people (members of the primary social network) think has caused your problem? As a group, are they in agreement about this?

- What do they say about its seriousness? Do they think it will take a long time or a short time to get over?

- How do they feel about your coming for help to me/this agency? Did they encourage you to do so or tell you it wouldn't help? Why do you think they feel this way?

Several other questions will elicit the network's reactions to the plans, methods, and goals that are established during the course of treatment:

- What do they say about your progress so far? Do they seem disappointed or encouraged by the changes you've made?

- What are they doing or saying to help you change in the ways we've talked about? Are they doing or saying things that undercut your attempts to change?

- Do they think we're on the wrong track about the nature of your present difficulty and about and how to deal with it, do they agree, or don't they say anything about these matters?

Questions of this order not only elucidate the network's definition of health, illness, and appropriate treatment, but they also demonstrate to patients the clinician's concern about the impact of professional treatment on the patient's relationships with significant peers. Fundamentally, they signal a recognition that effective clinical care must be integrated with the lay system of beliefs and care. In his forceful paper, "The Concept of Personal Network in Clinical Practice," Erickson (1975, p. 496) summarizes his view of the general significance of the lay system for the field of community mental health:

> The current task in relating network to the field. . . . is to discover how particular configurations, content and connections vary with

respect to a range of phenomena: specific mental health problems, the definition of problems, course of treatment, hospitalization and rehospitalization, corrective activities, and the reduction and amplification of pathology. Overriding importance is the development of concepts that actually link and bridge the three network sectors: kinship, friendship, and caregiving.

## CHARACTERISTICS OF PATIENTS' PRIMARY SOCIAL NETWORKS

Several recent studies of the social networks of diagnosed samples have varied the assessment procedure described below. I selectively review the findings of these studies in order to illuminate some of the actual properties of patients' primary networks.

Tolsdorf's (1976) comparative study of the social networks of two groups of ten male Veterans Administration hospital patients, one hospitalized for medical reasons, and one for psychiatric reasons, was one of the first to depict the distinctive properties of the mental patient's social orbit. It is noteworthy that Tolsdorf's data closely resemble those included in the assessment I have outlined, except that he did not delve into the network's ongoing reactions to the initial diagnosis or the course of the patient's treatment in the hospital. Instead, he interviewed patients only once, shortly after their admissions. Moreover, his study is important because it identified a dispositional variable that distinguished between the two groups' access to supportive social resources.

While there were no statistically significant differences between the sizes of the two patient groups' intimate networks, the psychiatric patients had networks composed of a significantly greater proportion of kin and characterized by a generally lower degree of intimacy. At an interpersonal level, the psychiatric patients also reported that they received much more support from their network ties than they returned. When Tolsdorf (1976) inquired into the two groups' attitudes toward the usefulness of calling upon their networks for support, advice, and feedback, he found that the psychiatric patients held a negative "network orientation" and the medical patients a positive orientation. In fact, upon follow-up with family members of the psychiatric patients, it seemed that they had not recognized any of the cues preceding their relatives' present psychotic episodes, thus giving some justification to the psychiatric patients' set toward them as helpers.

Tolsdorf (1976, p. 413) minimizes the possibility that the psychiatric patients' illnesses and present hospitalization colored their reports about the supportive character of their networks, stating that "it was clear from follow-up reports that the negative network orientations preceded the onset of the schizophrenic symptoms and that they in fact frequently dated back to the early childhoods of the subjects." But since these reports were based on the opinions of family members who may have been eager to deflect blame from themselves for the patients' present circumstances, they too must be considered cautiously. While prospective research is necessary to determine these causal relations, the present findings nevertheless highlight the complex interplay among patients' primary group relations, their help-seeking orientations, and their levels of adaptive functioning.

A second study comparing the networks of psychiatric patients to those of a general population sample replicates several of Tolsdorf's (1976) findings. However, in this study Froland et al. (1979) also attempted to discern differences among the social networks of psychiatric patients who participated in alternative treatment contexts: an inpatient sample, a day treatment sample, and an outpatient sample. Comparison of the characteristics of the general population sample's networks with those of the entire group of psychiatric patients revealed that the latter's networks were smaller, contained fewer kin ties, fewer long-term ties, and fewer ties drawn from different spheres of life such as school, work, and the neighborhood. Generally, the patients reported less interaction with intimate peers and voiced sentiments of depleted support from their networks more frequently than the general sample. This last finding may reflect a process referred to earlier, namely, that the social networks of those who enter treatment trigger professional help seeking when their members are no longer able to sustain their efforts to help one of their number.

In comparing the networks of the three groups of psychiatric patients, the authors found that each of these deficiencies was more pronounced with increasing degrees of institutionalization. Further, evidence suggested that receipt of professional help disrupted ongoing friendships in the patients' networks, thus depleting even further the informal supportive provisions to which they had access. Commenting on this finding and its implication for professional intervention, Froland et al. (1978, p. 92) observe:

> Repeated requests for help lead to further disruption of such relationships. Casual acquaintances and relatives would appear to be limited in their ability to provide continued or stable support. Thus, for the chronic client the sole remaining source often becomes a public agency. Service providers may play a central role in reducing the disruptiveness associated with the client's continuing need for support and assistance. Part of this task may be accomplished by expanding or mobilizing the skills and resources of the parts of the social network that the client does not view as support resources.

The authors also note, as did Tolsdorf (1976), that the erosion of stable patterns of helping by network members is, in part, a consequence of the absence or low level of support reciprocated by the patient. As long as the patient continues to call for support through words and deeds, and fails to return it, interaction becomes less satisfying, more burdensome, and eventually so draining that network members are forced to withdraw, if only to protect their own well-being. The findings of other studies also converge on this inequity in the mental patient's interpersonal transactions (for example, see Blackman & Goldstein, 1976; Sokolovsky et al., 1978). However, research has not determined whether it stems from poor social skills, from the tendency of network members to induce dependency on the part of the distressed individual, or from such low levels of self-esteem that the individual comes to believe that he or she is incapable of extending rudimentary supportive provisions such as companionship and practical aid.

Hammer and her colleagues at the New York State Psychiatric Institute have surveyed much of the literature bearing on the social networks of schizophrenic patients (Hammer et al., 1978). They have found that these networks tend to be smaller than those of nonpsychotic controls, less symmetric in their interpersonal helping exchanges, and relatively loosely knit. Thus schizophrenics inhabit a fragile interpersonal world that can easily disintegrate and that is not likely to provide consistent feedback. Its vulnerability stems from the lack of structural solidarity of a system in which the parties are not connected to one another. Hammer (1982, p. 238) states her point in this way: "Thus if we come back to consideration of schizophrenic individuals, it seems likely that one of the ways in which the schizophrenic patient's network becomes depleted is that it lacks sufficient cross-connectedness among the individuals in the network to assure the maintenance of connections."

Hammer (1982) illustrates how an individual's network might collapse due to insufficient connections to other members by presenting the case of a woman who relies on her relationship with her spouse to access social ties. Upon his death or upon divorce she will be left socially adrift because all her ties were mediated through her spouse. Had she maintained a circle of direct ties, his departure would have been less isolating. A second advantage of more tightly connected or dense social networks is the wider spread of communication through the cross-cutting links of the network, resulting in a higher level of mobilization and greater unison of action. Here, the parties can use their multiple channels of communication to agree about how to intercede. In sum, the structural patients' social networks play a part in determining their adequacy as support systems.

A final study comparing the social networks of schizophrenic subjects with the networks of nonpsychotic controls was conducted within the context of a single room occupancy (SRO) hotel in Manhattan (Sokolovsky et al., 1978). Three groups of tenants were studied: schizophrenics with moderate or severe chronic residual symptoms; those without such residual symptoms; and tenants with no known psychotic history. A total sample of 44 tenants was randomly selected from these groups, including both male and female occupants who had been residents for at least 10 consecutive months. The findings are generally consistent with the studies reported above: Both schizophrenic groups had significantly smaller networks than the nonpsychotic tenants, and both engaged in significantly more asymmetric aiding interactions than the nonpsychotic sample, the asymmetry stemming from their tendency to depend on others for help. Additionally, the schizophrenics' interactions with network members tended to revolve around a single type of helping exchange, rather than a variety of exchanges, signifying that these relationships tended to be less intimate or emotionally intense. The more impaired individuals also tended to form the sort of loosely knit networks that Hammer (1982) described. Sokolovsky et al. (1978, p. 14) also related the patients' network characteristics to their rates of rehospitalization, finding that "those with and without residual deficits, who have small, nonmultiplex networks with a low degree of connectedness, will exhibit higher rates of rehospitalization than schizophrenics with more extensive networks."

Considered as a group, these and several other recent studies (for example, Pattison, Llamas, & Hurd, 1979; Kleiner & Parker, 1974; Pattison et al., 1975; Silberfeld, 1978; Ratcliffe, Zelhart, & Azim, 1975; Baker, 1979) suggest that in comparison either to nonpsychotic control groups of patients or to general population samples, the networks of psychiatric patients are smaller, characterized by less interpersonal intimacy, greater asymmetry in helping exchanges, and less stability. There is less agreement, however, about some of the more complex structural features of their networks, particularly their overall density or cross-connectedness. In addition, there is scant knowledge about whether relations with network members from different spheres of life (role partners) are more or less significant to the affective well-being of the patient, and whether satisfying interaction with at least one very close significant other in the network can compensate for disordered or minimal feedback from the remainder. On the latter topic, Henderson, Duncan-Jones, McAuley, and Ritchie (1978) investigated the presence of and attitudes toward "principal attachment figures" in the primary networks of neurotic psychiatric patients and compared these data with those provided by a demographically matched general community sample. While members of both groups had access to close attachments and spent equal amounts of time interacting with them, the patients reported more negative interaction with and a greater insufficiency of support from their attachment figures. Moreover, the patients had fewer alternative attachment figures than the controls, which may explain the patients' dissatisfaction with the amount of support their principal attachment figures rendered and why interaction may have become so negatively colored.

Collectively, these studies of patients' primary social networks illuminate the reciprocal interplay among human distress, interpersonal dialogue and exchange, and characteristics of the enveloping social orbit. They reveal that contractions and expansions of the social field are not random, but occur systematically, in conjunction with interpersonal events unfolding inside its boundaries and environmental events affecting its members singly or collectively. It is also evident that members of the social network bring varying social skills, needs, and helping resources to their interactions with one another and that these factors shape the character and structure of the social aggregate as a whole, determining its resilience and its stability. The studies reviewed above represent preliminary efforts to capture these complex patterns in relation to only one social phenomenon — the mental disability of an individual in the primary network. Their dual relevance to clinical practice, however, is: (a) the instruction they offer regarding the nexus between the patient's personal adaptation and the organization and processes of the primary social milieu, and (b) the perspective they afford on the interplay between the professional's and the social network's influence on the patient's adaptive strivings. Depending on the degree of direct involvement clinicians wish to have with members of the patient's primary social field, they will differ in the practical uses to which they put this social-ecological viewpoint. Hence, in the following section, I briefly outline several types of interventions into the patient's close network, each differing in the degree to which the professional becomes directly involved with network members.

## A SPECTRUM OF CLINICAL INTERVENTIONS INTO SOCIAL NETWORKS

Family therapy and its most recent extension to "network therapy," as described by Speck and Rueveni (1969), Rueveni (1975), and Speck and Attneave (1973), are modes of intervention that cast a portion or all of the patient's primary network into the client role. In fact, network therapy evolved from family therapy when it was observed that primary group members with whom the family interacted regularly — close friends, extended family members, neighbors, and workmates — exercised a great deal of influence over the family's functioning and its interactions with the patient. Gradually, these significant parties were brought into the therapeutic enterprise and eventually the sessions were attended by the entire network of influential actors in the family's life. As the number of clients grew, so did the number of therapists and the number of innovative techniques necessary to accomplish the six phases of the group's work.

These phases begin with the process of "retribalization," which aims to revitalize lapsed or weak network ties, then proceed to the process of "polarization," then "mobilization," "depression," "breakthrough," and culminate with the "elation/exhaustion" phase.

In the polarization stage, the network is encouraged to air and confront differences among subgroups' perceptions of the current family crisis, and then to mobilize its resources to develop new solutions to different aspects of the crisis. The depression phase is characterized by collective feelings of frustration about apparently irreconcilable differences among members and by a recognition of the network's fragmentary quality. In this stage, the therapists are challenged to buoy up the group's energies by helping members to identify areas of common ground and sources of interpersonal support and cohesion. The breakthrough phase usually is signified by the emergence of several key "activists" in the network who identify new solutions to the present crisis and rally the group's helping resources. Once this stage is reached, the therapists withdraw so that network members can take ownership of their accomplishments. The final elation/exhaustion phase is accompanied by feelings of competence and confidence in the network's own strengths.

Network therapy has been used mainly as a last resort, after other therapeutic approaches have failed. The case studies presented by Speck and Attneave (1973) and by Reuveni (1975, 1977) suggest that it is appropriate in extreme cases of psychosis, in the face of repeated suicidal behavior, and when the patient has alienated virtually all potential allies in the primary network. It has been noted that network therapy is contraindicated among families who are unwilling to open themselves to the scrutiny of their entire network of close contacts, fearing that the process will not only prove embarrassing but that it will place them at a greater distance from their kith and kin. Moreover, network therapy has been neither widely practiced nor extensively evaluated. It makes heavy demands on the therapist's time and skills, each network session requiring approximately six to eight hours of planning, implementation, and follow-up. Additionally, many therapists have been dissuaded from practicing it because of its reliance on encounter group techniques such as "sculpting" and role plays of symbolic family rituals, as well as its dependence on a charismatic leadership style.

Three additional therapeutic interventions also rely on the mobilization of network resources during a crisis, but, unlike network therapy, they do not involve the entire network simultaneously in the psychotherapeutic process. Pattison et al. (1975) and Pattison (1973, 1977) have outlined the conduct of "social systems therapy," viewing it as an extension of family therapy. Here, the network unit is the "psychosocial kinship system," a more delimited social aggregate consisting of the ties with whom the client has frequent interaction, strong feelings of attachment, and mutual exchanges of positive affect and aid. Normal populations usually include 20 to 30 individuals in their psychosocial kinship system, neurotic samples tend to nominate about a dozen members, and psychotic patients nominate 4 or 5 people, typically family members. The intervention process is not as clearly demarcated by stages as it is in network therapy; it moves from the initial data collection about the system's functioning to a diagnosis of its dysfunctional qualities (such as its modes of interpersonal communications and defense, or its structural configuration), culminating with one or more professional interventions affecting subsets of the social system. The therapist may attempt to restructure the psychosocial kinship system and/or develop more effective patterns of communication. Except for the presentation of several case vignettes (Pattison, 1973), there is little empirical basis for assessing the efficacy of this approach to network intervention. However, as I report later, other practitioners who have been involved in the creation of community support systems for the mentally ill have drawn heavily upon Pattison's (1973, 1976) theoretical base in planning and accounting for the success of these support systems (Budson & Jolley, 1978).

Polak (1971, 1972) has also described yet another form of "social system intervention" that shares much with Pattison's approach. It too emphasizes work with significant parties in the patient's milieu, employing a range of intervention strategies to promote more accurate communication among network members, the ventilation of feelings, and greater overall integration and interpersonal support. Typically, the approach has been used in crises intervention. In one controlled evaluative study, social system intervention was extended to families who had experienced the death of a loved one. In comparison to an untreated control group, there was no improvement in their coping behavior or in their levels of social functioning at both a 6-month and 18-month follow-up (Polak, Egan, Vandenbergh, & Williams, 1975). However, despite prior matching of the two groups on appropriate demographic variables, the treatment group had experienced more sudden deaths and more deaths by suicide than the control group.

Hansell's (1968, 1976) and Garrison's (1974) "Screening-Linking-Planning Conference" (S-L-P) offers a third network-based strategy of therapeutic intervention that also has been mainly practiced in crisis intervention. It assumes that people have a hierarchy of needs or "environmental attachments," including access to biological supplies and an adequate income, a need for both dyadic and group role relationships, and the need to establish a comprehensive set of meanings about their place in relation to others. At times of crisis, these attachments are threatened or lost, resulting in a fragmentation of the individual's personal identity. Intervention seeks to restore equilibrium by mobilizing feedback from the intimate social network through a process that unfolds in seven stages resembling those outlined by the network therapists. However, the S-L-P approach is not a form of group psychotherapy. It is more directive, more clearly centered on shoring up the patient's coping abilities, and more intent on restoring the patient to adequate role functioning in a network that offers consistent and appropriate feedback. To date, the method has been applied in a variety of crisis contexts (Hansell, 1976), and has been used to help drug offenders make the transition from inpatient to community settings (Callan, Garrison, & Zerger, 1975). However, it has not been subjected to rigorous evaluation.

These four network strategies of clinical intervention operate from varied theoretical bases but have a great deal in common: Each interprets the patient's difficulties within the context of the immediate social ecology, sometimes casting the entire network in the client role and sometimes viewing it mainly as a resource to an individual or family. Collectively, they aim to reweave the social fabric so that it can provide more consistent feedback to its members, and they concentrate on ways of reestablishing mutually satisfying role relationships following a crisis. They share the challenge of embedding the patient in a network that neither suffocates nor encapsulates, and, to this extent, they directly confront a fundamental human task, namely, achieving a satisfying balance between independence and interdependence.

Each of these network interventions also poses a challenge to the professional. Venturing into a system that is currently under stress involves considerable risk. The actors in the network may be threatened by the invitation to play a part in the therapeutic process, and they may be uncertain about their willingness to commit themselves to it. However, the fact remains that the parties have played and will continue to play a part in the patient's life even when they withdraw entirely. Professional involvement with the social network ultimately signals a recognition of the interplay between the patient and his or her network, and it entails active efforts to guide and optimize the quality of this interplay. By doing so, the therapeutic enterprise becomes even more complicated and the role of the practitioner becomes more ambiguous and public, changes that typically occur when old boundaries no longer serve. These network approaches thus urge us to change our perspective from viewing patients as individuals to viewing them as fragments of networks and to shift our work from the individual level to the small ecosystems in which people are anchored.

## INTERVENTIONS WITH FAMILIES ENMESHED IN MULTISERVICE NETWORKS

The approaches described above are essentially concerned with forging inroads into the social networks of patients and families involved in professional treatment. However, they assess the client's network mainly by examining the informal sources of actual or potential support that bear upon coping and adaptive functioning in the community. To this extent, they may overlook the influence that other institutions and professional helping agents exert on the client's predicament, and the dilemmas ensuing from multiple, potentially contradictory pressures from the service sector (Hoffman & Long, 1969; Auerswald, 1968). Erickson, Rachlis, and Tobin (1973) noted that this problem frequently occurs among low-income populations who are dependent on several forms of public and agency assistance. They cite as an example the case of a single mother with several dependent children who was simultaneously receiving services from the city welfare department, the Canadian provincial Department of Health and Social Development, a children's aid society, a local public health nurse, a social worker from a "comprehensive" family care program, a school guidance counselor, a physician, a medical resident, a district public health nurse, and a student social worker. The authors interceded in this situation by developing a strategy that blended elements of family therapy with a coordinated approach to the family's involvement with the representatives of these several institutions. Their "combined family and service network intervention" thus offers yet another means of untangling and reorganizing clients' social contacts, especially when these contacts entail extensive involvement with human service organizations.

Erickson et al. (1973, p. 281) carefully point out some of the distinguishing factors between their approach and such traditional means of service coordination as the case conference: "The traditional case conference is marked by communication patterns which focus on deviance and pathology among the family members. This differs from family service network sessions in that they focus in on immediate problem-solving and whatever positive trends seem to exist in the family and environment." "Coordination of agencies and service can be viewed perhaps as a by-product of the interaction between the family and the organizations" (p. 278). Indeed, from these authors' points of view, the "case" itself is composed of the family *and* its agency service providers, and the contracts that result from their joint discussions include revised obligations on the part of *all* actors.

Gatti and Colman (1976) apply a similar approach to families in which a child is referred for treatment. Following referral from a school counselor and a decision to extend family therapy, they simultaneously involve themselves with all other parties — both professional and informal — who are currently important to the child's well-being and whose resources can be more effectively brought to bear in the course of intervention:

> By having access to many systems we are able both to receive and to share relevant information and to mobilize change at all points. . . . Our intervention strategy is based on our ongoing assessment of the major familial and community forces affecting the child, with an eye toward which of these forces might be made an ally for change. In as much as we make contacts concerning many children over time, we increase our access to, and the effectiveness of, our network building [p. 611].

Gatti and Colman (1976) discover which key subsystems have the greatest impact on their clients by sampling the opinions of key informants and by directly observing the client's interactions in a range of community settings. Later, they share their perceptions with members of the family's network, not in one large gathering, but by holding a series of small meetings with subgroups of the network. In part, this choice is dictated by their small-town practice, residents being especially sensitive to public disclosure of private problems, and in part by the fact that fewer actors, and especially fewer professionals, are concurrently involved with their clients. The small size of the host locale is itself an advantage in the practice of "community network therapy" since identifying and cultivating working relationships is easier in a more truncated human services network than it is in the more extensive, urban, multiservice context addressed by Erickson et al.

## ON THE DESIGN OF "COMMUNITY SUPPORT SYSTEMS"

One of the most profound changes that has occurred during the two decades following passage of the Community Mental Health Centers Act is the shift in the locus of care from institutional setting to a variety of community-based treatment arrangements. This movement took a number of forms, including programs that diverted new patients from hospital admission at the point of initial intake, programs that transplanted chronically ill psychiatric patients from hospitals to settings in the open community, and programs that emphasized shorter inpatient stays and partial (day or night only) hospitalization. "Deinstitutionalization" became the code word for progressive, humane care of the mentally ill. In 1975 the director of the National Institute of Mental Health defined its meaning in three ways: (1) prevention of inappropriate mental hospital admissions through the provision of community treatment alternatives; (2) discharge of institutionalized patients following adequate preparation for such a change; and (3) creation and maintenance of community support systems for noninstitutionalized patients in need of mental health services (Bachrach, 1977). As a graduate student, I was assigned a small part in fostering the second of these objectives. In retrospect, my experience points to several of the detrimental features of the movement as a whole. In particular, it highlights the pernicious consequences that result when inadequate attention is paid to the social resources that are necessary to sustain the community life of psychiatric patients who have spent years in a mental institution.

My internship placed me in a bridging role between a geriatric milieu therapy ward of a state hospital in Michigan and two treatment settings in Detroit. My assignment was to help prepare elderly inpatients whom the staff deemed ready to return to the community by taking them on periodic visits to the city, introducing them to a professionally staffed social club for ex-mental patients, and paving the way for their entry either into a group or an independent living arrangement. In addition, I was charged with the task of improving the patients' community living skills, a task that entailed teaching them how to use the city's public transportation, how to budget and shop for their food and clothing, how to take advantage of the recreational and leisure facilities offered in the city, and how to seek help from agencies when the need arose. Further, I was asked to develop and implement a job readiness program to be delivered in the group setting where many of the still employable patients would eventually reside.

Only two of the fifteen patients with whom I worked eventually left the hospital. One entered the home of a family in a carefully planned foster-type arrangement, working during the day as a caretaker in a local church. The other lived with relatives. The remaining thirteen patients expressed their gratitude to me for arranging the pleasant trips they had taken to the city. Nevertheless, they agreed that, as much as they longed for the independence and the diversion of community life, they preferred either to live out their days in the hospital's milieu ward or to defer their move out of the hospital until comparable arrangements were available to them in the community. When I compared the quality of life they experienced in the hospital with the quality of community life led by those who had already been discharged and those who had been initially diverted from the hospital, I concluded that these elderly patients had made wise decisions to stay in the hospital.

A variety of forces, including their present institutional circumstances and the community circumstances they would face, combined to dampen the patients' motivation to leave the hospital. First, the very fact of their assignment to the milieu therapy ward in which they lived constituted a reward for their prior therapeutic progress. The ward served the best functioning geriatric patients, and, as a demonstration project itself, hedged its bets on success by recruiting those who were best able to adapt to its democratic and progressive social milieu. Relations with staff were informal; decision making was a joint product of discussions between representatives of the patients' governing council and staff representatives; a work program paid patients for finishing the nameplates for automobiles manufactured in Detroit; a crafts workshop had been outfitted on the ward; and the patients had a great deal of access to local communities for recreational purposes. In addition, community volunteers actively participated in the ward's round of activities. All of these programmatic features and the homelike physical plan and decor of the ward resulted in an attractive, secure, and challenging milieu that was a microcosm of ideal community life. Indeed, its idyllic character no doubt contributed to its residents' disinclinations to leave.

The life that they saw for themselves in the community was a deplorable contrast. Those lacking relatives who were willing to take them in faced the specter of living in a cheap, overcrowded motel located in a semicommercial section of Detroit. It had very little programming, few staff, and no patient government. My assigment to develop a job readiness training program for the younger motel residents gave me a closer view of the setting. Two or three patients to a cramped motel unit, a basement room used as both lounge and cafeteria, and a single multipurpose room that could potentially be used for group activities but was mainly reserved for caseworkers to meet with patients. The motel's proprietors, who did not live on the premises, greeted my project with a mixture of skepticism and dismay. They were chiefly interested in ensuring that it not disrupt the patients' daily routines. In fact, their real concern was with the project's effects on their own ability to keep track of the patients' whereabouts, since the pattern of custodial care would, no doubt, be disrupted if patients actually ventured beyond the block in an effort to find a job. In fairness to these proprietors, however, their need to contain patients was prompted by economic realities: They received such paltry recompense for their board and care and had access to so few outside agency services that, in order to show a profit, they were forced to restrict the patients' movements while meeting their basic needs for food, shelter, and medication. Lamb's (1979) discussions with the residents and staff of several board and care homes located near downtown Los Angeles led him to the following conclusions about the dilemma faced by the operators of such facilities and the appropriate remedies:

> Operators are seen as regarding their board-and-care homes almost solely as a business, squeezing excessive profits out of it at the expense of the residents. Whether or not this is true is far from clear, but having this situation overseen by a strong licensing and monitoring agency as well as patient advocate groups would do much to reassure staff, residents, and outside professionals. This applies to the physical structure, food, staff (both numbers and quality), and the provision of an arrangement for treatment and rehabilitation services. . . . there needs to be striking of a balance so that the board-and-care home operators make a fair return on their investment and at the same time provide adequate service to the residents.

There also needs to be more careful initial screening of the operators so that only the ethical and competent are allowed in [p. 132].

The second community facility available to the patients with whom I worked was a recently opened "social club" for ex-mental patients. It was staffed by a handful of energetic and dedicated social workers who were intent on optimizing the independent living skills of ex-mental patients and fostering their mutual reliance. They established a governing council among the patients attending the club, held group sessions focusing on daily living problems, organized numerous outings and recreational activities, and coordinated the care provided by the several agencies serving the patients. Unfortunately, the program did not meet the special needs of my cohort of patients because they already functioned at a higher level than those whom they met at the club and because, in the agency's short history, it had not developed housing and job arrangements as attractive as those available in the hospital.

My unsuccessful effort to place elderly long-term psychiatric patients in the community brings to light a number of important themes submerged beneath the deinstitutionalization movement. First, it reveals that certain types of hospital care can be far more beneficial to patients than certain types of community care. Second, it suggests that certain hospital settings offer less restrictive treatment surroundings than certain community settings. Third, it points out that "adequate preparation" for deinstitutionalization entails preparation of the environment in which patients are received, as well as preparation of the patients for that environment. Fourth, and most important to my present emphasis on the psychosocial dimension of patient care, it reveals that the patient's primary group has a critical impact on treatment outcomes and that the patient has an impact on the immediate social field. On the latter score, while I have little doubt that my charges' experience of the hospital's work program, its crafts room, its "open" door to the outside world, and its comfortable surroundings contributed to their reluctance to leave, unquestionably the primary losses they would suffer upon their move out of the hospital entailed severing long-standing social ties, vacating a position in a meaningful social system, and sacrificing a psychological sense of community that took years to cultivate. Even those patients who had spent an average of 26 years in the state hospital had developed a satisfying pattern of interdependence and a sense of shared history that was now threatened by an abrupt order to transfer the hospital's patient population to the community. *While the logic of deinstitutionalization was unassailable, its actual practice was devoid of a coherent ideology about the social circumstances that foster community care for the mentally ill.*

Maxwell Jones (1976), the architect of the therapeutic community, emphasizes the need to pay as much attention to the patient's social field in the planning of community-based treatment and rehabilitation programs as to the medical treatment of the individual. He maintains that we should assign "at least equal importance to a social system that can give its members a feeling of identity and of belonging, along with as active and creative a role in the system as the potentialities will allow" (pp. 97-98). The patients with whom I worked no doubt had greater potentialities than those of most long-term mental hospital patients, and their expectations for community life were higher than most. Indeed, these characteristics were cultivated through their active involvement in a carefully planned social organization that met their needs for independence and interdependence.

## STRUCTURING SUPPORTIVE SOCIAL MILIEUS IN COMMUNITY TREATMENT PROGRAMS

In what follows, I review several community-based treatment and rehabilitation programs that highlight special ways of mobilizing informal social resources on behalf of adult psychiatric patients. In addition to reviewing programs for formerly hospitalized mental patients, I also examine settings that divert patients from the hospital. My purpose is not to review critically the effectiveness of the deinstitutionalization movement as a whole. Bachrach (1977) and Braun, Kochansky, Shapiro, Greenberg, Gudeman, Johnson, and Shore (1981) have already addressed this broader task. Rather, my purpose is to analyze ways of structuring the patient's social field, including relations with family members, other patients, and treatment staff, so as to optimize the social support available to patients. In addition, I pay special attention to the creation of "support systems" for those family members who provide community care to the mentally ill, and review important recent work on certain deficiencies in the patient's family relations that precipitate relapse and rehospitalization.

### The Community Lodge

The Community lodge, developed by Fairweather and his colleagues (Fairweather, Sanders, Maynard, & Cressler, 1969), exemplifies how a cohesive support system developed among patients in the hospital can be transferred and preserved in the community. In fact, the lodge program was initiated following the discovery that patients who were prepared for community living after participating in small, autonomous problem-solving groups in the hospital did not adjust successfully when their community placement denied them continued access to the group's resources. The lodge program thus aimed to keep this small social system intact by transferring the group en masse to an independent living arrangement in the community. The move itself constituted the group's "graduation" from the hospital, signaling that all its members had successfully performed the prerequisite steps. These steps included the daily completion of specific work assignments, involvement in group decision making, and responsible communication with staff. Once settled in the community facility, the group continued to function autonomously while staff supervision was gradually reduced. The lodge was not intended to serve as a transitional living arrangement, but as a permanent one, although members could elect to move to other community facilities or to private homes.

Patients' social statuses in the lodge society depended primarily on what they were able to contribute to the maintenance of the social system as a whole rather than on their degree of psychological impairment. Higher social statuses and leadership roles were predicated on the assumption of greater levels of responsibility; foremen who supervised the lodge's janitorial business were accorded a higher status than were workers, and the bookkeeper's position was elevated above the kitchen worker's. Patients who displayed psychiatric symptomatology were tolerated within the lodge, but they were notified by the group that deviant behavior was not acceptable in the community. The group was also collectively responsible for monitoring members' adherence to medication regimens.

The major accomplishments of the lodge program were to increase the patients' length of stay in the community and their productivity. It failed, however, to reduce the rate of recidivism, defined in terms of the number of patients who returned to the hospital. At follow-up, 40 months after discharge, comparison of the lodge group with a control group of patients who received traditional aftercare services and medication showed that the former spent about 80 percent of the time in the community and the latter 20 percent. The lodge residents were involved in full-time employment 40 percent of the time compared to virtually no full-time employment among controls (Rappaport, 1977). The two groups did not differ on standard measures of psychiatric impairment and psychosocial adjustment, a finding that suggests that the lodge did not offer a better "cure" for psychiatric illness, but largely effected a longer and more productive adjustment to community life. One additional finding bears spotlighting because it touches on an issue to which I will return. The lodge residents who did return to the hospital rarely cited pressure from significant others among the factors causing their return. In contrast, 41 percent of the control group gave this reason for their return.

## Berkeley House

A second model for the systematic development of a social support network capable of sustaining the community life of psychiatric patients has been described by Budson and Jolley (1978). Strongly influenced by Pattison et al.'s (1975) formulations (reviewed earlier in this chapter within the context of clinical interventions into patients' social networks), they sought to develop an "extended psychosocial kinship system" among the residents of a psychiatric halfway house in Boston called Berkeley House. This network of close ties germinates spontaneously during the residents' stay in the facility and is composed of relationships with those co-residents who are sought out "because of affinities of interest and temperament" (Budson & Jolley, 1978, p. 612), and with one or more paraprofessional house managers, as well as whatever relationships develop through the residents' contacts in their places of work, their neighborhoods, and the social clubs and day centers they attend. In addition, residents are encouraged to reestablish ties to nearby family members, but, because these relationships are often the most difficult to deal with, the halfway house staff and close associates become actively involved in helping to modulate their intensity. In the following description of the ideal network in which a resident is embedded when he or she prepares to leave the halfway house, Budson and Jolley (1978, p. 613) reveal the hallmarks of a robust psychosocial kinship system:

> If the halfway house nuclear family system has not isolated itself from the community, and has done its job within its own interactional milieu, the resident preparing to move out can do so with the support of a healthy psychosocial network of relationships. This matrix is composed of a variety of people from different settings with whom frequent contact occurs. He can expect instrumental help in a variety of ways in finding an apartment, securing a proper lease, getting a job or learning about social security benefits to which he may be entitled. There is a range of reciprocity in these relationships, with the professionals having somewhat less need of

the resident than the resident has of them, but otherwise the network of friends potentially approaches symmetrical reciprocity.

The program also encourages former residents to maintain continuing contact with Berkeley House. Weekly meetings are organized for ex-residents; an extra bed is always reserved in case an ex-resident needs to return temporarily due to a crisis; and visits at any time without charge are permitted. Residents often leave the halfway house in pairs or in small groups and take apartments together, thus maintaining their closest relationships. Once settled, they reach out to the next generation of ex-residents, helping them to find housing and meet other needs surrounding the transition.

Budson and Jolley (1978) state that this psychosocial kinship model is particularly appropriate for two types of patients: patients who have been hospitalized so long that their family and friendship circles have atrophied, and young adults with a history of social isolation except for their connections to nuclear family members. Evaluation of the program's outcome among 78 of these latter ex-residents revealed that, one year after leaving the halfway house, 91 percent were living independently, 74 percent were at work or in school, and almost 60 percent had continuing contact with other ex-residents (Budson, Grob, & Singer, 1977). A second study that investigated the relationship between community tenure and involvement in the house's ex-resident program revealed that almost three-quarters of the 182 residents who were served over a 7-year period continued to affiliate with the house (Lynch, Budson, & Jolley, 1977). Unfortunately, in the absence of information about the efficacy of alternative forms of halfway house rehabilitation — particularly alternatives that place little of no emphasis on developing the social system among comparable residents — there is little basis for judging the relative superiority of this type of treatment. Short of precise measurement, however, these findings compare favorably with Rog and Rausch's (1975) follow-up studies of the residents of 26 halfway houses. Generally, they found 20 percent of ex-residents were rehospitalized, 58 percent showed successful, independent living in the community, and 55 percent were employed or in school.

## The Community Network Development Project

The Community Network Development (CND) approach, implemented by the Florida Mental Health Institute in Tampa, Florida, places as much emphasis as does Berkeley House on the creation of a peer support system among formerly hospitalized mental patients

(Edmunson, Bedell, Archer, & Gordon, 1982). It differs, however, by basing its operation in four catchment areas in the Tampa region, rather than in a single mental health facility such as a group home or a halfway house. That is, since clients are dispersed in a variety of living arrangements throughout the four locales, the project's main goal is to organize a variety of decentralized programs and activities that offer occasions for the development of new peer ties and the expression of mutual support. Only one of the geographic zones served by the CND project contained a congregate living facility housing eight persons who jointly managed their household.

The services and activities offered by the CND project include: areawide meetings that center on recreational and leisure pursuits; group problem-solving sessions that address the members' individual and collective problems in living; networkwide meetings that draw together members from each of the four catchment areas; business activities that focus on the fund-raising needs of the entire project; and educational and growth-oriented activities. These last activities involve programmed instructional modules on community living skills, job hunting, leadership, communication, and problem-solving skills, as well as group goal-planning activities that identify the necessary skills for dealing with specific problems of needs. The major purpose of all these activities is to create a social fabric "whereby former mental health clients who reside in the community form a helping network for each other and provide each other with emotional, instrumental, and recreational support in their daily lives" (Edmunson et al., 1982, p. 133).

In order to animate an active, informal, peer support system, a staff composed of both professionals and paraprofessionals is necessary. It coordinates all network activities and plans outreach strategies to potential new members and to those who require extra help in sustaining involvement in the network. The mental health professionals serve as staff area managers, hiring, training, and providing ongoing consultation to community area managers, who, in turn, supervise member leaders, member volunteers, and members themselves. The community area managers are part-time paraprofessionals who are either current or former mental health clients and who are paid to offer peer counseling and to organize social activities within their geographic areas. They carry major responsibility for ensuring a high level of member involvement, planning the agenda for weekly area meetings, and facilitating the formation of ties among area members. The member leaders and the member volunteers assist the community area managers in these activities.

The CND approach is essentially fashioned in the mold of mutual-help groups. Members are oriented toward dealing with their difficulties through small group problem solving rather than by seeking professional help. The incorporation of paraprofessional peer counselors within the network also resembles the inclusion in mutual-help groups of veteran models who have successfully managed the same hardships as ordinary members of the group. Members have "round-the-clock" access to the network's resources, and, because they already live in the open community, the network they develop can continue indefinitely. In contrast, the residents of both Fairweather et al.'s Community Lodge society and Berkeley House risked losing important network contacts at the time they left their temporary placements or when the placements themselves closed. On the other hand, the CND model does not include a work component or a vocational preparation program and is therefore less comprehensive in its rehabilitation effort. It also began by serving patients whose functioning was not severely impaired: Initial clients had been hospitalized for less than four months, did not require constant supervision, and were capable of group participation (Edmunson et al., 1982). Preliminary evidence comparing 40 CND members' use of mental health services over a period of 10 months to the use made by a randomly selected control group of 40 patients who received only traditional aftercare services indicated that the CND clients required significantly less mental health treatment and had significantly fewer hours of outpatient contact. While the figures are not statistically significant, the two groups also differed in the total number of hospitalized days, the CND clients reporting 40 days and the control group 136 days. These data ought to be judged cautiously, however, because they are based on clients' self-reports and do not take into consideration the amount of individualized professional and peer counseling the CND members received.

## Fountain House and Fellowship House

Fountain House in New York City (Beard, 1978) and Fellowship House in South Miami, Florida, are two additional examples of psychiatric rehabilitation programs that foster the development of peer support networks while also offering a more comprehensive set of services than those provided by the CND project: Both programs attempt to repopulate former mental patients' networks with new peer relationships by involving them in abundant recreational and social activities, and both offer housing and vocational rehabilitation services. Fountain House, the older of the two psychosocial rehabilitation centers, has a bank of approximately 40 apartments accommodating small groups of former patients (who are referred to as members), while Fellowship House offers a more elaborate choice of housing arrangements, ranging from a closely supervised halfway house that has a high measure of internal structure to satellite apartments suitable for those who are more capable of independent living. Both Fountain House and Fellowship House hold the leases to these housing units and group meetings are held among the residents to discuss housekeeping problems and to forestall interpersonal difficulties. Both facilities also offer a prevocational training program for members who are not ready for employment outside a sheltered context. The programs focus on upgrading work skills by involving the members in the maintenance of the physical plant of the houses, involving them in clerical and research/educational activities, and in the food service area. A team approach similar to the one implemented in Fairweather et al.'s Community Lodges is taken, except that here, staff work alongside the members. Finally, both houses have developed placements for their members in a variety of local businesses. They have secured entry-level, half-time positions that are rotated among their members every four to six months, each position first occupied by a house staff member who learns about its demands, trains members in the necessary work skills, and remains on the job alongside the member until competent performance levels are attained. Both individual and group placements are available.

While both of the rehabilitation programs make a less concerted effort than the CND project and Berkeley House to build a coherent peer group network among their members, they nevertheless seem to accomplish this end by planning all rehabilitative activities within a social matrix. The hallmark of their common approach to both social and vocational recovery in the community is to foster interdependence in living arrangements, employment preparation, and on-the-job skill development. Two studies that examined rates of Fountain House member rehospitalization generally revealed that, compared to ex-mental patients referred to other aftercare facilities, members who received active outreach services had significantly lower rehospitalization rates in the short run (two years in one study and five years in the other), and spent 40 percent fewer days in the hospital than controls. In short, participation in the full spectrum of Fountain House programming delayed, but did not prevent, rehospitalization (Beard, Malamud, & Rossman, 1978).

## THE ROLE OF NONPROFESSIONALS AND FAMILY MEMBERS IN COMMUNITY TREATMENT PROGRAMS

One general observation about the selection and role of the staff in many of the preceding rehabilitation programs is warranted. Virtually all of these programs have incorporated nonprofessionals either as primary care managers or as house staff. In some cases, ex-mental patients who have achieved successful vocational and social rehabilitation occupy these positions, and in others the staff positions are filled by individuals who share the socioeconomic background of the patients, are interested in people with psychiatric problems, and show exceptional ability in working with them. In the Philadelphia Enabler Program (Weinman & Kleiner, 1978) which I have not described in detail, housewives who had little prior experience or training in dealing with mental patients but who were particularly motivated to work with a chronic population were the primary treatment agents. Working on a one-to-one basis with patients, their role involved training and assisting patients in such daily life activities as housekeeping, food preparation, and shopping, as well as ensuring that they took their medication and attended appropriate community activities and agencies. Similarly, Mosher and Menn (1978) used specially trained nonprofessionals as the primary staff in an intensive and unorthodox approach to the treatment of schizophrenics who were acutely disturbed. The residents of Soteria House were given minimal or no medication during the course of their psychotic episodes, but were allowed to experience the crisis in the company of nonprofessionals who offered a trusting and supportive relationship. Mosher and Menn's (1978, p. 87) preference for using nonprofessional treatment agents stems from their belief that

> relatively untrained, psychologically unsophisticated persons can assume a phenomenological stance vis-à-vis psychosis more easily than highly trained persons (e.g., M.D.s or Ph.D.s) because they have learned no theory of schizophrenia, whether psychodynamic, organic, or a combination of both. Because they lack the preconceived ideas of professionals, our nonprofessional staff members have the freedom to be themselves, to follow their visceral responses, and to be a person with the psychotic individual. Highly trained mental health professionals tend to lose their freedom in favor of a more cognitive, theory-based, learned response that may invalidate a patient's experience of himself if the professional's theory-based behavior is not congruent with the patient's felt needs.

A second noteworthy feature of the programs I have reviewed is that they neither involve the patient's nuclear family members in the process of building a supportive social milieu nor generally include them in the reconstituted network. There are several reasons for their exclusion. First, in many cases nuclear family ties have been severed many years earlier as a result of lengthy hospitalizations. Second, family members may not reside proximal to the rehabilitation setting in which the patients participate. Third, relations with family members who are nearby may be so conflictual and guilt-ridden that they are usually either addressed separately or actively discouraged. In commenting on their approach to the families of patients who participated in the Training in Community Living project, a program that diverted patients from the hospital and substituted intensive training in daily living skills, Stein and Test (1978, p. 47) write:

> Work with families is primarily directed toward breaking pathological dependency ties. With married patients structured meetings with patient and spouse are held to facilitate increased symmetry in the relationship. Most of the patients however are unmarried. In these cases families (parents, parent surrogates, siblings) are evaluated to determine whether the patients' problems are significantly contributed to by a pathological family relationship. When this is found to be the case a highly specialized treatment approach termed constructive separation is utilized.

The message that is communicated to family members in this process of constructive separation is that their contact with the patient would only undermine his or her ability to accomplish the program's goals and, consequently, it should be curtailed. While the staff provide support to the family in making the separation, either on a case basis, as in the TCL program, or on a group basis, as in Chicago's Thresholds program (Dincin, 1975), the fact remains that family members are left with little direct involvement in the therapeutic enterprise. Only much later — "when the patient has gained sufficient independence to relate to his family in a more adult to adult fashion" (Stein & Test, 1978, p. 48) — is contact reestablished.

Continued empirical research will determine whether or not the patient's rehabilitative progress is advanced by strongly restricting continuing contact with immediate family members or by improving the quality of their interaction via the clinical approaches outlined earlier. In the meantime, the many needs of those family members who are accessible demand the attention of the rehabilitation programs serving their relatives. Moreover, those families who actually carry the burden of caring for a severely psychiatrically disabled relative at home are in even more desperate need of support and guidance. Family care of the mentally ill, either on a partial or full-time basis, has increased dramatically since the beginning of this era of de-institutionalization, yet, until recently, few initiatives have been taken by professionals to support caretaking in this informal sphere. These new initiatives have been sparked by two developments: (a) the emergence of mutual-aid and advocacy organizations composed of family members of schizophrenics and patients themselves who seek more support for their informal caregiving activities; and (b) the refinement of scientific knowledge about the attributes of the schizophrenic's family environment that predispose to relapse during aftercare. Knowledge gained about relatives' "expressed emotion" has, in turn, formed the basis for intervention programs that guide the family toward interactions with patients that foster their recovery.

## Parents of Adult Schizophrenics

Parents of Adult Schizophrenics is a mutual-help and advocacy group that was launched in 1973 by a group of fifteen parents of adult schizophrenics who not only needed ongoing contact with others facing similar stressful circumstances, but also required supplementary services including periodic respite from caregiving. Their early contacts with one another also helped them to identify and subsequently overcome attitudes held by professional service providers that undermined their confidence in their own helping abilities. For example, they realized that such terms as the "schizophrenogenic mother" and the "identified patient," a term suggesting that the entire family, not just the patient, was disturbed, had the effect of raising the family's doubts about the adequacy of its healing and caring provisions (Lamb & Oliphant, 1978). Further, they were able to discuss the adverse emotional fallout of certain advice proffered by mental health professionals about methods of coping with their relatives' disturbance. This advice usually directed them either to give up on the patient because the sacrifice was too great or to insulate themselves from the emotional concomitants of their interactions with the patient. Unwilling to comply with the former advice and incapable of the latter, the families gradually developed a set of guidelines that were more realistic and more effective. The advice the group now shares with other parents of schizophrenic adults and conveys to professionals is summarized by Lamb and Oliphant (1978, p. 805):

Goals for patients should be realistic; it is important for professionals and relatives to determine together what a patient can achieve. Then, if a relative can maintain objectivity and emotional overinvolvement does not cloud his judgment, he can apply pressure to counteract the patient's social withdrawal. However, the patient must not be pushed to achieve standards beyond his capability, and he must be left with a good deal of control over what he actually does.

The group also educates new members about current research on the causes of schizophrenia, emphasizing the fact that biochemical, hereditary, and social factors interact in determining its onset and course. The group's advocacy work has been directed toward expanding the range of services that are available to long-term patients and educating legislators and mental health professionals about how to structure services in a way that leaves a meaningful role for the family members who wish to participate in their relatives' rehabilitation. Since its beginnings in California, Parents of Adult Schizophrenics has become a national organization. Its Canadian counterpart, ARAFMI (Association of Relatives and Friends of the Mentally Ill), is equally active.

## The Quality of Emotional Responses in the Families of Schizophrenic Patients: Research on Expressed Emotion

Recent empirical studies of the quality of the schizophrenic's interactions with family members at home give credence to the approach recommended by Parents of Adult Schizophrenics. In the previous quotation the group advises family members to guard against emotional overinvolvement with the patient, to recognize that the patient must not be pushed, and to allow the patient a good deal of control over his or her actions. Similar phrases appear in the writing of Brown, Birley, and Wing (1972) and Vaughn and Leff (1976a, 1976b), researchers who have found that the most powerful predictor of relapse and hospital recidivism among schizophrenic patients who are discharged to the home of a relative is the extent to which a key family member in the home is highly critical of or emotionally overinvolved with the patient. Relatives who frequently engage in this type of interpersonal influence are categorized as high EE (expressed emotion), and patients who are exposed to their influence during the nine months after hospital discharge are significantly more likely to relapse than patients who have had contact with low EE relatives (Brown et al., 1972; Vaughn & Leff, 1976b). Furthermore, this relationship held even when controls were introduced for the degree of the patient's behavioral disturbance and work impairment.

showed that it largely reflected three aspects of the key relative's attitudes toward the patient: the number of critical remarks that were made about the patient (based on content and tone of voice); the expression of hostility toward the patient; and the expression of emotional overinvolvement or excessive concern about the patient. Each of these three domains was measured in an interview with a key family member (usually a spouse, but sometimes a parent) shortly after a patient had been readmitted to outpatient or inpatient care, and appropriate measures of interrater reliability were taken and were deemed satisfactory. The resulting index of EE showed that 58 percent of the schizophrenic patients from high EE homes relapsed during the nine months after their discharge from treatment, compared to only 16 percent of the low EE group. Furthermore, Vaughn and Leff's (1981) inquiry into the beliefs that distinguish high EE from low EE relatives revealed that the former do not tend to view schizophrenia as a legitimate illness over which the patient has little control and therefore are less tolerant of the patient's disturbed functioning, placing more conformity pressures on him or her.

Several intervention programs have recently been mounted to reduce the rate of patient relapse by modifying the expressed emotion in the patient's home and by educating the family about the nature of schizophrenia and its treatments (Anderson, Hogarty, & Reiss, 1981; Berkowitz, Kuipers, Eberlein-Frief, & Leff, 1981; Falloon, Boyd, McGill, Strang, & Moss, 1981; Snyder & Liberman, 1981). The programs differ in the approaches they take to lower the elements of expressed emotion among family members, some adopting a more unstructured support group approach in which high and low EE relatives are combined, the latter modeling a calmer, more accepting, and tolerant manner of dealing with patients (Berkowitz et al., 1981). By contrast, Falloon et al. (1981) have deployed a strict behavioral strategy of intervention, consisting of family therapy in the home, communication and problem-solving training, and education about the principles of behavioral change and about schizophrenia. Preliminary results of these two controlled trials show that, in the short term, both approaches lower the relatives' levels of expressed emotion and prevent relapse. A third approach has concentrated on fashioning a new form of family therapy that focuses on high EE patterns of communication and modifies them (Snyder & Liberman, 1981), and a final approach taken by Anderson, Hogarty, and Reiss (1981) offers families a series of workshops imparting both "survival skills" and knowledge about schizophrenia and patient management. All four approaches incorporate pharmacological regimens for the patient. Berkowitz et al.'s (1981) intervention differs from the other three in excluding the schizophrenic patients from the family program.

Goldstein's (1981, p.2) comments aptly summarize these intervention programs' shared perspective on the family's role in the informal care of a schizophrenic relative. He writes that the programs' designers

> do not deny that families of schizophrenics frequently are disrupted and disordered but that they do not see these negative patterns as a basis for family rejection or isolation. Instead, [they] see beyond these acrimonious relationships to latent strengths in the families of patients — strengths that can be mobilized under the right circumstances as a constructive force for change. Rather than isolating or rejecting relatives of schizophrenics, [they] try to involve them as allies in the aftercare of the patient.

## CONCLUSION

This chapter brings a social-ecological perspective to bear on clinical interventions with outpatient clients and with the chronically mentally ill. It discusses how the patient's social network can influence the course and outcome of professional treatment and it lists several types of clinically relevant information that can inform the professional's assessment of the client's social milieu. Several methods of directly intervening in the patient's social network are also described but await evaluation. Their common aims are to restructure the network and to improve communications among members in order to reestablish stability and reciprocity following crises. The chapter also considers alternative ways of structuring the social ties and mobilizing informal support on behalf of chronic mental patients living in community-based facilities. Community rehabilitation programs differ most sharply in the relationships they prompt patients to cultivate; some place an emphasis on creating a "psychosocial kinship system" composed of former associates and family members, while others insist on severing family ties because they are deemed psychologically destructive to the patient. In many instances the close relatives of the mentally ill have either been left without a meaningful role to play in the rehabilitation process or they have not received adequate support in their informal caregiving roles. Some relatives have attempted to redress this problem by organizing mutual-aid associations, while others are benefiting from new family intervention programs that combine education and training based on principles gleaned from "expressed emotion" research.

**Part III**

# *SPECIFIC APPLICATIONS*
# *OF SOCIAL SUPPORT*

Chapter 5

# MEDICAL AND WORK CONTEXTS

The concept of social support was first introduced in this volume through descriptions of three empirical studies whose subjects were undergoing contrasting types of life stressors. While all three studies pointed out the protective effects of social support on health and morale, two of them also bore important implications for institutional practices. Hospitals, for example, could revise policies regarding patient contact with supportive family members and friends, and job termination might have fewer adverse psychological consequences if employers ensured that supportive contacts in the community were available to workers during job transitions. Both studies point out that opportunities for mobilizing social support exist outside the traditional purview of mental health practice.

This chapter focuses on two of the contexts represented among the volume's introductory studies. First, it enlarges on strategies of mobilizing social support to improve coping with the psychosocial problems that arise during rehabilitation from medical illness. Specifically, it considers the adaptive demands faced by cardiac patients and by women diagnosed with breast cancer, demands that arise following the acute phase of their medical crises, and it reviews types and outcomes of supportive group interventions on their behalf. Second, the latter half of the chapter provides an overview of recent studies examining the role of social support in the workplace. It outlines the types of inquiries that have been undertaken by occupational stress researchers and "burnout" researchers, spotlighting differences in their approaches to this topic.

## SOCIAL SUPPORT IN MEDICAL REHABILITATION

In their seminal papers on social support's role in protecting health, Cobb and Cassel concentrated far more on the variety of physical health outcomes, medical conditions, and health behaviors that were susceptible to the influence of social support than on mental health outcomes. For example, Cobb (1976, p. 30) summarizes his review with this observation:

> The conclusion that supportive interactions among people are important is hardly new. What is new is the assembling of hard evidence that adequate social support can protect people in crisis from a wide variety of pathological states: from low birth weight to death, from arthritis through tuberculosis to depression, alcoholism, and other psychiatric illness. Furthermore, social support can reduce the amount of medication required and accelerate recovery and facilitate compliance with prescribed medical regimens.

Similarly, Cassel (1976, p. 121) concludes his review of the literature on the health protective effect of social support as follows:

> Taken alone, then, not one of these studies is entirely convincing. Taken together, however, the results are more impressive . . . the health outcomes have spanned a spectrum from self-reported symptoms and sickness behaviors to levels of blood pressure, complications of pregnancy and death.

Each of these quotations also touches on the authors' own epidemiological inquiries; Cobb mentions arthritis because he and Gore (1978) found that, following job loss, men with low levels of support from members of their own social networks had a much greater probability of having two or more swollen joints than men with high levels of support. Cassel mentions pregnancy complications because he and his colleagues found that, among expectant mothers who had experienced high life stress before and during their pregnancies, those who had high "psychosocial assets" suffered fewer complications in labor and delivery than those with low psychosocial assets (Nuckolls, Cassel, & Kaplan, 1972). In sum, both of these epidemiologists based their keystone formulations on a large body of medical evidence suggesting that unmet needs for psychological and material support increase human vulnerability to physical disease and disability and prolong recovery from illness episodes.

Social support has a powerful impact on the latter domain of health behavior because the process of rehabilitation from acute illnesses and adaptation to chronic illnesses usually unfolds after the patient has been discharged from the hospital and its course and outcome are therefore strongly influenced by those persons who inhabit the patients' social environment. In particular, their accommodations to the patient's rehabilitative regimen and their responses to the patient's own emotional and behavioral changes following the period of intensive medical intervention have critical effects on patient adjustment and health status.

Extensive study has been made of the ways patients' networks influence adaptation to various illnesses. Doehrman (1977) has reviewed the literature pertaining to the psychosocial aspects of recovery from coronary heart disease, Dushenko's (1981) review pertains to cystic fibrosis, Johnson's (1980) deals with juvenile diabetes, Meyerowitz's (1980) addresses breast cancer, and King's (1980) focuses on asthmatic children. In contrast, knowledge of practical methods that can be used to foster psychosocial adaptation has lagged far behind. Only two recent reviews have considered the design and effects of planned support group interventions in medical rehabilitation (DiMatteo & Hays, 1981; Hackett, 1978), and only the second offers details about the practical matters of group composition, leadership, and process. Hence, I begin with a brief account of the psychosocial needs that patients experience in the stage of medical rehabilitation, and then concentrate on ways of implementing and evaluating patient support groups. I include within my scope both professionally led support groups and mutual-help groups, illustrating their application in the rehabilitation of patients suffering from two medical conditions: patients with chronic and acute heart ailments and women who have developed cancer of the breast and who may have undergone mastectomies.

## Psychosocial Needs of Patients in the Rehabilitative Process

Although different types of illnesses and medical interventions arouse different adjustment needs, at least six kinds of threat are more or less imposed by all illness experiences: (a) threats to life itself; (b) threats to bodily integrity and comfort; (c) threats to self-concept and future plans; (d) threats to emotional equilibrium; (e) threats to the accomplishment of customary roles and social activities; and (f) threats associated with the demands of adjusting to a new physical or social environment (Cohen & Lazarus, 1979).

Stern (1978) and Doehrman (1977) have described the specific forms that these threats take during the immediate recuperative period of heart disease, and Meyerowitz (1980) and Thomas (1978) have outlined their character in relation to breast cancer. Stern (1978) reports that the majority of cardiac patients experience intense feelings of anxiety and depression in the aftermath of their heart attacks; they worry about their ability to resume regular work, to fulfill their obligations in their family roles, and retired heart patients in particular dread the curtailment of leisure activities that have represented important sources of satisfaction and interpersonal support. In addition, patients are concerned about the present and future financial burden incurred by their medical problem, their ability to adhere to the physician's advice regarding new patterns of eating and exercising entailed by their present condition, and ultimately, their most profound fear is imminent death. Stern, Pascale, and McLoone (1976) also observe that virtually all previous reports of heart patients' post-hospitalization distress include mention of the patients' fears of a second, potentially fatal heart attack. Whether or not they see themselves as personally responsible for triggering their heart ailment, they also experience a diminution of self-esteem because they are no longer able to meet former (usually high) levels of work output, sexual functioning, and physiological resilience. Those patients in particular whose precoronary behaviors conformed to the Type A pattern of functioning — extreme aggressiveness, easily aroused hostility, a sense of time urgency, and competitive achievement strivings (Rosenman, 1978) — tend to make self-deprecating attributions that compound their recuperative difficulties. Stern (1978, p. 44) notes that their prior aggressive style not only predisposes them to depression following their heart attacks, but also tends to give them little experience in giving or getting emotional support:

> Pre-infarct, they manage by functioning as human dynamos — spending long hours at work and having little time for human intimacy and recreational comforts. Post-infarct, however, their hyper work activity is curtailed, and their independence of action sharply limited by medical restrictions. . . . they find themselves, frequently for the first time in their adult lives, dependent on their relationships with others, particularly their physicians and families. For many

patients with these personality characteristics, the shock is too much and regression into a state of brooding depressive passivity is the result.

Doehrman's (1977) extensive review of the literature on the psychosocial aspects of recovery from heart disease confirms Stern and his colleagues' observations about the psychological and social threats patients face, adding information about the strains that arise in their interactions with family members. Fearing another heart attack, patients' wives tend to behave too solicitously toward them, causing patients to react to their spouses' overprotectiveness by dominating them. Doehrman (1977, p. 214) also notes:

> The emotional distress of most CHD patients reaches a peak after hospital discharge during convalescence at home. Some patients become very depressed at this time. Family tensions are common. Nonetheless, one study suggested that patients seek and receive most of their social support from relatives, friends and their doctor and very little from institutional or professional services.

Doehrman's last reference is to Croog, Lipson, and Levine's (1972) study of informal helping resources in the recovery process. They found that different actors in the network specialized in the types of help they rendered; both kin and nonkin sources of assistance were highly valued for their moral support, neighbors were more highly valued than were kin for the concrete services they provided to the patients, and kin were deemed most helpful by virtue of the financial aid they rendered.

The social and emotional repercussions of breast cancer and mastectomy are strikingly similar to those of heart ailments. However, women requiring mastectomies also must come to terms with bodily disfigurement and attendant fears of loss of femininity (Ray, 1978). Meyerowitz's (1980, p. 114) review of the psychosocial impact of breast cancer points to three problems requiring attention in the rehabilitation process:

> To summarize, most women can be expected to experience (a) some degree of depression, anxiety, and/or anger; (b) some disruption in everyday life patterns, including marital and/or sexual relationships; and (c) considerable fear regarding the danger and mutilation of cancer and mastectomy.

Evidence that these problems are not generally attended to by the medical care staff comes from a recent study of patients' unmet needs 3 to 24 months after their mastectomies. Kagan, Olsson, and Shalit (1980) administered a semistructured questionnaire to 142 women and found that, of the 228 unmet needs they deemed of moderate or critical importance to their adaptation, 85 (almost 30 percent) were needs for advice about medical or psychological care, 36 (13 percent) were needs for both general support and specific opportunities to ventiliate their feelings and gain reassurance about the future, 32 (11 percent) were needs for advice about problems that had surfaced in their relationships with their husbands, families, or friends, and 115 (40 percent) pertained to needs for information about their health or health care. The latter no doubt reflect problems or uncertainties about permissible health behaviors in the recovery period, that is, questions of adherence to an appropriate health regimen. The authors concluded that approximately 80 percent of these women's unmet needs could be addressed by providing individual or group programs of support. Similarly, Mitchell and Glicksman (1977) found that 28 of 50 cancer patients undergoing radiation therapy could not nominate an individual with whom they could discuss their emotional problems and 86 percent of the patients wished they had such an outlet. Parenthetically, the potential value of peer support groups was indicated by patients who had disclosed their concerns to one another in the waiting room; they expressed a desire for more opportunities to discuss problems with other cancer patients.

Meyerowitz (1980) finds much agreement in the literature about the importance of emotionally supportive relationships in fostering psychological adjustment to cancer, adding that key sources of support include "support from their doctor or other medical personnel, from spouse and family, and from other patients who either have been or are concurrently in a situation similar to that of the patient" (p. 123). One study that inquired into the psychosocial factors that distinguished between women who reported better and worse adjustments to their mastectomies revealed that the former received significantly more emotional support from doctors, surgeons, nurses, spouses, and their children than the latter (Jamison, Wellisch, & Pasnau, 1978).

Thomas (1978) has outlined the psychosocial problems of mastectomy patients and their families during ten critical phases of the diagnostic and treatment process. She points out that the coping responses of patients and family members are congruent during certain phases and conflict during others, creating even greater stress for both parties. For example, in the "prediagnostic period" when symptoms are first discovered and medical specialists have not yet been consulted, both patient and husband are likely to deny the possibility of cancer and to delay seeking expert diagnosis. However, later, when the patient is hospitalized for a breast lump biopsy and even after a malignancy is confirmed, she typically copes by denying the gravity of her situation while family members and the spouse in particular try to face up to the threatening situation and urge the patient to do so too. This clash of coping patterns makes the parties angry with each other, confused about how best to meet each other's emotional needs, and apprehensive about the impact of the illness on future family functioning. Thus supportive interventions must not only address the patient *and* the family's emotional needs, but they also must teach both parties how to render support to one another in a way that does not undermine the coping behaviors that are of adaptive value to each.

Patients with heart ailments and women who have developed breast cancer thus face a common set of psychosocial adjustment challenges. Initially they experience intense emotional reactions to their illnesses, usually anxiety and depression, and they must grapple with the long-term threat to their health. Second, they must develop new patterns of living that accommodate their changed physical health, some of which are clearly prescribed by medical authorities and some left to the patient's own discretion. They must also contend with the reactions of their families and social intimates, whose coping strategies may be at odds with their own. Typically, network members are either overprotective or too demanding during the recovery process. Patients must also come to terms with changes in their self-perceptions and regain their self-esteem, which has often been damaged because they are either temporarily or permanently unable to function at pre-illness levels. Finally, the disfigurement of mastectomy and the enforced reduction of activity among postcoronary patients may bring into question their attractiveness and their capacity for physical intimacy.

## Using Support Groups to Foster Rehabilitation from Illness

Programs addressing the psychosocial needs of patients in these two diagnostic categories have been initiated by physicians, rehabilitation psychologists, and social workers. In addition, mutual-help organizations have created hospital- and community-based support group programs that address the needs of both patients and family members. The most comprehensive approaches unite the efforts of medical personnel and self-help groups, thus ensuring that patients' needs for emotional and medical aftercare are met.

Professionally organized support groups for heart patients are usually referred to as "therapy groups." However, this label does not accurately reflect the ways members engage in the groups' processes. Indeed, group leaders report that heart patients (the majority of whom are men) are particularly resistant to exploring their feelings about the emotionally threatening aspects of the illness. For example, in one of the earliest group approaches to the rehabilitation of the postcoronary patient, Adsett and Bruhn (1968) held ten "psychotherapeutic" sessions with six patients and their wives and found that the patients fended off their feelings of anxiety and depression by engaging in such counterphobic behavior as joking about their predicaments. Relative to a matched control group of patients, those in the therapy group had higher serum cholesterol levels, an adverse physiological outcome. In a study involving a larger sample of patients, Rahe, Tuffli, Suchor, and Arthur (1973) also report that four to six group therapy sessions had no beneficial effects in comparison to a no treatment control group, findings largely substantiated in two earlier anecdotal case studies (Bilodeau & Hackett, 1971; Mone, 1970). One controlled study yielded positive physiological outcomes of group therapy, but showed few effects on the patients' psychosocial adaptation (Ibrahim, Feldman, Sultz, Staimin, Young, & Dean, 1974). After one year of weekly group psychotherapy sessions, patients had higher survival rates and shorter periods of hospitalization relative to the controls. Those patients who were more seriously ill at the outset of the study appeared to benefit most from the intervention.

Nor is the term "therapy group" justified on the basis of the substance of the intervention. For example, in the "group therapy" that Rahe, Ward, and Hayes (1979) extended to myocardial infarction patients, peer support and educational input from medical staff figured most prominently:

> The major approach to the group sessions was educational. Discussion centered upon the problems inherent in optimal rehabilitation. The beginning of each session often included a didactic presentation

of educational material; an active discussion followed where patients were encouraged to report their experiences with the topic. Some confrontation of patients' coronary behaviors was allowed, but the sessions were generally supportive rather than critical of long-standing life styles [p. 231].

Collectively, these studies show that patients attend the group sessions at a high rate, welcoming the opportunity to talk about their illnesses with one another, but preferring not to disclose their feelings about their illness experience. Hackett (1978) observes that the group's chief contribution was the assistance patients rendered one another in their efforts to gain control over their health by smoking less, altering their diets, and gradually resuming work and leisure activities. Moreover, he recommends abandoning the label "group therapy" because it suggests to patients and cardiologists alike that the group members suffer from psychiatric disturbances. Instead, he suggests that the term "support group" conveys a more accurate impression:

> that the group is structured around education and the sharing of experiences. Cardiac patients want to know the facts of their illness and to have someone in authority whom they can question. Practical questions are asked having to do with medication, the limits of activity, the frequency and duration of sexual intercourse, among other things. Furthermore, they want to compare notes with other patients about how problems common to their group have been overcome [p. 128].

Hackett's (1978) personal experience in conducting such groups for cardiac patients led him to the following conclusions about their format and emphasis: (a) Because the process of social comparison is constrained by the presence of the spouse, spouses should receive separate group sessions, ancillary phone contacts, or periodically participate in the patient groups. (b) A staff leader with some medical training in heart disease and disorders should attend in order to meet the group's needs for information about cardiac problems and their treatment, and to reassure members who fear a cardiac emergency. Moreover, the leader should know enough about group processes to prevent undue hostility or passivity, but should not interpret subterranean emotional currents. (c) Groups should be initiated in the hospital and introduced as an element of routine medical (as opposed to psychiatric) rehabilitation. (d) Once discharged, the patients can form or join self-managed coronary clubs that offer a continuing reference group of similar peers and afford access to medical specialists who serve as group sponsors. Group members' anxiety and depression can be dispelled through an equal emphasis on didactic presentations from medical personnel and opportunities for ventilation of patients' feelings about their medical conditions and recuperative progress.

In their review of group approaches to the psychosocial rehabilitation of cardiac patients, neither Blanchard and Miller (1977) nor Hackett (1978) could identify a single controlled study documenting a reduction in anxiety or depression following group involvement. Patients report less emotional strain and prize the group sessions, but objective measures show few ameliorative effects. As noted earlier, Ibrahim et al.'s (1974) controlled trial of group psychotherapy resulted in some physiological gains and less social isolation in the treatment group after one year, but it does not testify to the influence of social support on psychosocial adaptation. Similarly, evaluations of support groups for heart patients (for example, Adsett & Bruhn, 1968; D'Afflitti & Weitz, 1974; Holub, Eklund, & Kennan, 1975; Jersild, 1967; McGann, 1976) rarely present objective evidence of their effects on the parties' psychosocial adaptation. They typically rely on participants' reports concerning the extent to which they shared difficult feelings, increased their knowledge about coronary risk factors and posthospital convalescence, improved their decision making about future plans, made more use of community health resources, and reconciled their own and family members' expectations for care and support. Finally, stroke clubs that combine expert and lay mutual help resources have not been subjected to adequate empirical evaluation (see, for example, Lesser & Watt, 1978).

There is stronger empirical evidence of the ameliorative psychosocial effects of supportive group interventions among the victims of breast cancer. Although case reports also dominate this literature (for example, Corder & Anders, 1974; Parsell & Tagliareni, 1975; Vachon & Lyall, 1976), several controlled studies incorporating objective measures of psychosocial functioning provide a stronger basis for assessing the nature and effects of social support strategies. Spiegel, Bloom, and Yalom's (1981) evaluation of the process and outcome of support groups arranged on behalf of 86 women with metastatic breast cancer is an excellent illustration. The group's aims were to moderate feelings of anxiety and depression in the face of terminal illness and to promote the members' self-esteem and sense of personal control over their situation.

Women with metastatic carcinoma of the breast were randomly assigned to three separate support groups, each composed of seven to ten patients, a psychiatrist or social worker, and a counselor whose breast cancer was in remission. A randomly selected control group of women received routine medical care and an equivalent amount of chemotherapy during the study year. The support groups met weekly for 1½ hours in outpatient settings and had no fixed termination date. Outcome data, collected at four three-month intervals, were based on the following six measures: (a) the Health Locus of Control Scale, a measure of the respondents' perceived control over their health; (b) the Profile of Mood States, a measure of affective arousal; (c) a self-esteem scale; (d) a measure of several habits reflecting maladaptive coping responses, such as eating too much and smoking; (e) an inventory of specific fears; and (f) a denial measure. Due to subject attrition, through death, over the course of the study, special statistical procedures were used to examine group differences in the average rate of change.

The support groups were structured informally and members were not prohibited from contacting one another outside the group sessions. Like the cardiac patients' "therapy groups," neither interpersonal confrontation nor exploration of the group's overall process commanded the members' attention. Instead, they shared mutual fears and concerns related to death and dying, family problems, treatment problems, communication with medical staff, and problems of living with a terminal illness. Having observed another group of cancer patients prior to their present involvement, the two group leaders discussed and evaluated their present groups' process following each group session. Spiegel et al. (1981, p. 531) note that "the skills to conduct such groups may be obtained by persons from many health disciplines over a few months' time through group observation and supervision."

After one year of weekly group sessions, the patients reported significantly less tension, less depression, more vigor, less fatigue, less confusion, less maladjusted coping responses, and fewer phobias. While there was a trend toward improvement in these psychological outcomes at four months and eight months, a full year's participation was necessary before significant group differences appeared. However, even at twelve months, no significant differences were found between the experimental and control groups' scores on measures of self-esteem, denial, and sense of personal control over their health. Comparisons among the three support groups revealed no significant differences, suggesting that any differences in the training or interventions of the groups' leaders had little influence.

Spiegel et al. (1981) identify five dimensions of the change processes that unfolded over the course of the group sessions. First, they observe that patients' discussions provided an occasion for pinpointing and clarifying several problems entailed by their illness and its treatment. Members were able to untangle the web of anxieties associated with their illness and take action, or at least identify the sources of their feelings of helplessness. Second, the basic companionship the groups afforded and the relief gained from venting fears and concerns mitigated the sense of physical and affective isolation the women experienced in their daily lives. Third, the group helped to "detoxify" dying. By witnessing the death of several co-participants and airing the intense fears and grief that attended their deaths, members gained the strength to confront their own imminent death, becoming less phobic about it. Fourth, the group experience helped them to consider more carefully how they wanted to spend their remaining days, some making plans to complete specific projects and some simply gaining a new perspective on ways of living out their family lives. Finally, the very fact of rendering aid to one another despite their present circumstances gave meaning to their lives. Indeed, the group was the one sphere of their lives in which they could see themselves contributing to the well-being of others, thus enhancing their sense of personal worth and usefulness.

Other group approaches reported in the literature on breast cancer provide fewer details about how the peer support process unfolds and conduct a less rigorous evaluation of its outcomes (Corder & Anders, 1974; Krant, Beiser, Adler, & Johnson, 1976, Vachon & Lyall, 1976). Only one study has evaluated the group's influence on recovery outcomes (Winick & Robbins, 1977), but it did not include a control group or control for the patients' preintervention levels of psychological functioning. Other methods of augmenting the social support extended to women with breast cancer have concentrated on the medical staff, encouraging them to help patients ventilate their stressful feelings (Creech, 1975; Holland, 1976). Some emphasis has also been given to reforms of medical care that promise patients continuing and personalized contact with one or two primary care providers (for example, Howard & Strauss, 1975). Bloom, Ross, and Burnell (1978) illustrate the latter approach. They modified the health care provided to cancer patients in order to embed them in a more supportive treatment context, incorporating a self-help organization's services.

Basing their intervention on the premise that mastectomy patients receive insufficient reassurance and fragmented care due to their multiple contacts with relatively anonymous medical personnel, Bloom, Ross, and Burnell (1978) mobilized and coordinated three sources of psychological support: a volunteer who was affiliated with the American Cancer Society's Reach to Recovery Program (Markel, 1971), an oncology counselor, and a social worker. The volunteer extended emotional support immediately preceding and following surgery, and provided information about everyday matters of living. Fundamentally, she served as a successful role model. The oncology counselor also provided support and information to the patient and her family before and after surgery, and maintained close communication with the patient's physician. The social worker's main responsibility was to coordinate the care the patient received during the transition from the hospital back to the community. Thus, beginning at the biopsy stage and extending to the final rehabilitation stage, continuing care was provided by three primary sources.

Two of the measures used in Spiegel et al.'s (1981) study were used to assess the efficacy of this intervention program: the Profile of Mood States and the Health Locus of Control Scale. These measures were administered to a control group of 18 patients admitted to the hospital prior to the new system of supportive medical care and to a group of 21 women admitted thereafter. Each group completed the measures within a week after surgery and two months later. Their findings revealed that the intervention group initially experienced stronger negative affective reactions, including greater tension, depression, and confusion, than those women who had earlier received routine medical care. This trend persisted two months later, but the group differences were no longer significant. Group differences in health locus of control scores were reversed; initially, there were no significant differences in the patients' perceptions of self-efficacy, but two months later patients in the intervention group scored significantly higher. In the absence of long-term follow-up data on the psychological functioning of the mastectomy patients assigned to the supportive medical care, judgment must be reserved about whether such an intervention augurs well for mental health. Indeed, the authors signal their uncertainty about the intervention's benefits by stating:

> Our data suggest that those who receive a support system within the medical-care setting express more extreme emotionality shortly after surgery. One may infer that the program group, in contrast to the comparison group, demonstrated less denial, but whether this reduction has long-term benefits remains to be seen [Bloom, Ross, & Burnell, 1978, p. 57].

The preceding study thus draws attention once again to the relationship between social support and individual coping preferences. It spotlights deficiencies in our understanding of the fit between the psychological means of coping and the supportive provisions rendered by the social milieu. Meyerowitz (1980) believes that it is possible to render support to women with breast cancer without necessarily disrupting a coping style based on denial. She defines support in terms of communications with medical staff that accurately disclose the patient's condition and that allow opportunities for dialogue and empathic exchanges. Bloom, Ross, and Burnell's (1978) approach may have erred by providing such intense continuous exposure to social support that it magnified the threatening aspects of the patient's illness experience, triggering greater mood disturbances. The inclusion of a patient education component may have conditioned a greater sense of control over their health. Thus the evidence from intervention studies involving the mobilization of support among both cardiac and breast cancer patients points to the need for intensive investigation of the interplay between psychological coping strategies and the social environment's contribution to coping.

The inclusion of a Reach to Recovery volunteer in the intervention mounted by Bloom, Ross, and Burnell (1978) is not unique to their work. The American Cancer Society has widely introduced this program in which a volunteer who has had a mastectomy renders emotional support, proffers information, and serves as a general model of successful adaptation. Several mutual-help groups also address the psychosocial needs of cancer patients and their families, including Make Today Count, United Ostomy Association, the Candlelighters (an organization of parents of children with cancer), and the International Association of Larnygectomies. These groups operate on the assumption that relief and practical information are gained through social comparisons with similarly afflicted peers. They offer a sense of fellowship and reliable alliance and, as Wortman and Dunkel-Schetter (1979, p. 144) have pointed out, they help members to reattribute the causes of the adverse reactions they encounter in the community: "By interacting with other cancer patients, it may become evident to the patient that the rejection or avoidance he or she experiences is a normal consequence of the disease, not a reflection of his or her own inadequacy and weakness." Wortman and Dunkel-Schetter also enumerate three conditions under which interaction with other patients may be damaging and that therefore should be closely regulated by professionals who lead patient groups: (a) if it results in self-deprecating social comparison; (b) if other group members model behaviors that reflect a loss of control over their feelings; and (c) if they encounter members whose recuperation takes a turn for the worse.

Adams (1979), Gartner and Reissman (1977), and Tracy and Gussow (1976) have comprehensively reviewed the types and functions of mutual-aid groups in diverse areas of medical rehabilitation. The last report is especially useful because it contains empirical data on the psychosocial benefits derived by members of several health groups. The authors interviewed participants and local and national officers of several organizations, observed group meetings, and attended state and national conventions. On these bases, Tracy and Gussow (1976, p. 388) conclude:

> Perhaps one of the strongest support components that self-help clubs offer is the opportunity for patients to get to know and interact with others who are similarly afflicted, with others who are also attempting to deal with similar adaptive problems, and with those who have already been successful. Members are quite explicit about the importance of role models in their efforts to attain "normalcy" within the limits of disability. This, they note, cannot be provided by physicians: it is something that only those who have gone through the experience can give to another human being.

## Summary

People who are diagnosed with serious illnesses such as heart ailments and breast cancer face numerous adaptive tasks. During the period of intensive hospital treatment, they must make emotional reconciliations to their condition and deal with the threat it poses to life itself and, later, they must adjust to a new pattern of living and reestablish their sense of self-esteem and control. Their interactions with medical practitioners, family members, and other lay helpers during and after hospitalization can complement or disrupt their adaptive strivings. Supportive interventions such as mutual-aid groups, sympathetic medical care, and patient clubs can be introduced to foster psychosocial adaptation and adherence to medical regimens. By combining emotional support and patient education, they can induce more benign appraisals of the threats imposed by illness, thus mitigating attendant anxieties, and teach self-care practices. The effects of support groups for cardiac and breast cancer patients are mixed; patients report some health and psychological benefits that are not always reflected in objective measures. No long-term outcome studies of support group interventions have been reported, nor have systematic comparisons been made of outcomes under varying conditions of group leadership and composition and length of member participation. Support groups have a strong impact on the emotional liability of breast cancer patients in particular, but their longer-term effect on mental health rests on their congruence with individual needs and coping strategies.

## SOCIAL SUPPORT IN THE WORKPLACE

The workplace is a second context that calls for the introduction of support-enhancing interventions. Given the sheer number of hours that people spend on the job and the amount of time they invest in thinking and talking about their jobs and job-related concerns outside working hours, the work sphere undoubtedly has a profound impact on their morale, their physical and mental health, and their personal identity. Especially during economic downturns, employees grapple with issues of job entry, job seniority, and job mobility, while supervisors and managers put on additional pressures for job productivity and efficiency. Workers, feeling squeezed by wage and fringe benefit concessions they must make at the bargaining tables, must also reconcile themselves to downgraded job reassignments, or contend with the threatened loss of the job itself. Even those whose jobs are protected by seniority or special skills show signs of exhaustion and "burnout" from the additional workload they must carry due to "reductions in force" (RIFs), while others are acutely demoralized by the arbitrary dismissal or relocation of trusted coworkers who enriched their work lives.

In short, the recent economic recession dramatizes and more fully exposes the entire range of possible job stressors, increasing their prevalence as well. These stressors include threats to workers' sense of security, job overload, time pressures, excessive demands from supervisors, job ambiguity resulting from successive reassignment, reduced monetary compensation, and poor prospects for job advancement and upward mobility. When these sorts of occupational stressors occur during economically stable and prosperous eras, as they do, they are more likely to reflect the special conditions of the workplace rather than the national economic scene. However, the distinctive feature of the present context of exposure to workplace stressors is its social dimension or, more precisely, the socially impoverished context in which exposure occurs. Three factors condition this state of social impoverishment: (a) the loss of supportive coworkers due to their dismissal or relocation; (b) diminished access to potential sources of support outside the work sphere due to the widespread demoralization and deprivations accompanying economic hardship; and (c) reluctance to cultivate supportive relationships with coworkers who remain in the workplace due to well-founded fears that they will be supplanted by further reductions in force or job reassignments.

This adverse combination of high exposure to occupational stressors in the workplace and low access to supportive relationships with coworkers and supervisors in particular is likely to hinder organizational productivity and worker health. Supporting this proposition is empirical evidence from several recent studies that deal with both the industrial and human service fields, showing that supportive relationships at work moderate job-related strains and ameliorate perceptions of diverse job stressors.

## Social Support and the Reduction of Occupational Stress

Research by Burke and his colleagues (Burke & Weir, 1975, 1976; 1978; Burke, Weir, & Duncan, 1976) and more recently by Cowen (1982) and Kaplan and Cowen (1981) documents the extent of informal helping that occurs among workmates in peer or supervisory relationships. Burke's inquiries into this topic were launched with a study that posed the following question to a sample of 250 engineers and accountants: "Let us suppose something happened to you while you were at work that made you feel extremely tense and anxious. Which one of the following people would you go to first?" Respondents then rank-ordered their preferred helpers from a list that included a spouse, an immediate supervisor at work, an equal-status coworker, a subordinate, a secretary, a close friend of the same sex and one of the opposite sex outside the workplace, a son or daughter, an immediate relative, or someone else. The study followed up this question with probes about the qualities that drew them to the helper of first choice, and ended by asking whether the respondents felt they had sufficient access to sources of support in times of adversity.

Despite the global nature of the initial question, the researchers found that almost one-fourth of the respondents nominated their superior at work as the first choice of helper, and 18 percent ranked an equal-status coworker first. Together, these two categories of workmates made up 45.5 percent of all the first-chosen helpers. Further, they found that 94 percent of the respondents cited someone at work among their first two choices of helpers. The most common reasons given for first choice of helper centered on the helping process this person established and the expertise, knowledge, and experience he or she brought to solving the problem. In short, respondents focused on both the socioemotional conditions created by the helpers and their problem-solving talents, two primary dimensions of informal support that are described in more complete detail in the classification scheme presented in Figure 2.1 (Chapter 2). Respondents were generally satisfied with the number of people to whom they had access for help.

In subsequent studies Burke and his colleagues explored some of the organizational characteristics that were conducive to the expression of social support in the workplace and also probed the kinds of problems typically addressed in these informal helping exchanges. On the latter score, Burke et al. (1976, p. 372) found that male managers tended to feel most comfortable helping their coworkers deal with "problems of a more impersonal nature, dealing with more objective issues and events" rather than with more intimate concerns such as personal relationships and unpleasant affective states. In particular, they were most comfortable helping with such job-related matters as work procedures and performance, material concerns (such as finances or housing), and personal development issues affecting their job or career advancement. Cowen (1982) has reported remarkably consistent findings among a sample of 97 industrial supervisors (mainly foremen). They typically fielded problems pertaining to advancement opportunities, coworker relations, and job restlessness, not domestic or general emotional problems. Kaplan and Cowen's (1981) description of the supervisors' methods of helping also accord with Burke et al.'s (1976) findings; most often, they listened, offered sympathy or empathy, and showed a willingness to help.

In order to assess the broader contextual factors distinguishing between organizations in which managers were more and less involved in informal helping relationships, Burke and Weir (1978) developed a measure of organizational climate that consisted of four empirically derived dimensions — Authentic Relationships, Minimizing Negative Feelings, Task Orientation, and Rational Orientation — and examined its relationship to several measures of informal helping in the workplace. Not surprisingly, they found that organizations that adopted a "participative-consultative" style of management tended to accord greater legitimacy to the expression of informal help among coworkers and, in practice, evidenced more lateral and vertical sharing of both personal and work problems, and more effective and valuable helping.

These noteworthy findings about the circumstances associated with supportive work relationships strongly imply that an organization's structural features and ongoing processes influence the social support norms and behaviors that workers adopt. That is, the extent of support that is expressed in face-to-face relations among coworkers varies in direct relation to the broader structure and social climate of the workplace, its manner of conducting human relations, and the attitudes it conveys regarding its acceptance of helping interactions among its members. Evidence of the benefits to the physical and psychological health of workers that arise from supportive exchanges with their work associates should convince us even further of the need to modify these organizational structures, norms, and processes.

The literature from group dynamics and from the human relations area of organizational psychology clearly demonstrates that cohesive, task-oriented work groups, supportive supervisors, and cooperative worker involvement in decision making about job-related matters favor positive morale and productivity (Kahn, Wolfe, Quinn, Snoek, & Rosenthal, 1964; Katz & Kahn, 1978; Likert, 1961, 1967; Seashore, 1954). In contrast, studies devoted to assessing the role of social support in mitigating *specific occupational stressors* have yielded inconsistent evidence. In fact, the research in this particular domain reflects in microcosm the very same conceptual and methodological ambiguities and the same uncertainties about social support's impact on health outcomes as those that plague research in the broader mental health domain. Chapter 2 identified the set of problems that attend this research, including remarkable disparities among operationalizations of the support construct itself, contrasting preferences for support sources studied, mixed findings regarding the buffering versus direct effects of social support, differential effects of support in the face of contrasting environmental stressors and symptoms of stress, and divergencies among choices of outcome measures of psychological and behavioral functioning. Studies by French (1974), House and Wells (1978), La Rocco and his colleagues (LaRocco, House, & French, 1980; LaRocco & Jones, 1978), and Wells (1982) reveal how these problems are manifested in the domain of occupational stress.

House and Wells's joint and independent reports on the effects of social support are based on a sample of more than 1000 male blue-collar workers in a large tire, rubber, chemicals, and plastics factory; French's research was conducted among a small sample of more highly skilled white-collar workers at the Kennedy Space Center; and LaRocco et al.'s data were collected from a stratified, occupationally diverse (blue- and white-collar) random sample of 636 men. Thus, while these studies are limited to samples of male employees, they cover heterogeneous occupational settings. Further, their measures of social support are highly comparable and some of their measures of occupational stressors and health outcomes also converge.

House and Wells (1978) and Wells (1982) probed workers' *perceptions* of both the instrumental and socioemotional dimensions of the support they received from coworkers and supervisors in the rubber factory (I omit those data also collected about perceived support from other sources in the workers' networks). All of their findings are thus based on a narrow definition of social support, indexed by three items that empirically tapped one dimension of the construct. They asked their respondents to rate separately (a) how much they could rely on supervisors and coworkers "when things get tough at work," and the extent to which these categories of workmates were (b) "willing to listen to your work-related problems," and (c) "helpful to you in getting your job done." Similarly, LaRocco et al. (1980, p. 208) used only four items "designed to tap the presence of psychological and tangible supports" from coworkers and supervisors. Although the report does not list the items, its discussion of findings in relation to the *perceived* effects of social support strongly points to the adaptation of measures very similar to those used by House and by Wells. In both studies, preliminary analyses of the two workplace sources of support showed that they were relatively independent; Wells (1982) found a correlation of .30 between respondents' ratings of support from supervisors and support from coworkers, while LaRocco et al. (1980) report a correlation of .39.

House and Wells (1978) and Wells (1982) related these measures of social support to the rubber workers' ratings of the extent of perceived stress associated with seven aspects of their work: work load, role conflict, responsibility, quality concern, job-nonjob conflict, occupational self-esteem, and job satisfaction. LaRocco et al. (1980) also included the first two of these occupational stresses, adding indexes tapping stresses associated with underutilization of skills and abilities, job future ambiguity, and participation. In order to achieve his particular aim of assessing whether perceived social support in the workplace moderates between objectively determined stressful job conditions and workers' subjective perceptions of occupational stress, Wells (1982) employed "expert" raters who were knowledgeable about jobs in the rubber plant to obtain objective measures of four of the seven occupational stressors. Dependent measures of the rubber workers' physical and mental health included symptoms of heart, ulcer, skin, and chest difficulties and a measure of neurotic symptomatology, while "mental health strain" measures tapped workers' somatic complaints and symptoms of depression, anxiety, and irritation. These dependent health measures, based purely on the self-reports of the workers, thus constitute measures of perceived mental and physical health.

While these studies have yielded relatively consistent general findings regarding social support's effects on occupational stress, there is no discernible pattern underlying their specific results. Thus we learn from these studies that perceptions of some job stresses, but not others, are moderated by the presence of supportive coworkers and supervisors at work, and that peer support moderates some stresses not moderated by supervisor support. In addition, the relationships between job stress and some health outcomes (both physical and affective) are buffered by perceived coworker support while perceived supervisor support protects workers from other potentially adverse outcomes of occupational stress. In short, perceived social support has been found to exert both direct and indirect (buffering) effects on self-reported worker health, but the evidence supporting this conclusion shows no meaningful configuration. In the absence of a coherent theory of social support, there is little basis for generating hypotheses about the kind of occupational and life stressors that are ameliorated by access to particular kinds and sources of social support, or about the types of stress-health relationships that are cushioned in the presence of different types and sources of support. Instead, post hoc explanations abound, invoking numerous implicit but unmeasured variables that make the quiltwork of empirical findings more plausible.

For example, LaRocco et al. (1980), in attempting to explain their finding that coworker support buffers the impact of perceived occupational stress on neurotic and ulcer symptoms but not on job-related strains such as workload dissatisfaction and boredom, invoke ideas about the norms that people subscribe to regarding appropriate occasions for extending and accepting support. They suggest that "only certain job strains and health outcomes would be seen by most people as reasons for seeking or offering social support. Specifically, we think neurotic symptoms and affects (depression, anxiety, somatic complaints) and ulcer symptoms are commonly thought to be both caused or exacerbated by psychosocial stress and potentially responsive to social support, especially the kind of emotional support operationalized . . . here" (p. 23). LaRocco et al. (1980) speculate further that attitudes toward job-related strains (that is, people do not view feelings of job dissatisfaction as legitimate occasions for providing or seeking support) accounted for the finding that neither supervisor nor coworker support generally buffered the relationships between perceived job stress and feelings of job-related strain. In this regard, they suggest that coworkers may perform a "negative buffering" function, exaggerating feelings of job strain. By negatively buffering some stress-strain relationships and positively buffering others, their overall effect may be washed out or at least concealed.

One clue to interpreting the differences between LaRocco et al.'s (1980) findings and those of House and Wells (1978) pertains to differences in the types of workers and work structures they studied. The latter study was conducted among rubber plant employees who were more dependent on their supervisors for feedback and more closely supervised by them. These conditions may have given rise to the superiority of supervisor support in attenuating work stress. In contrast, LaRocco et al. (1980) examined the effects of social support among professionals, managers, and supervisors who were not subject to close hierarchical control and feedback and who therefore relied more on peer workmates for support. Here, strong buffering effects were produced mainly by coworker support. Research by LaRocco and Jones (1978) among a large sample of U.S. Navy enlisted men also points to the greater relevance of leader, as opposed to coworker, support in conditioning feelings of shipboard job satisfaction. Further, Caplan (1971) found that job-stressed NASA professionals who reported poor relations with workmates showed a variety of physiochemical symptoms of strain. Working in the same organizational context, French (1974) reported that employees who maintained supportive working relationships with their subordinates were protected from the physiological strains resulting from work load stress, but supportive relations with peers, supervisors, or subordinates failed to condition the effects of job stress on psychological strains.

Finally, in Wells's (1982) separate analysis of the conditioning effects of workplace support on the relationship between objectively assessed job stress and the rubber workers' subjective perceptions of stress, the importance of the supervisors' support in this kind of work environment was underscored once again. Specifically, Wells found that support from supervisors conditioned four of nine possible relationships between *objective* work conditions and the workers' *perceptions* of stress, including the domains of work-load responsibility and three domains of job dissatisfaction (intrinsic rewards, extrinsic rewards, and importance rewards, the latter having to do with the workers' sense of his job's importance, prestige, and influence). In contrast, coworker support only conditioned perceptions of pressures stemming from work-load responsibility.

House (1981) has recently summarized the general findings of studies of social support's influence on perceptions of occupational stress and on the actual health of workers who are exposed to stressful workplace conditions. His agenda for future research in this area echoes some of the recommendations made in the final section of

Chapter 2, following my review of studies relating social support to broader life stressors and transitions:

> Social support can reduce work stress, improve health, and buffer the impact of work stress on health. Although not large, the body of data reviewed here is remarkably consistent. But not any and every form of social support will reduce every form of work stress or enhance all aspects of health, or buffer all relationships between stress and health. Indeed, the major task for both future research and application is to specify under what conditions what kinds of social support will have what kinds of effects on stress and health [p. 83].

In addition, it is necessary to gain a better understanding of the processes or mechanisms whereby the social support expressed by work associates accomplishes its stress-moderating and stress-ameliorating functions. As I have noted before, there is a shortage of intensive studies of the ways social support is mobilized in the coping process to prevent psychological strain, and the forms that it takes. In addition, information is lacking about the personal and organizational forces that militate against and for the expression of social support in the workplace. On the latter score, Burke and Weir's (1978) discovery of higher levels of interpersonal support in organizations characterized by a "participative-consultative" style of management suggests that organizational redesign and development can complement interpersonal training approaches to create more supportive workplace conditions. For example, Goldenberg's (1971) Residential Youth Center offers a model for the design of institutional settings that place a premium on collaborative and mutually supportive work relationships.

One type of organizational transformation that merits study because of its potential impact on supportive processes is employee ownership. In some cases, the shift to employee ownership entails little more than a buy-out with no changes in organizational control. Other instances involve a wholesale transfer of responsibility for decision making to the employee-owners, increasing their participation in the executive functions of the organization, enlarging their investment in the quality of their life at work, and conditioning workplace relationships so that they contribute to the development of supportive exchanges. Indeed, these natural experiments in employee ownership provide an occasion for assessing how changes in organizational structure and behavior enhance employee embeddedness in a cooperative and supportive social milieu.

Klein (1982) and Tannenbaum (1982) have discussed the effects of various forms of employee ownership — workers' cooperatives, employee stock ownership plans (ESOP), and "social ownerships" — on organizational productivity and participation. Tannenbaum (1982, p. 19) concludes that "the limited evidence that is available suggests that compared to conventionally owned firms, employee owned firms are likely to be more equalitarian, participative and supportive." The research examples he cites show that, as contrasted with employees of conventional companies, employee-owners are involved in a higher level of participative decision making, are less subject to autocratic supervision, and engage in more cooperative relations with coworkers. He argues that the more supportive tendencies of managers in employee-owned firms stem from the fact that their subordinates, who are also worker-owners, elect or hire management personnel. Klein (1982) views participation as the critical process that mediates between employee ownership and workplace social support. She cites evidence revealing that employee ownership increases organizational commitment and the joint monitoring of coworker performance. For example, an increase in worker feedback was observed following the transition to employee ownership at South Bend Lathe, a machine tool manufacturing firm that was bought out by its employees when the company faced liquidation and the loss of 500 jobs. After takeover, the performance of new probationary employees was assessed by other workers, not by a select group of management personnel. The owner-employees' greater pride in their work showed up in huge reductions in expenses formerly resulting from poor workmanship; productivity increased as well, partly because workers had a greater stake in each other's job performance. One tool and cutting grinder at South Bend Lathe captured the collective sentiment at the plant as follows; "Hey, you've got your hand in my pocket if you don't do your job" (*Time,* October 4, 1976, p. 80). These and other experiments in industrial democracy certainly warrant further study because they represent large-scale organizational innovations that promise to foster cohension and support in the workplace.

## Social Support as an Antidote
## to Burnout in Human Service Organizations

A second stream of research on the topic of occupational stress also merits attention because it links social support to job morale and productivity. However, the approach taken by this group of studies yields information of an entirely different order than that produced by the survey studies reviewed above. Taking a more intensive and qualitative approach, largely based on participant-observation, interviews with a small number of respondents, and case studies, this research brings a phenomenological perspective to the study of the organizational and personal processes leading to low worker morale and low productivity. It thus conveys a more holistic appreciation of the experience of work stress.

The research to which I refer has been designated by the term "burnout." As yet there is some disagreement about whether this term refers to a *state* of worker demoralization or the *process* whereby this state is brought about. Cherniss (1980, p. 18) describes burnout as a "process in which a previously committed professional disengages from his or her work in response to stress and strain experienced in the job"; Maslach (1976, p. 81) defines it as the "loss of concern for the people with whom one is working"; and Pines and Aronson (1981, p. 15) define it as a state ensuing from "constant or repeated *emotional pressure* associated with an intense involvement with *people* over long periods of time." Pines and Aronson's emphasis on the strains arising from involvement with people reflects the fact that burnout has been studied almost exclusively within the human services field. Hence these studies of burnout yield insights about the causes and consequences of work stress that are not highly generalizable to industrial, traditional bureaucratic, and nonoccupational settings. However, they enrich our understanding of aspects of the process of support that merit closer scrutiny in the latter contexts.

Cherniss (1980, p. 118) calls upon the impressions of a clinical social worker employed by a community mental health center to illustrate his thesis that the supervisory process best insulates workers from burnout when it strikes a balance between providing support without requiring subordinates to relinquish their autonomy:

The other day I had an emergency, a client, a couple of clients, and I was feeling upset about things. But supervision means we get into stuff about clients very objectively and analyze it. And in a way, it feels like my supervisor's show, like she's doing a performance. The main thing that happens in supervision is she analyzes the client. And that's great for her. She really gets off on it. It can be exciting momentarily for me. And you know, she can help me see a little more clearly what's happening. But for me that takes a lot of the fun out of it. My attitude is, "So you take that client then." I don't want my supervisor to take it away from me, the joy of discovering how to work with this person.

This social worker's sentiments reflect a pervasive theme in this volume's treatment of social support, namely, the regulation of support in a manner that recognizes the helpee's simultaneous needs for meaningful interdependence and independence. It also points out the limitations of inquiries into social support that takes only superficial swipes at the phenomenon. How faithfully can questions of the sort House and Wells (1978) and LaRocco et al. (1980) asked their respondents record this social worker's judgments of the support her supervisor extended? Surely, questions like "How helpful is your supervisor to you in getting your job done?" demand unconditional responses that blur critical distinctions among various supervisor, job, and worker-related contingencies. These questions demand global judgments that are products of complex psychological calculations, each of which, if exposed, tells us about an important contextual dimension of supportive exchanges. In the case of this social worker, such calculations might take the following expressions: "Yes, my supervisor is quite helpful in *telling me* how to proceed with certain clients"; "No, my supervisor is not helpful because she robs me of a sense of ownership of my work."

Pines and Aronson (1981, p. 129) also caution researchers "to think of social support not in a global sense, but as separate functions." In their cross-sectional case study approach to the investigation of burnout, they discerned six basic supportive provisions: listening, technical support, technical challenge, emotional support, emotional challenge, and feedback regarding social reality. While different people offer different provisions, burnout occurred when these provisions were not forthcoming.

The literature on professional burnout has also focused attention on the organizational and personal barriers inhibiting the expression of peer support. The privacy associated with human services work, particularly in the mental health sphere, also tends to isolate professionals from one another, and when group activities are structured into the workday, they rarely satisfy staff needs for support. Cherniss (1980) and Pines and Aronson (1981) describe the sense of disappointment and disillusionment of human service professionals in the quality of interaction that takes place in staff meetings and case conferences. Participants come to these meetings in the hope that they will provide opportunities for meaningful sharing of work-related concerns and a genuine exchange of ideas, but leave feeling stifled by their perfunctory character and embittered by their colleagues' and their own defensive and self-protective reactions to job challenges. In fact, one study of 76 mental health professionals found that more frequent staff meetings were associated with more negative staff attitudes toward patients (Pines & Maslach, 1978). Additionally, differences arising from personal values and theoretical orientations, perceived status differentials, and competition for scarce organizational resources create barriers to personal and professional development.

Deficiencies in social support among human services professionals may also stem from a more fundamental dilemma created by professional norms. In Glidewell, Tucker, Todt, and Cox's (1982) penetrating analysis of the professional norms hindering the expression of support in the teaching profession, the cross-pressures arising in this context are illuminated more clearly than in any other study of professional support systems. The researchers conducted their investigation of "the constraining and facilitating effects of social norms on professional support" (p. 34) in three settings chosen to highlight different aspects of the process of collegial exchange among teachers. The first study simply documented the content of verbal interactions among teachers in two elementary schools by observing their daily communications for several days and then content coding them in four simple categories: (1) description, (2) direction, (3) evaluation, and (4) orientation. After the data were compiled, they were fed back to half the teachers who had been observed, who were asked to interpret the findings.

The findings largely revealed that "description" was the predominant type of communication and "direction" the least frequent. Further, within the latter category of communication, a small proportion of directions involved advice, suggestions, or assistance regarding the tasks of teaching, and 60 percent of all directions given were expressed in a way that "implied autonomy for the other teacher" (Glidewell et al., 1982, p. 18). That is, directions were usually couched in language that left the final decision about its merits to the receiver. Subsequent feedback from teachers about these findings revealed a pervasive "professional norm of constraint against requesting or offering advice about the practice of the profession" (p. 18). A final noteworthy finding of this first study bears directly on the teachers' preferred means of exchanging support. Much of the content of the "description" category of communication consisted of "experience swapping"; one teacher offers a verbal description of a teaching experience and the other responds with one of her or his own. From the authors' viewpoint, these exchanges provided support in a manner that did not imply a status differential between the two parties. In particular, their dialogue did not signal an elevated status for the advice giver.

Glidewell et al.'s (1982) second and third studies of the norms, constraints, and needs surrounding the expression of support among teachers largely confirmed and extended these early findings. The second study drew upon observations and interviews with a larger sample of elementary school teachers and the third was conducted in a resource center explicitly established to render advice and support to teachers. The interviews focused more sharply on the extent of the teachers' endorsement of norms concerning status equality and autonomy, their beliefs about the effects of informal helping transactions on these status- and autonomy-related issues, and their requirements for support in their work. These data provided firm evidence that direct requests for and offers of professional assistance were highly constrained by the teachers' norms of equal status and autonomy, while experience swapping was largely unconstrained by these norms, occurring six to eight times more frequently than requests and offers. Indeed, these two norms facilitated the expression of experience-swapping exchanges, thus reinforcing this adaptive alternative means of meeting the teachers' needs for support. Interestingly, the authors found that teachers who were involved in team teaching not only expressed less commitment to the norms that constrained the more direct channels of obtaining professional aid, but engaged in these channels of aid at a rate that far exceeded their proportion of the sample of teachers studied. This exception to the prevalent pattern of support seeking and giving suggests that supportive teacher exchanges can be increased by introducing new forms of interdependence that are naturally conducive to their expression. Team teaching seems to legitimize collegial helping by supplanting the norms that proscribe its expression.

Glidewell et al.'s (1982) third study, conducted in a teacher resource center, was based on observations of the interactions between teachers and staff members. Even here they found that the staff members were reluctant to provide direct advice to their teacher-clients despite the fact that their roles specifically entailed this function. They justified this stance in the following terms: To offer advice was to derogate the client's status and undermine the client's professional autonomy. Instead, they preferred to swap experiences, serve as teacher-models, recommend teaching materials, and simply offer a setting for "autonomous experimentation."

Although Glidewell et al. (1982) did not set out to examine the topic of occupational stress and "burnout," their findings about the normative structure that conditions the expression of social support among teachers clearly bear on this topic. They prompt a number of questions about the extent to which professional socialization proscribes collegial support seeking and support giving. These studies also provide leads about ways of promoting peer support through job changes that call for cooperation and coordination (such as team teaching, cotherapists, or outreach teams).

Other strategies of developing more robust workplace support systems (other than the wholesale changes brought about by the employee ownership movement) include initiation of training programs that impart skills in expressing social support (House, 1981), organization of support groups composed of employees who do similar work in the same or different organizations (Maslach, 1976), and introduction of "burnout workshops" in which human service professionals plan ways to optimize the support they give and receive at work. For example, in the workshops conducted by Pines and Aronson (1981, p. 196),

> emphasis was put on techniques for recognizing, establishing, and using support systems among colleagues. Recommendations included employee-oriented staff meetings, open communication, active listening, providing of technical support and technical challenge, open discussion of disruptive emotional experiences, looking for positive aspects in the interaction with clients, and work sharing.

## CONCLUSION

I have reviewed evidence that the support available from work associates can ameliorate occupational stress, prevent demoralization on the job, and contribute to personal and organizational effectiveness. These studies reveal that the quality and quantity of support that is expressed reflects the complex interplay among the social climate of the workplace, its structure, and its ongoing processes and norms. Mental health professionals can initiate consulting and training programs in collaboration with the staff of existing employee assistance programs in industry that reach into the interpersonal sphere of organizational functioning and enlarge its supportive provisions. Indeed, since supervisors, coworkers, and other long-standing work associates make up the organization's informal help-giving sphere, they have a more immediate and powerful impact on the morale and health of employees than does the professional system of assistance. Although we have yet to learn which people at work have the most impact on different types of job stress, and what types of structural changes are most conducive to the expression of social support, the knowledge currently at our disposal offers promising leads for programs and policies to enhance social support in the workplace.

Chapter 6

# INFORMAL CARE AMONG THE ELDERLY

Two views of the elderly compete for adoption in North America. The majority believes that isolation, inactivity, dependence, and depression inevitably dominate the elderly's lives. According to this view, biological aging and the psychosocial transitions of later life gradually erode the elderly's capacity to contribute to society and progressively limit their ability to fend for themselves. As the frailties and chronic illnesses of old age take their toll, and as major family and work roles are shed, the elderly "disengage" themselves (Cumming & Henry, 1961) or they are shunted aside from the life of the community. Further, restricted physical mobility leads to a contracted social world, while psychological and social deficits supplant their existing relationships, also preventing the formation of new ties. The minority and more romantic view of the elderly is that they turn inward, gaining new satisfactions from a more contemplative existence, reviewing their life trajectory, monitoring news from the "outside world," and contenting themselves with one or two family relationships that have become more dependable if not emotionally closer. Regardless of which view is held, there is little evidence that advancing years reduce the need for affiliation or lessen the importance of its rewards.

This chapter reviews recent research that belies the stereotype of the elderly as isolated, dependent, and deficient in support. It surveys present knowledge about the extent and quality of the elderly's interactions with their kith and kin networks, paying special attention to their impact on morale and adjustment. It also highlights several features of the helping relationships established between the elderly and their family members and friends, emphasizing their reciprocal nature. The chapter pays detailed attention to the family's role in preventing the institutionalization of the elderly population's most vulnerable segment — those whose serious physical and/or mental disabilities require almost continuous care. Here, consideration is given to the shaping of programs and policies that reinforce informal care and reduce the burdens that fall upon the elderly's caregivers. The chapter concludes with ideas about ways mental health practitioners can promote more supportive arrangements on behalf of the elderly in the community.

## THE SOCIAL NETWORKS OF THE ELDERLY

### Intergenerational Relations

Both census data and survey research studies document the proposition that the elderly maintain ties to nuclear family members and that these ties prevent and postpone institutionalization. Using the most recent available U.S. Census figures, Sussman (1976) and Bengtson and Treas (1980) show that regardless of age, sex, or race, the family context (usually consisting of an aged man and his spouse) is the most common living arrangement among persons aged 65 and over. In 1970 only 4 percent of the aged population was institutionalized, mainly the "old-old," as fewer than 1 percent of those in their 60s were represented in this segment. The elderly who resided neither in a family household (with a spouse or children) nor in an institution tended to be women; almost 40 percent of elderly women, compared to 15.4 percent of aged men, lived alone. Since women marry older men, live longer than men, and are less likely to remarry, this discrepancy becomes sharper with increasing age: in 1975 almost half of the white women over the age of 75 who resided in the open community lived alone, compared to only 21 percent of their male counterparts. Moreover, those living alone at this advanced age were more likely to be childless or to have never married, since the vast majority of their age peers were taken in by a daughter who tended to be single.

The protective effect of the elderly's connections to nuclear family members can be seen from a second statistical vantage point. U.S. Census data comparing the marital status of the institutionalized elderly and those residing in the community have shown that three times as high a proportion of the former than of the latter have never married and almost twice as high a proportion are widowed. It follows that a much greater proportion of the institutionalized elderly have no children and, therefore, are less likely to be diverted from such placement.

Given that the majority of the elderly reside in the community, how isolated are they from their kin? Numerous studies have shown that they tend to live near a close relative whom they see rather frequently (Rosenberg, 1970; Rosencranz, Pihlblad, & McNevin, 1968; Rosow, 1967; Shanas, 1962, 1979; Stehouwer, 1968; Youmans, 1962). Rosenmayr (1976) aptly characterizes this pattern of interaction as "intimacy at a distance." For example, a cross-national survey that was conducted in 1962 showed that in Denmark, Great Britain, and the United States one-third of the elderly lived within 10 minutes of one of their children; less than one-fourth of the sample resided more than 30 minutes away from their children. Cantor (1975) reports similar data regarding the proximity of children to the elderly of New York City: 28 percent of all their children are within walking distance, while another 26 percent live within the five boroughs of New York. Proximity of family members, particularly children, also leads to high levels of interaction. In fact, Rosenberg (1970) found that proximity determined interaction to a greater extent than did consanguinity among an elderly working-class sample. Cantor's (1975) and Shanas, Townsend, Wedderburn, Frits, Milhaj, and Stehouwer's (1968) reports on the frequency of the elderly's intergenerational contacts show that 90 percent of older Americans have seen one of their children in the past 30 days and about 50 percent report that they have had face-to-face contact with a son or daughter during the past 24 hours. These rates differ by ethnicity (Bengtson & Manuel, 1976; Cantor, 1979; Guttman, 1979) and by socioeconomic status, middle-class elderly tending to have less contact with children than the working class (Hill, Foote, Aldous, Carlson, & MacDonald, 1970; Riley & Foner, 1968). Notably, the elderly who suffer poor health receive more frequent visits from their children (Rosencranz et al., 1968) a finding that relates to the informal care the family extends to the aged, discussed later in this chapter.

Lowenthal and Robinson (1976) have raised doubts about whether the elderly's attitudes regarding involvement with their children are true expressions of their needs. Specifically, they question the results of surveys showing that the actual amount of intergenerational interaction matches the expressed preferences of the elderly. They suggest that the elderly may be constrained by cultural norms dictating proper intergenerational relations and reconcile themselves to a less desirable degree of interaction with their children, who "have to lead their own lives." Lowenthal and Robinson (1976, p. 438) address this issue as follows:

> It is not quite clear whether involvement with middle aged or aging parents is construed by adult children as precluding the possibility of living one's own life, or whether the kind of attitudinal and behavioral research which our methods by and large ordain prevent adequate understanding of the complexity of the relationship between adult children and their parents and vice versa. Our current norms do not sanction older people making demands on the young except in matters of illness and other dire necessity. Possibly reacting to this norm, most older persons report that they see their children and grandchildren as often as they would like (Riley & Foner, 1968, p. 547).

While cultural norms may prevent the elderly from making greater claims on the affection and support of their adult children, thus engendering feelings of disappointment, relations with peers may be more satisfying because they are voluntary, freed from obligations. Indeed, evidence reviewed later provides indirect testimony that family relationships are less important to the morale of the elderly than are relationships with close friends. The friendship network and the family network fulfill different support functions for the elderly and, similarly, the family network receives a different contribution from the elderly than does the peer network (Rosow, 1967). These issues await more detailed discussion following my review of research on the elderly's friendship ties.

## Peer Relations

The elderly who reside in the community have substantial peer contacts, although they are less frequent than their interactions with family members. Cantor (1975) reports that, among her sample of elderly New Yorkers, 68 percent of close friends are seen at least weekly and 39 percent are seen daily. Shanas et al.'s (1968) cross-national study reveals that 39 percent of the elderly living alone in the United States visited friends during the previous day, while 27 percent of those in Britain and 29 percent of those in Denmark did so. Typically, those of higher socioeconomic status interacted more frequently with friends, as did those in better health (Riley & Foner, 1968). Neighboring relations seem to be influenced by a variety of environmental factors, high crime rates, social heterogeneity, and varying marital status of residents each suppressing the degree of social interaction (Blau, 1961; Bultena & Wood, 1969; Rosenberg, 1970; Rosow, 1967). Rosencranz, Pihlblad, and McNevin (1968) report that widowhood constricts the peer network of elderly men and that retirement of both men and women who have pursued lifelong careers diminishes the network of close associates (Lowenthal, Berkman, et al. 1967). Lowenthal and Robinson (1976) note that retirement does not necessarily entail the severing of relationships with workmates, but depends on the individual's involvements in leisure pursuits and voluntary associations, and on his or her prior pattern of involvement with work associates. Apparently, professional, managerial, and highly skilled workers tend to maintain more active contact with coworkers following retirement than do blue-collar workers (Moore, 1963; Rowe, 1973). Some preliminary evidence also suggests that women find adjusting to retirement more difficult than men because they have established closer relationships at work, having had less time to participate in voluntary organizations due to the greater domestic burden they carried while they worked (Fox, 1977; Jaslow, 1976; Levy, 1980-81).

Several studies have inquired more closely into the quality of the elderly's peer network, distinguishing between the extensivity and the intensity of relationships. Notably, Lowenthal and Robinson (1976) draw attention to the "subjective saliency of the social network" and Lemon, Bengtson, and Peterson (1972) underscore the importance of the quality or type of interaction that the elderly maintain with peers in determining their feelings of life satisfaction. Close companionship with one or two agemates who serve as confidants appears to satisfy needs for integration and socialization. As Weiss (1974) has observed, different relationships offer different supportive provisions and are, therefore, not substitutable. As detailed below, abundant evidence demonstrates that the elderly's morale depends more on the quality of their peer relationships than on their family relations, and that, within the peer social field, the most intimate ties, rather than the weak, more abundant peer ties, undergird personal adjustment and well-being.

## SOCIAL TIES, MORALE, AND ADJUSTMENT

Early investigations of the link between the elderly's social integration and their morale and adjustment were largely inspired by Maddox's (1963) activity theory. According to Maddox, those elderly who maintained or developed extensive social ties in the community that compensated for the bonds severed during late-life role transitions had a more positive self-concept and higher morale. In general, empirical inquiries have amply supported this proposition, showing more specifically that family interaction is less significant to the well-being of the elderly than peer relations, and that general activity levels are more closely associated with the well-being of the poorer elderly than of the more affluent. That is, the higher the socioeconomic level of the elderly, the less likely they are to have extensive contacts with their children and the less dependent is their morale upon a high level of social integration.

Larson (1978), however, in his review of these studies, has pointed out that correlations between life satisfaction and social activity have been moderate, rarely exceeding $r = .30$. He further notes that most of these studies have adopted objective measures of social integration such as global indicators of activity, role counts, and frequency measures of informal activities shared with others. An exception is Liang, Dvorkin, Kahana, and Mazian's (1980) recent study, which presents convincing evidence that the "subjective sense of integration" is a stronger predictor of the elderly's morale than is their objective integration. Specifically, they demonstrate that measures of the amount of interpersonal interaction, organizational participation, and interpersonal helping are only indirectly related to morale because they are mediated by the elderly's sense of subjective integration. They measured the latter construct by items tapping the elderly's feelings of loneliness, feelings of integration with or isolation from their networks, and reports on their access to significant others. Moreover, their subjective perceptions conditioned the relationship between objective integration and morale even when statistical controls were introduced for the health and socioeconomic status of the respondents.

Lemon et al.'s (1972) empirical refutation of hypotheses drawn from activity theory and Lowenthal and Haven's (1968) exploration of the role of intimacy in the elderly's adaptation have also strongly influenced others to assess the elderly's morale by examining their perceptions of the quality of their social relations. Indeed, Lowenthal and Haven (1968) discovered that access to a confiding social bond safeguarded the mental health of the elderly even when they experienced certain types of life events that reduced their contact with less intimate network ties. That is, in the face of such traumatic life events as widowhood and retirement and more gradual declines in social activity, the presence of a stable confidant had a health-protective effect. Yet, there were limits to the capacity of an intimate social bond to buffer adversity in old age. Serious physical illness brought on symptoms of depression even among those with access to a confidant, a finding that Lowenthal and Haven (1968, pp. 27-28) interpret in three ways:

> One possible explanation is that serious physical illness is usually accompanied by an increase in dependence on others, which in turn may set off a conflict in the ill person more disruptive to his intimate relationships than to more casual ones. . . . A second possibility is that the assumption of the sick role may be a response to the failure to fulfill certain developmental tasks. In this event, illness would be vitally necessary as an ego defense, and efforts of intimates directed toward recovery would be resisted. A third possibility is that illness is accompanied by increased apprehension of death. Even in an intimate relationship, it may be easier (and more acceptable) to talk about the grief associated with widowhood or the anxieties or losses associated with retirement than to confess one's fears about the increasing imminence of death.

In the same study, characteristics of those elderly who reported having at least one confidant are consistent with other reports. Women are less dependent on remarriage to achieve intimacy than are men (Blau, 1961; Blood & Wolfe, 1960; Lowenthal, Thurnher, Chiriboga et al., 1975; Lowenthal et al., 1967); the socioeconomically advantaged elderly are more likely to report having a confidant; and, as noted earlier, men in white-collar occupations are more likely than those in blue-collar jobs to report having a confidant. Although men invariably nominate their spouses as their confidants, women rarely do so, choosing instead a son, daughter, or friend. Neither sex chooses siblings or extended kin, including grandchildren, as confidants with any frequency.

To summarize, numerous studies have shown that social interaction has a positive but moderate effect on life satisfaction, while other studies have failed to support this proposition (Cohler & Lieberman, 1980; Conner, Powers, & Bultena, 1979; Edwards & Klemmack, 1973; Lemon et al., 1972; Markides & Martin, 1979). The evidence is less equivocal, however, when measurement shifts to the qualitative aspects of primary group ties, particularly to the elderly's "sense of involvement" (Lowenthal & Robinson, 1976), access to a confidant (Lowenthal and Haven, 1968), and "subjective sense of integration" (Liang et al., 1980). These phenomenological measures prove to be more robust predictors of life satisfaction and psychosocial well-being than are the composite indices of social interaction, contact, activity, or integration. Intimate, confiding social bonds may be most important in warding off feelings of emotional isolation by providing opportunities for ventilation and validation (Dunkel-Schetter & Wortman, 1981), and in maintaining positive self-concepts during periods of adversity. In contrast, more casual relationships with peers may offset feelings of social isolation and encourage sustained involvement in community life (Weiss, 1974). Conner et al. (1979, p. 120) advocate qualitative assessment of the elderly's social ties in the following terms:

> Attention should be shifted from questions of "how many" and "how often" to the meaning of social relationships and the interactional process. Concern should be focused more on identifying personal needs that are met by interaction, the meanings attached to various social relationships, the extent to which social relationships are substitutable, and the circumstances under which substitution can and does occur.

The evidence reviewed thus far also suggests that marriage offers the greatest intimacy for both sexes, and that the morale of the elderly, particularly of the more affluent and of widows, depends more upon their relationships with close friends than with family members (Adams, 1971). Indeed, there is near consensus in the literature that interaction with friends sustains or boosts the morale of the elderly while family ties do not (Adams, 1971; Creecy & Wright, 1979; Lowenthal & Robinson, 1976; Wood & Robertson, 1978). However, for methodological reasons, the latter proposition should be viewed cautiously because it may be an artifact of the cross-sectional approach of these inquiries. It is conceivable that interaction between the elderly and their family members increases when the former are in special need of care and support, and that interaction with peers is intensified when good health permits it, hypotheses supported by research reviewed earlier. Thus the finding in several studies of low or inverse correlations between life satisfaction and intergenerational contact may reflect the process of mobilizing the support of the family network *during times of illness or adversity.* Similarly, the stronger, positive relationship between interaction with friends and life satisfaction or happiness attests to the importance of friendship ties in sustaining the elderly's self-image and role identity *under conditions of stable health.* In the absence of longitudinal studies on the relationship between kin and friendship interaction and the health status and morale of the elderly, these dynamic interactions remain unexamined.

## THE ROLE OF KITH AND KIN IN THE HELPING NETWORKS OF THE ELDERLY

Evidence of the elderly's differential interaction with family members and friends, along with the significance of this interaction for their well-being, highlights the fact that the elderly do not withdraw from their peers nor are they alienated from their children. Further, while their expressed satisfaction with life and their sense of well-being hinge in part upon their social connections, the nature of their interactions in these relationships must be gauged if we are to answer questions about the quantity and quality of support they give and receive. To what extent are the elderly dependent on others for support and to what extent can they meet the supportive needs of others? Does the ability to reciprocate support and aid decline with advancing years? Are the elderly less capable of forming viable support systems because they have little to offer others in return for the demands they make?

General research findings on the supportive functions of the elderly's social networks establish three propositions:

- The elderly who reside in the community have a viable informal support system composed primarily of geographically close family members and friends.

- The support provided by the kith and kin segments of their networks is somewhat specialized and complementary in terms of satisfying the elderly's various needs for support.

- So long as their health permits, the elderly are actively involved in equitable exchanges of support, thus participating in naturalistic support arrangements. With declining health, the family assumes virtually all support for the elderly who become less able to reciprocate.

Several large-scale studies detail the kinds and extent of support that the elderly receive from and give to family members and friends. In a widely cited study, Cantor (1975, p. 25) reports that about two-thirds of inner-city elderly New Yorkers "receive substantial assistance from their children in the chores of daily living," half reporting that their children shop for them, 40 percent that their children do household repairs, and almost one-third that their children provide mobility services. The older and poorer the respondent, the more help of these sorts they received. In contrast, neighbors are relied upon extensively to meet the elderly's need for companionship and to respond immediately to sudden medical or environmental emergencies (Cantor, 1975). Litwak (1980, pp. 97-98) has pointed to some of the factors underlying the differences in the support rendered by kin and neighbors:

> Kin have long-term commitments to the subject. Neighbors have immediate access and deal with problems requiring geographic proximity but not necessarily long-term commitments. Peers who are friends have the unique understanding of the problems of aging that ensures a commonality of interests as well as a unique ability to communicate about leisure activities and problems. Thus the kinship system can take care of an aged relative for illnesses that require some home nursing care. Neighbors can ward off muggers, warn the police if the home or apartment is being burglarized, exchange information on inexpensive places to shop and . . . provide each other with companionship.

Johnson (1971) and Hochschild (1973) provide some evidence that friends and neighbors can substitute, if only temporarily, for the care provided by relatives, but when problems become serious or chronic, the elderly seek help from or are channeled to formal service organizations.

Sussman (1976) and Bengtson and Treas (1980) have recently reviewed the literature on patterns of intergenerational support and mutual aid. They converge in depicting the elderly as highly involved in exchanging goods, services, and financial resources with their children, belying the stereotype of the elderly as dependent recipients of assistance. Both reviews show that socioeconomic and ethnic variables account for differences in the frequency and nature of the support that is exchanged, although they identify a universal feature of the elderly's family-based support network: the provision of care, usually by a daughter, during times of illness.

Guttman (1979) and Cantor (1979) agree that the use of family members and friends as sources of support differs as a function of ethnicity. The former investigation examined the use of both formal and informal help sources among samples of relatively healthy and prosperous white ethnics from Eastern, Central, and Southern Europe, while the latter examined these patterns among low-income Black, Puerto Rican, and Caucasian inner-city New Yorkers. In both studies a small minority of the respondents lacked an informal support system. In New York the Hispanic elderly reported the highest levels of reciprocal helping exchanges with their children, followed next by the Black respondents, and then by the white elderly. These findings suggest that the extended family system in the Hispanic and Black cultures offers the strongest structural unit for the provision of social support (Sussman, 1976). Guttman's (1979) samples of white elderly ethnics reported much lower levels of informal support from children. Of the Greek respondents, 39 percent reported receiving help from their children, the highest percentage of all the ethnic groups he surveyed, while the Estonians reported receiving the least help from children (20 percent).

Finally, the gerontological literature converges on two structural features of the elderly's support system. First, the primary form of mutual intergenerational support consists of children sharing a household with their parents. Sussman (1976) found that 16 percent of elderly women and 8 percent of elderly men live in a household headed by another relative, usually a son or daughter. Murray's (1976) survey of Americans who were approaching retirement age revealed that 54 percent of unmarried men and 43 percent of unmarried women shared their homes with an elderly parent. Smaller but significant proportions of this retirement age group lived in their elderly parents' home. Second, the marital relationship is the unit of social structure that offers the most intense support to the elderly, particularly to elderly men. Indeed, recent research shows that elderly men perceive that they obtain more support from their spouses than women report providing to their spouses (Depner & Ingersoll, 1982), perhaps because they have fewer close relationships than do women and rely on them more. Since they receive less support from fewer intimates than do women, elderly men may have lower standards for judging the amount of support they receive from their wives. In contrast, relative to the greater amount of support older women receive from a larger circle of intimates, they may underplay the amount of support they render to their spouses. These data point out, once again, how people's requirements for and perceptions of support differ as a function of the characteristics (such as size and supportive provisions) of their wider network of social ties.

Much of the preceding evidence regarding the nature of the support systems available to the elderly in the community has been gathered in a perfunctory and episodic way. Typically, the elderly are asked to report on the kind and frequency of help they exchanged with members of their networks during a recent interval. Reliability checks are rarely taken, perhaps reflecting the researchers' belief that the lives of the elderly follow a constant rhythm. As I have noted elsewhere in this volume, the process of network formation and change has received very little attention. The steps people take to draw themselves into supportive relationships have not been examined, nor has research probed people's preferences over time for varying degrees of social involvement versus withdrawal. With rare exception (for example, see Wentowski, 1981), researchers have not attended to the cultural norms surrounding the expression of social support in different settings and by people in different life stages and circumstances.

A serious shortcoming of these studies of the elderly's support systems is their failure to take a systems view. They give separate treatment to the family's versus friends' contribution to support, skirting an assessment of the elderly's perceptions of their network as a whole, its density, or solidarity, and relations between sectors. Little wonder, then, that the present evidence suggests that the elderly tend to compartmentalize their relations with kin and friends (Hochschild, 1973; Johnson, 1971). Admittedly, differences exist in the bases of these two types of relationships, relations with friends being based on voluntarism and reciprocity, while affect and obligation govern relations with kin. Nevertheless, a network-analytic approach can reveal the extent of encapsulation or integration of the kith and kin sectors of the elderly's support systems. In short, studies are needed that *systematically* assess the elderly's supportive milieu, analyzing the entire structure of their network of supportive social ties, and documenting changes in the network's overall configuration resulting from changing needs of its members and changing environmental events. Along these lines, Kahn (1979) has advocated a life-span approach to the study of attachment and support. Such an approach is capable of gauging support system changes in relation to the process of aging by taking into account the joint effects of the personal and situational variables that determine the support system's structural characteristics over time. He has used the term "convoy" to capture the idea that "each person can be thought of as moving through life surrounded by a set of significant other people to whom that person is related by giving or receiving of social support" (p. 84). He adds that the convoy "is a structural concept, shaped by the interaction of situational factors and enduring properties of the person, and in turn determining in part the person's well-being and ability to perform successfully his or her life roles" (p. 84).

## THE FAMILY'S ROLE IN AVERTING INSTITUTIONALIZATION OF THE VULNERABLE ELDERLY

Evidence shows that the family and the peer group tend to make different contributions to the elderly's support system. Friends provide outlets for socializing, thus moderating feelings of loneliness; they provide information about local services and are consulted about health practices involving self-care; they occasionally serve as confidants; and when they reside nearby, they can respond quickly and flexibly to emergency, time-limited needs. The family's support is complementary. The elderly's children provide care during periods of illness, give as much financial support as they can, share their households when no other satisfactory housing options are available to their parents, and offer reassurance and emotional support on a continuing basis. Ultimately, it is the elderly's children, particularly their middle-aged daughters or daughters-in-law, who devote themselves to sustaining the community life of the elderly, thus preventing or postponing their institutionalization. Family care thus dominates current discussions of social policy regarding services for older people. Recent demographic trends, however, and studies that probe the costs and burdens associated with this informal means of care raise doubts about how long this arrangement will last. This section provides an overview of family care for the vulnerable elderly, highlighting priorities for social policies that recognize its limits.

The magnitude of the family's involvement in the care of the elderly has been documented in two ways: by examining the factors that distinguish between the elderly who reside in institutions and those residing in the community, and by surveying those among the latter group who are infirm or bedfast and inquiring into the sources and means of care on which they depend. Several studies have found that the institutionalized elderly differ from their counterparts in the community mainly by virtue of their lack of a family support system. Lawton (1981) cites data collected by the National Center for Health Statistics revealing that 12 percent of the institutionalized elderly are currently married, compared to 54 percent of community residents, and that the proportion of the never-married institutionalized elderly is 2.5 times greater than their proportion who reside in the community. The latter data, in turn, suggest that the institutionalized elderly have fewer children than those in the community, and therefore are less likely to be diverted from institutional placements. Indeed, Lawton (1981) reports·census data revealing that, conrolling for age, the probability of institutionalization is inversely related to the number of children ever born, a statistic that overshadows predictions based on socioeconomic data.

Further, the elderly's level of physical impairment does not distinguish between the institutionalized and those who reside in the community. Smyer (1980) found that the variable that discriminated most strongly between an institutionalized and a community sample of elderly who were matched on their level of impairment was their family's self-reported ability to care for them as long as needed. In a similar vein, Brody, Poulshock, and Masciocchi (1978) note that the presence of a "family caring unit" accounted for the placement of chronically ill/disabled elderly persons in the community rather than in private and public nursing homes. Tobin and Kulys (1981, p. 146) observe that "impairment is characteristic of those who live in institutions but a greater percentage of those with similar impairments live outside of institutions." They support this statement by citing data revealing that 17 percent of community elderly suffer from impairments that interfere with their ability to carry out daily living tasks and that 47 percent of those in the community are partially incapacitated by a chronic impairment. Moreover, when the elderly experience a major disability or chronic illness requiring a new living situation they typically move into the household of a family member (Newman, 1976). Those lacking family networks face institutionalization.

Among the elderly who reside in the community — 95 percent of those over the age of 65 (Tobin & Kulys, 1981) — Shanas (1979) has estimated that 3 percent are bedfast and 7 percent are housebound. In short, twice the proportion of the elderly who are seriously impaired live in the community than reside in institutions. An additional 6-7 percent of the elderly in the community need mobility assistance. Estimates of the overall proportion of the elderly population in need of home care services have ranged from 25 percent to 41 percent (Brody, 1981). At present, their needs are being addressed primarily by family members. Tobin and Kulys (1981, p. 147) describe those who care for the sick and frail elderly in terms of the following hierarchy:

> If married, the respondent named the spouse unless the spouse was ill or newly acquired; respondents who were unattached or whose spouses were ill or newly acquired named a child; if a spouse or child was not available, a sibling was named; if none of these was available, an extended family member (niece, nephew, grandchild or other) was named; if not a family member, a friend; and rarely, a professional.

Similarly, Shanas's (1979) national survey of the noninstitutionalized impaired elderly revealed that spouses were the main sources of help for both the bedfast and those who had been bedridden for a brief interval. Often supplementing the spouse's care was a paid helper, rather than one provided through social services, and children ranked next in importance as sources of care. Further, the family did not merely provide intermittent care to the aged; the National Health Survey study revealed that about one-third of the elderly who received home care from a family member residing in the household required constant, prolonged attention (U.S. Department of Health, Education and Welfare, 1972).

## THE LIMITS AND BURDENS OF FAMILY CARE

Recognizing the extensive role that the family assumes in meeting the health needs of the elderly, a number of researchers have attempted to assess the quality of the care that is rendered as well as the costs incurred by the caregivers. For example, Newman (1976) estimates that 40 percent of children caring for aged parents in their homes spent the equivalent of a full-time job in this capacity, and Sanford (1975) points out that institutionalization is often triggered when the family feels exhausted by its efforts to provide continuing care to an impaired relative. Describing the wife's role in caring for a disabled husband, Golodetz, Evans, Heinritz, and Gibson (1969, p. 390) observe:

> In her work situation, she bears a heavy emotional load, but no colleagues or supervisor or education to help her handle this. Her own life and its needs compete constantly with her work requirements. She may be limited in her performance by her own ailments.

Similarly, Fengler and Goodrich (1979) report that elderly wives who care for their disabled husbands suffered from intense feelings of loneliness, tended to become socially isolated, and experienced a high degree of role overload and economic hardship.

Brody (1981) has focused attention on the cross-pressures and strains experienced by the middle generation of daughters and daughters-in-law who assume the bulk of the responsibility for the care of an elderly relative, particularly the widowed. According to Brody's data, the adult daughters and daughters-in-law of the impaired elderly are their principal caregivers, a fact that reflects "the cultural assignment of gender-appropriate roles" (p. 474). The husbands of these middle-aged daughters do not become involved in the day-to-day household maintenance tasks associated with the care of their elderly mothers or mothers-in-law; instead, typically, they help with finances and funeral arrangements. Yet they are indirectly affected by their wives' caregiving since it may instigate family and marital tensions. Brody (1981) has labeled these caregivers the "woman in the middle," and attributes their plight to the competing role demands they face at this time of their life. In particular, they experience cross-pressures from the traditional value of filial responsibility and the emerging value of career and extradomestic involvements. Noting the multiple demands that these "women in the middle" must face, Brody (1982, p. 9) writes:

> It is becoming apparent that theoretical formulations of the family life stages ending in the peaceful, responsibility-free Empty Nest stage must be re-thought. For many of the middle aged, the traditional Empty Nests are being refilled with impaired older people, either physically or figuratively in terms of increased responsibilities for parent care. . . . the hidden costs are becoming visible [and] may be converted to dollar costs if the stress on the middle aged and aging caregivers triggers their own physical and mental breakdowns.

Several recent studies have focused more sharply on the degree of burden and the emotional impact experienced by the elderly's family caregivers. These inquiries are critical because they can inform the planning of community services that fortify informal care and, in doing so, both preserve the family's helping efforts and prevent the institutionalization of the elderly. Zavit, Reever, and Bach-Peterson (1980) have attempted to quantify the degree of burden experienced by the spouses and daughters who were primarily responsible for the care of an aged family member with senile dementia. The "Burden Interview," surveying 29 problem areas identified in the literature and in prior interviews as being most frequently mentioned by caregivers, included the caregiver's health, psychological well-being, finances, social life, and relations with the impaired older person. The caregivers rated each of the 29 areas of potential burden in terms of its degree of discomfort to them, and a total burden score was then derived from the sum of the ratings. The results of this study closely mirror earlier findings reported by Sanford (1975) and Sainsbury and Grad de Alarcon (1970). The areas of greatest burden to the caregivers included lack of time to pursue personal interests and needs, excessive dependency of the elderly, and fears about further deterioration in the patients' behavior.

Of special note in this study, the researchers found that the level of burden experienced by the caregivers was most strongly and inversely correlated with the frequency of family visits received by the elderly. Level of burden was not associated with the degree of the elderly relative's physical or mental impairment. However, the data do not speak to the quality of the interaction that occurred during the family visits and therefore leave unanswered important questions about the kinds of family support that attenuated the caregivers' feelings of burden. Did the visits simply offer the caregivers respite from their tasks, did they have a reassuring effect on the elderly because they signaled that they had not been abandoned by their other kin and would not be abandoned if the primary caregiver could no longer attend to them, or did the visitors communicate their appreciation of the caregiver's role? Furthermore, these correlational data invite an alternative interpretation: Family members who sense that they would not be blamed by the (unburdened) primary caregiver for their relative lack of involvement in the care of their relative would visit more frequently.

Other evidence cited by Brody (1982), Gurland, Dean, Gurland, and Cook (1978), and Cantor (1980) reveals that family care of the infirm elderly restricts social and leisure activities, reduces income, and has adverse effects on marital relationships and the quality of the caregivers' family life. As Tobin and Kulys (1981) show, the elderly's institutionalization is frequently triggered by stressful life events that alter the family situation of the caregivers (such as geographic moves necessitated by employment or retirement, or an illness in the caregiver's own family generation), as well as by abrupt declines in the health of the elderly person to whom help has been extended over the years.

Family support is critical to community tenure, especially among the frail and chronically ill elderly, but programs and policies for the aged must be formulated in light of the emotional and physical strain placed on the caregivers and their families. Similarly, social policy must take into account present demographic trends, pinpointed by Treas (1977) and Brody et al. (1978), that pose new constraints on the family's caregiving role and will limit it even more in the future. These trends include: (a) increasing longevity and declining fertility rates; (b) increasing participation of women in the labor force; (c) increasing incidence of marital disruption and rising rates of remarriage; and (d) reduced economic power of the elderly to ensure the support of their children. I briefly elaborate on each of these trends before addressing the programmatic initiatives that can buttress the elderly's informal system of care.

Since the turn of the century, demographic trends show that the proportion of the elderly population in the United States has grown while the proportion of the younger population has shrunk. Consequently, there is an increasing imbalance between those in need of care and the children who can provide it. The first trend, then, increasing longevity, results in a greater pool of very old persons whose children are in the middle-age group and entering old age. In short, the elderly as a group are much older than they were early in the century, they have fewer children who can share the tasks of caregiving, and those who are available tend to be the "young-old" whose energy, health, and finances are more limited (Treas, 1977). A second trend has been the dramatic increase in the number of married women currently in the labor force, thus either reducing the pool of women who can provide extensive care to the elderly or compounding the stress these women experience as a result of their existing work and domestic responsibilities. Alternatively, as Treas (1977) suggests, these working women may use their income to purchase care for the elderly. The third trend, rising divorce rates and the attendant increase in the proportion of female-headed households, will surely limit the capacity of families to render financial and personal support. Divorced mothers with limited resources will inevitably place their own children's needs ahead of their elderly parents' and when these divorced women reach older age themselves, their single status will place them at greater risk of institutionalization. The increasing prevalence of "reconstitituted" families — families that tend to have a greater number of children combined from the partners' earlier marriage(s) — also deplete the resources that can be devoted to the couple's parents. Finally, Treas (1977) has suggested that the expansion of welfare and entitlement programs for the elderly may reduce the generations' financial dependence on one another. Increasing reliance on the provisions of the state will gradually replace reliance on the family as the source of care.

## SUPPORTING THE FAMILY'S CAREGIVING ROLE

Various ways of strengthening the informal support system available to the elderly in the community have been suggested, and several demonstration projects have already been mounted. Recommendations for action range from providing tax and other financial incentives to family caregivers to initiating support groups on their behalf and offering them supplementary agency services to sustain their efforts. In addition, numerous proposals for new types of services have been circulated that directly meet the elderly's need to live independently in the community, including provisions for increased income and medical benefits, and an expansion of social services and housing options. A comprehensive and humane policy to ensure the social welfare of the elderly must take into consideration both their needs and desires, differences in their families' capabilities and willingness to render care, and the fundamental freedom of both generations voluntarily to determine their personal and mutual responsibilities. In instances where intergenerational support is unavailable or too psychologically or financially costly, societal means of support must be available.

New initiatives that support the family's caregiving efforts emphasize ways of mitigating their emotional strains and providing tangible goods and services to supplement the family's contribution. The Community Service Society of New York City has pioneered a

"Natural Support Program" (NSP) that exemplifies these dual objectives. It attempts to enhance and shore up the care rendered by the family by providing supplemental home care, respite care, counseling services, mobility assistance, and information and advocacy programs. In addition, it offers "support groups" for the caregivers (Rzetelny, Kasch, Topperman, & Hudis, 1980). Mellor, Rzetelny, and Hudis (1979) report that two types of groups have been created on behalf of the caregivers: (a) socioeducational groups that provide information about the psychological and physical aspects of aging, and instruction in the care of the chronically ill elderly; and (b) mutual-aid peer support groups "in which participants learn from each other and provide each other with recognition and support in their caring roles" (p. 6). In these groups, discussions tend to focus on alleviating the caregivers' stress and guilt and on balancing personal needs with caregiving responsibilities.

Based on their experience with these groups, Rzetelny and Mellor (1982) have developed a training manual for group facilitators that outlines the steps involved in creating a group, salient topics for group discussion, the role of the group leaders, and methods of transferring group leadership to the members and transplanting the group in the community. These caregiver support groups were initiated following a needs-assessment study conducted by Hudis and Buchsbaum (1978), revealing that 26 percent of caregivers' requests for services reflected a desire to share their experiences with others. In addition, the study found that 40 percent of the requests were for information about community resources, particularly entitlements for elderly relatives; 32 percent were requests for information to help the caregivers anticipate their role — by obtaining information about illnesses, disabilities, and resources; and 22 percent of the requests concerned needs to learn how to provide care to multiply disabled and mentally impaired adults.

Data from the NSP also confirm Brody's (1981) observation that it is the middle-aged daughters of the elderly who assume the bulk of the caregiving role: 54 percent of the elderly's primary caregivers were daughters. The following case example dramatically illustrates the extensive care given by these women to their parents, and the way in which the NSP attempts to supplement it to ensure its continuation:

> For the past 4 years Ms. P, age 51, has been the major caregiver for her 90 year old father who suffers from a prostate problem, is hard of

hearing, has poor eyesight and has become forgetful and confused. His general condition is deteriorating. She works full-time, leaving home at 8:00 a.m., after preparing breakfast and lunch for her father. In the evening she prepares supper, spends time talking with her father who has no other companionship and changes her father's catheter bag and helps him bathe. Frequently she has to take him to the hospital clinic (often at night) because of a clogged catheter. On weekends she cleans, does household chores and takes her father out for a walk. She also visits her 92 year old mother who has been in a nursing home for many years. Ms. P. was physically exhausted and emotionally depressed when she learned about NSP. NSP provides this family with: 1) twice a week *homemaker* service which gives Ms. P more time to relax in the evenings and attend to her own needs on weekends; 2) *respite* for Ms. P to occasionally spend a day or two with a friend away from home; and 3) *counseling*, since Ms. P tends to become depressed and feels great ambivalence about leaving her father's care to anybody else [Zimmer & Sainer, 1978, p. 7].

The Community Service Society has recognized the value of mobilizing peer support to sustain the family's caregiving efforts. In light of the empirical findings cited earlier in Fengler and Goodrich's (1979) and Zavit et al.'s (1980) studies of the factors alleviating the caregivers' feelings of burden, such recognition gains greater importance. Both studies found less strain on the caregivers the more frequent their contact with family members in particular and close network associates in general. Fengler and Goodrich (1979) asked a subsample of caregiving wives about their interest in participating in group meetings with one another. All of them expressed an interest in becoming involved in this way. Similarly, Zavit et al. (1980) outline several ways of enriching the supportive contacts among the caregivers of the elderly suffering from Alzheimer's Disease, including the extension of counseling services to the caregivers' entire family systems, mobilizing neighborhood contacts, and organizing the caregivers into mutual-aid groups. In fact, one of the authors, Karen Reever, subsequently mounted an intervention program at the Philadelphia Geriatric Center involving the creation of 30 "support groups" for the caregivers of relatives with senile dementia. In addition, a partnership between professionals and concerned citizens has recently resulted in the establishment of the Alzheimer's Disease and Related Disorders Association based in Chicago, with 36 chapters nationwide. The association publishes scientific information about the disease and helps to catalyze local caregiver support groups. Practical guidelines for the creation of these groups are also available from the National Support Center for Families of the Aging located in Swarthmore, Pennsylvania, and in Mace and Rabins's (1981) useful book, *The 36-Hour Day*.

In an effort to help agencies plan services to support the informal sector's contribution to the care of the elderly, the U.S. Administration on Aging has commissioned several organizations to undertake syntheses of present work. For example, a firm called Community Research Applications, Inc., has generated seven guidelines to aid agencies in implementing support programs for informal caregivers, guidelines distilled from their observations of nine model programs, including the NSP described above. The guidelines suggest, among other considerations, that agencies "should expand the traditional definition of 'client' to include actual and anticipatory informal supports" (Dichter, Alfaro, & Holmes, 1981, p. III-2); that they should "direct and maximize outreach to the informal support target population" (p. III-10), and "include informal supports in case management functions, as both clients, and, if possible, case managers" (p. III-12); and that they should develop specialized staff expertise in problems of informal support networks and techniques for involving and helping them in caring for the elderly" (p. III-20).

Agencies can render other services to sustain the informal sector's caregiving efforts. Day hospital and day-care programs with service components could ensure adequate social and cognitive stimulation in addition to appropriate medical and nutritional resources (Rathbone-McCuan, 1976; Cohen, 1973; Robins, 1974). Fengler and Goodrich (1979) report on a Swedish arrangement in which a "service house" reserves one floor to accommodate approximately 20 elderly and impaired persons while their caregivers are ill or on vacation. Additional respite and supplemental care services include in-home household help, personal care services, transportation aids, and some sort of financial relief. On the last subject, many proposals have touched on financial incentives that might reduce some of the economic burdens associated with family care. For example, Sussman (1976, p. 238) has proposed five economic benefits to assist families:

(a)  a direct monthly allotment of funds;

(b)  specific tax write-off for expenses incurred;

(c) a low-cost loan to renovate or build an addition to their home in which the elderly person can maintain independence in a physical setting which would have few architectural barriers;

(d) the provision of income tax relief for assuming this responsibility;
    . . .

(e) property tax waiver with some formula proportional to dwelling usage.

Sweden has implemented a system of tax-free payments, with a maximum of $450 per month, to families who care for a chronically ill or handicapped person at home. And Butler (1977-1978, p. 72) has argued that significantly fewer people would be institutionalized "if even a fraction of the sums used to support older people in nursing homes were available to help families provide for their elders." Financial incentives, however, are not likely to motivate families to care for their aging relatives when they have been unwilling to do so in the past. Indeed, as Sussman (1976) has shown, 19 percent of a sample of respondents who were asked about their willingness to take an elderly relative into their home said they would not do so regardless of the availability of cash incentives and services. Indeed, families spurred into caregiving solely by the promise of such benefits would probably not provide a desirable quality of care. Instead, financial benefits should be directed toward those who would, except for financial problems, be ready to fulfill the caregiving function.

The private sector has also developed several new arrangements that directly benefit the elderly by making it easier for them to remain in independent living arrangements in the community. Recognizing that more than 70 percent of the elderly in the United States have meager incomes, but own their homes, a plan initiated in California allows them to sell their property to investors while continuing to live in it as tenants for as long as they wish. Typically, the home is sold for somewhat less than market value, and the elderly resident receives mortgage payments from the buyer that exceed his or her monthly rental, thus providing additional income. The investor, who gains tax benefits through the purchase, contracts to permit the elderly resident to stay as long as he or she wishes or until the time of his or her death. Shared housing plans offer a second means of assisting the elderly who wish to stay in the community. These include both house or apartment sharing and group living arrangements. While administrative and regulatory changes are necessary to facilitate home sharing, this arrangement allows small groups of elderly persons to maintain themselves in a more supportive and financially feasible situation. The initial experiment in group living — and a legal test of its zoning classification — was demonstrated by the Share-A-Home Association of St. Petersburg, Florida.

## INTERVENING DIRECTLY IN THE SUPPORT NETWORKS OF THE ELDERLY

Present efforts to enhance the support and prevent institutionalization of the elderly are largely centered on preserving the family's caregiving efforts. Other approaches have focused on optimizing the quality and extent of support the elderly receive through their relations with peers in neighborhoods and in congregate living arrangements. Foremost among these *network-building approaches* are strategies of organizing and developing neighborhood-based associations among the elderly, usually referred to as "natural helping networks" (Collins & Pancoast, 1976). Reflecting ongoing patterns of social participation in the community, these networks are usually maintained by certain resourceful and energetic "central figures" in the neighborhood, and they provide their members with both concrete services and outlets for socializing. Smith (1975) has developed a practical handbook that outlines methods of scanning neighborhoods to identify these networks and forging mutually beneficial agency links. Froland, Pancoast, Chapman, and Kimboko (1981) have also described a set of roles that professionals can assume in working with these networks, emphasizing that professionals and human service organizations must modify their customary practices when working with natural support systems. They visited 30 agencies that were combining informal and professional approaches to service delivery, using these site visits as the basis for generating a useful typology of program strategies that proved most effective in working with the elderly's helping networks.

A second approach to strengthening the elderly's neighborhood-based support system is educational, "combining principles and techniques of primary prevention, informal support system intervention, community organization, outreach and older adult education" (Crowe & Middleman, 1982). The Elder Program is a model demonstration project funded by the Administration on Aging and mounted by a team of action-researchers at the University of Kentucky's Kent

School of Social Work. The program drew predominantly black, female, elderly residents from six contrasting neighborhoods into a series of educational sessions that taught life skills, helping skills, and advocacy and group-building competencies. Next, each group pinpointed pressing needs or problems of elderly residents in its neighborhood and assumed the functions of a local "task force," working with neighbors to resolve these concerns. The groups continued to be active locally well after the formal training and educational sessions terminated. The project also disseminated a "Leader's Guide" and a workbook to other agencies serving the elderly and to organizations of seniors across the country.

A number of more circumscribed group approaches have also been extended to the elderly, their common aims being to foster higher levels of social interaction and to expand the elderly's networks. Pilisuk and Minkler (1980) describe six programs of this sort, concentrating on the ways they were tailored to the functional capacities and ethnic backgrounds of the elderly populations they served. Nickoley-Colquitt (1981) has reported on seven different "preventive group interventions" with the elderly, providing a useful outline of the needs addressed by the groups as well as their formats and processes. Small group techniques have also been used to impart problem-solving skills in the areas of interpersonal relations (Spivack, 1982) and late-life health difficulties (Petty, Moeller, & Campbell, 1976), as well as to foster more positive self-concepts among the elderly (Nickoley, 1978; Leavitt, 1978) and enhanced morale and personal growth (Lieberman & Gourash, 1979; Berland & Poggi, 1979). The latter objective has been accomplished by involving the elderly (usually the more educated, healthy, and psychotherapeutically oriented) in encounter group and psychotherapeutic experiences. Nickoley-Colquitt's (1981) review of many of these group interventions shows that a small minority of them incorporated evaluation methods that adequately tested their effectiveness (such as inclusion of control or comparison groups or use of psychometrically sound evaluative measures), the majority relying on leaders' or members' descriptive reports.

Much less effort has gone into creating programs that provide a more supportive milieu for the institutionalized elderly, a greater proportion of whom lack family ties than their counterparts in the community. Improved support for this group might consist of initiatives to foster some degree of integration with the elderly residing in the community and to enhance their institutionally based social system. Existing evidence in the former domain reveals that the extent of contact the institutionalized elderly have with the outside world depends in large measure on the policies and social climate of the setting in which they live. For example, Dobroff (cited in Tobin & Kulys, 1981) reports that the amount of interaction between the elderly and their families in five long-term care facilities in New York City depended on the staff's attitudes and the reception the family received upon visiting, while David, Moos, and Kahn (1981) show that low levels of community integration of residents in skilled nursing facilities was associated with program policies that precluded much resident control over decision making and with a social climate that failed to encourage resident self-sufficiency and self-direction. They also found that facilities characterized by a cohesive social climate fostered higher levels of resident interaction with the external social environment. Moreover, these policy and social climate dimensions were more strongly associated with community integration than was the facility's proximity to community resources.

Although there have been attempts to "remotivate" and "resocialize" the institutionalized elderly by bringing in friendly and youthful visitors — high school students (Wallach, Kelley, & Abrahams, 1979), college student companions (Arthur, Donnan, & Lair, 1973), and elementary grade children (Thralow & Watson, 1974) — these programs generally have aimed to maintain the cognitive abilities of the elderly (Reinke, Holmes, & Denney, 1981; Schulz, 1976). They fail to meet their needs for intimacy and meaningful relationships, nor can they compensate for a social climate that is otherwise unsupportive. The quality of the elderly's everyday life in an institution depends in larger part on the social relations they maintain with one another and with the staff, and there is reason to believe that the support extended by the latter is particularly deficient. For example, Kastenbaum and Aisenberg (1972) found that nurses and orderlies typically avoided open communication when their elderly charges disclosed their feelings about death. The staff tried to avoid the subject, denied the implications of the disclosure, or prematurely terminated discussion of these feelings. Nor do institutional policies foster a cohesive social system among the residents. Most care facilities do not have resident governing councils, do not permit residents to plan their own recreational activities, and do not let them select their roommates (Austin & Kosberg, 1976). To the degree that they undermine feelings of choice and control, they also condition a sense that residents have no responsibility for one another, thus suppressing prosocial behaviors. Seeing how little influence they have on the everyday routines of the institution, they become equally passive in their social behavior.

Efforts to optimize the supportive dimension of institutional life must be leveled at the staff, the residents, and the administration. Residents need a greater voice in decision making, more influence on the selection of staff and roommates, and more involvement in activities that enhance their sense of community. Staff training should emphasize the importance of providing opportunities for the elderly to express their feelings both to the staff and to one another. The peer support group approach could be fruitfully introduced among both staff and residents. Administrative policies inhibiting interaction and undermining residents' perceived control over day-to-day events and social relations should be discarded and replaced by policies that increase opportunities for environmental control. Instead of importing friendly visitors and temporary companions, efforts should be made to cultivate the social resources and enlarge the fund of support from within.

Part IV

# CONCLUSION

Chapter 7

# SOCIAL SUPPORT AND PROFESSIONAL PRACTICE
## A Broader Perspective

This volume documents the progress made in advancing our appreciation of the nature and effects of social support. Early theoretical formulations pointing to the protective power of human dialogue and the health advantages of social integration have been refined, bringing greater precision to the measurement of the social support construct and a clearer understanding of its ameliorative impact. The scientific study of social support's role in moderating stress has broadened our perspective on the provisions extended by the enveloping social network. Exposure to adversity prompts a need for contact and social comparison with similar peers who augment or redirect the individual's coping efforts by marshaling cognitive, affective, and material resources. A multidimensional view of social support thus dominates current empirical inquiry, the challenge being to ascertain which supportive provisions carry the greatest adaptive value for different people in different stressful circumstances.

Preceding chapters have shown that support is expressed in a variety of social aggregates and arises spontaneously in diverse community settings. It finds expression in the intimate relationship between husband and wife, and in the mutual aid exchanged among a group of nursing mothers. It is entailed in the transactions occurring among a collection of unemployed men who inhabit a single room occupancy hotel and among a group of female executives who meet biweekly to compare notes about career strains and share information about useful job contacts and resources. Social support is also evident in an informal association of neighborhood mothers who have established their own cooperative day-care system, and it is implicitly communicated when co-congregationalists greet one another at services.

Limitations on the prosocial quality of human relationships have also been acknowledged in preceding chapters. Indeed, I have advocated abandoning the term "support system," since it betrays a false, excessively romantic view of the social network's influence on mental health. Much of the clinical treatment enterprise is fundamentally directed toward undoing destructive relationships, teaching human relation skills, and assisting people to recover from social rejections or losses. However, once we grant that there is conflict in the network and recognize the demoralizing influence of certain actors, we can concentrate on ways of reconstituting the patient's social orbit and enlisting it in the therapeutic enterprise. For example, Chapter 4 discusses how research on the quality of "expressed emotion" in the schizophrenic's family interactions has been used to plan family interventions that decrease the likelihood of the patient relapsing. My review of psychosocial treatment programs also underscores the importance of weaving the patient into a meaningful social system. Moreover, when people face life events and transitions that challenge their coping skills, social support can be mobilized in several ways that are detailed in Chapter 3: (a) by upgrading the quality of support rendered in social networks; (b) by fostering affiliation among people facing similar stressful circumstances; and (c) by attempting to reanchor people in a network that is more responsive to their present needs for emotional ventilation and personal validation or reorienting them to sectors of their network containing more appropriate psychosocial resources. Finally, approaches to primary prevention that involve optimizing the support available from people's networks include: (a) training workshops that enlarge the repertoire of helping skills and extend the reach of informal community caregivers; and (b) network development workshops that provide opportunities for planning support-enhancing changes, especially at times when life transitions (such as marital separation or job or residential changes) disrupt network ties.

## THE SOCIAL NETWORK'S BROADER INFLUENCE
## ON THE HELP-SEEKING PROCESS

Although this volume spotlights the social network's role in mitigating stress and promoting mental health, it also brings to bear a unique perspective on the broader process of help seeking. This social-ecological perspective calls attention to the influence of primary group members on stages of the help-seeking process that precede and follow the actual provision of support and guidance. Accordingly, members of the help seeker's social network perform two functions prior to their mobilization as a support system. Initially, they engage in informal diagnostic functions and subsequently in informal referral functions. Through their involvement in the former activities, they lend shape to the initial definition of the help seeker's problem and judge its significance for well-being. Through the latter activities, they control the direction of help seeking and condition expectations about how help will be given. Close examination of the network's informal diagnostic and referral functions also reveals its influence on professional practice.

Help seeking actually begins when an individual first recognizes signs of demoralization or decrements in functioning. This departure from steady state may be precipitated by exposure to an acute stressor such as job loss, or it may be gradually amplified by continuous exposure to hardship, such as chronically stressful workplace conditions. Often, the affected party fails to recognize that something is awry, or prefers to ignore it until a close associate brings the matter into the open. Hence, at this earliest stage of the help-seeking process lay parties may intervene by calling attention to unfamiliar, potentially serious changes in the help seeker's behavior. For example, work associates may take note of a coworker's persistent irritability, increased consumption of alcohol at lunch, and depressed mood. After conferring among themselves, one of them will find an opportune moment to broach the topic, and the ensuing discussion will typically reveal the network's views about the help seeker's condition and courses of action. Specifically, this dialogue will communicate the network's attributions concerning the causes of the problem, its estimate of the problem's seriousness and probable duration, and network members' ideas about available remedies. Discussion may conclude with a decision to "wait it out" in the hope that the problem will prove self-limiting, or to seek further help from expert or lay consultants, or a combination of the two. While it is important to recognize that the help seeker may also confer with other members from different sectors of the network, they share a common purpose at this earliest stage, namely, to lend shape and meaning to the help seeker's problem, and to speed or delay movement to the next stage in which appropriate helping resources are identified. In sum, the social network's informal diagnostic activities set the stage for its informal referral activities once a decision is reached to seek outside resources.

When people recognize that they cannot come to terms single-handedly with a health-related problem but must find outside resources, they typically do not browse through the Yellow Pages of their phone directory or call the local information bureau. Instead, they consult family members, friends, workmates, and neighbors, calling upon them for advice about community resources that are best matched to their needs, their definitions of the problem, and their preferred styles of helping. For example, a woman who has recently moved to a new town and is seeking obstetrical care for her first pregnancy will consult other women she has met, either at work or in the neighborhood, outlining to them the special qualities of the physician she wishes to see and her preferences for certain labor and delivery practices. In this way she uses her social network to screen potential physicians, trying to identify the medical resources that are best suited to her health beliefs and special needs. Moreover, once she reaches a practitioner she may confer once again with her female associates, now seeking their opinions about a referral her physician has made to the prenatal classes offered by the local public health unit. Not only will they influence her decision to attend, but they will also condition her expectations. They may clarify misconceptions about the content and the structure of the classes, or they may advise her to attend selected sessions, such as the visit to the hospital. Once again, it is important to underscore the fact that the help seeker may receive different, even contradictory, messages about the use of services from different parties in her network. Moreover, structurally contrasting networks may have quite opposite effects on decisions about service use. On the former score, McKinlay (1973) has shown that the spouses of expectant mothers typically encourage attendance at prenatal classes, while their mothers and mothers-in-law discourage attendance. On the latter score, both McKinlay (1973) and Birkel and Reppucci (1981) have found that participation in close-knit or dense social networks is associated with low use of parent education services.

The lay referral network also channels the help seeker to informal sources of support. Indeed, recent usage of the term "network" carries the connotation of people using their contacts to gain access to new contacts and hidden resources in the environment. To extend the previous example, an expectant mother who plans to breastfeed her newborn will be directed to a mother who is currently nursing her infant, and this contact, in turn, may lead the expectant mother to participate in the local La Leche League chapter. Referral to informal sources of care is more typical of ethnically based networks and more generally of networks that do not intersect with the middle-class culture of the professional community networks in which "the prospective clients participate primarily in a indigenous lay culture and in which there is a highly extended lay referral structure" (Freidson, 1960). For mental health-related problems, the spiritualist in the Puerto Rican community, the *curandero* in the Hispanic community, and the root worker in the black community carry sizable caseloads. Moreover, these caregivers, in turn, may refer the help seeker to other informal sources of support, thereby adding several links to the referral chain until the problem is resolved or becomes so aggravated that professional help is needed or imposed.

One additional example clearly illustrates the way lay networks channel patients to professional practitioners and provide advance instruction about professional practice. Kadushin (1966) examined the routing of patients to certain prestigious psychoanalysts in New York City and discovered that entree was gained largely through the sponsorship of members of a socially elite circle. Referring to the latter as the "friends and supporters of psychotherapy," Kadushin found that they attended gallery openings, went to the opera, theater, and concert halls of New York, and proudly counted themselves among those currently or formerly patients of the city's most eminent psychoanalysts. Acceptance as a new patient of one of these therapists was predicated upon acceptance into this sophisticated social set, which also taught prospective patients how to present their symptoms in a manner that fit the analysts' practice orientations. For example, prospective patients were taught to present their difficulties in terms of an existential crisis rather than in specific behavioral terms. Kadushin points out that this social circle was, therefore, a real boon to these psychotherapists because it flawlessly recruited and socialized patients.

The stages of informal diagnosis and referral naturally give way to the network's involvement in rendering aid and support directly. This volume chronicles the sources and nature of this aspect of the network's contribution to the help seeker's adjustment. However, it touches only briefly on the final stage of the help-seeking process, the stage in which the network is enlisted in reintegrating the individual and normalizing life once again. One of the most critical aftercare functions assumed by the network is its accommodation to the help seeker's new plan of living. Whether such a plan has been prescribed by a professional, entailing changes in medication, diet, and exercise, or proposed by members of a mutual-aid group, it can be either undermined or reinforced by family members and other close associates. They may have to change the scheduling of the family meals, reduce their coworker's load, or moderate their emotional involvement in a family member's life. In addition, this stage calls for the network to monitor any adverse side effects of the help rendered during the intensive period of treatment or support and to neutralize whatever stigma surrounded it. The network's foremost role in the aftercare stage is restorative; it reintegrates rather than closes ranks against the help seeker.

By dividing the help-seeking process into four career stages and magnifying the social network's influence at each stage, I have tried to enrich our appreciation of the larger context in which the lay system operates. The primary group is not only the milieu in which direct support and mutual aid are extended, but also the forum in which people make meaning of their difficulties, find avenues for resolving them, and regain a sense of stability and identity following intensive intervention. Once recognition is given to the wider social ecology in which the help-seeking process occurs, it becomes easier to see the network's impact on many other aspects of clinical and community mental health practice. First, the network controls the flow of clients to practitioners. If the network proscribes use of certain services or deems them too psychologically costly, it can have a "blackballing" effect. On the other hand, it can promote attendance by endorsing other services. Second, by conditioning accurate expectations about the type of help rendered by professional practitioners, it can avert the likelihood of patients dropping out of treatment. Third, it can speed or delay use of professional services by involving the help seeker in a protracted or brief period of informal referral. Fourth, network members can contradict or concur with the professional's diagnosis of the problem and attributions about its cause. Fifth, in the aftercare stage, the network can improve or interfere with the patient's ability to adhere to professionally prescribed regimens.

## RESHAPING RELATIONSHIPS BETWEEN PROFESSIONALS AND CITIZENS

As the preceding discussion has demonstrated, the social network has both a direct and an indirect impact on the help-seeking process. It extends tangible and emotionally sustaining resources that augment the individual's coping efforts, and it conditions interactions with the social institutions of the community. Recognizing the importance of the network's latter function, the community's social institutions, in turn, have attempted to manipulate it. They have tried to attract public favor by using media channels, including citizens on their boards, and creating new staff positions involving community liaison activities (Litwak & Meyer, 1966).

The mental health field has devised its own strategies of shaping public opinion to achieve greater social control of the community's networks. Recognizing in the late 1950s that many citizens from ethnic and low-income communities were alienated from the mental health delivery system, a concerted effort was made to bridge the cultural gap using indigenous nonprofessionals to effect a rapprochement. Local opinion leaders and informal helpers were identified and recruited from the social networks of these communities, for the purpose of linking citizens to professional services. Some of these nonprofessionals were also trained to provide direct clinical services and proved to be highly effective practitioners. Many launched new careers in the health and welfare fields, gaining both personal satisfaction and upward mobility from their work.

Yet, viewed from a social-ecological perspective, the paraprofessionals who formerly occupied central positions in local social networks were misused. Instead of reinforcing and extending their help-giving activities, or supplementing their resources, professionals encouraged them to channel help seekers into the formal service delivery system and absorbed the paraprofessionals into that system. Meeting the needs of the underserved in this manner had the unintentional effects of depleting these social networks of valuable human resources and of reorienting their members to institutional rather than indigenous solutions. In these ways professionals imposed hegemony on the informal helping systems of the community.

The President's Commission on Mental Health (1978) recently proposed quite the opposite approach to the social networks of the community. Recognizing the important role of these support systems in sustaining indigenous helping practices, the commission advocated cooperation and partnership rather than annexation:

> Mental health services should be offered to individuals which would build first on their own assets and strengths, maintaining and cultivating their membership in social networks and natural communities in the least restrictive environment. This would mean developing methods which could identify and assess the functioning of an individual's natural support systems, and establishing, where appropriate, linkages between the natural support systems and the professional caregiving systems based on a respect for privacy and on genuine cooperation and collaboration, not cooperation and control. . . . Helping people where they are and assisting them to help themselves allows entry into the help giving and receiving system without requiring that a person be labeled patient or deemed "sick" [Vol. II, p. 154].

Indeed, cooperative relationships are beginning to develop between the professional and natural helping systems and both parties appear more willing to engage in mutually instructive activities rather than pressuring for use of their own approach to helping. For example, in a recent study I asked members of mutual-aid groups about their present use of professionals for the same problem or condition addressed by their groups (Gottlieb, 1982). I learned that almost half of those attending groups composed of persons with clinically diagnosable conditions such as mental illness and alcohol addiction were concurrently receiving professional treatment and most of them had been referred to the group by the professional practitioner. Equally important, all but one of those dually involved in treatment actively discussed their self-help group experiences with the professionals. The large majority perceived no conflict between the help they received from the group and the help proffered by the professional. At the same time, these self-help group members were wary of professional encroachment. When asked to rate the appropriateness of several different roles that professionals might assume in relation to their groups, they expressed strong preferences for indirect rather than direct involvement. Specifically, the roles they viewed as more suitable for professionals included those of consultants, referral agents, trainers, and group initiators; those deemed less appropriate were the roles of evaluator, researcher, and group leader.

Professionals have actively initiated mutual-aid groups as well. They have helped to form stroke clubs, support groups for the widowed, and weight-loss groups, among others. Where they have expert knowledge about the nature of the disorder or condition shared by group members, their contribution is invaluable. An experienced neurologist can calm the fears of a group of multiple sclerosis patients by explaining that symptom remission can occur as suddenly as the flare-up that has placed one of their members in a wheelchair since the last meeting. Professionals are also germinating mutual-aid groups by bringing together patients with similar conditions, helping them to gain group cohesion, and then withdrawing to allow them to carry on independently in the community. The growth of groups attended by those who live with someone who has a mental or physical disability, such as the National Alliance for the Mentally Ill and Al-Anon, has also alerted professional caregivers to the radiating social impact of their patients' illnesses and their treatment.

The Presidential Commission's prescription for cooperation between professionals and lay helpers has also been heeded by numerous health and welfare agencies in North America. Collaborative strategies of service delivery have been invented, their collective experience most recently documented by Froland et al. (1981). Their study of the ways that "shared care" was managed by thirty agencies yielded a set of practice guidelines as well as recommendations for organizational and managerial changes to foster these practices. Furthermore, their discussion of the changes in the role of agency staff and in their orientation to practice required by their work with citizens has direct implications for professional training.

First, work in the community was clearly impeded by the staff's reliance on a professional frame of reference regarding the meaning of help. They failed to appreciate the full range of practical services and verbal exchanges that sustained community relationships. In particular, they were unaccustomed to a helping style predicated upon direct involvement and reciprocity. A second, related point is that they were unprepared to shift their perspective from a deficit to a strengths viewpoint. They approached the community with a mind to identifying unmet needs, greeting citizens as potential service recipients, instead of identifying local resources and viewing citizens as providers of support and care. Third, they had received little training in outreach activities and found that their formal agency role did not gain them the community acceptance they desired. They were uncomfortable outside the structure of their agencies and uncertain about how to engage in the reconnaissance that would lead them to local informal helpers. Fourth, they were uneasy with an indirect, consultative role in the community. As Froland et al. (1981, p. 156) observe, "The process of working through informal helpers gives rise to a conflict between staff feeling responsible for the adequacy and appropriateness of the help given to the client, and feeling that the informal system should continue to work autonomously according to its own standards." The tension produced by the process of working *through* the local networks rather than *on* them was also compounded by agency supervisors who were reluctant to transfer the accountability for outcomes to the community. Finally, nothing in the staff's prior training had prepared them for the difficulties involved in gauging the limits of informal helpers and determining the right balance between the agency's and the voluntary sector's responsibilities for care. They feared that the partnership might collapse either because excessive burdens were placed on lay helpers or because the responsibility for change was transferred to the professional partner. This strain on the agency worker was never resolved but was mitigated through staff discussions and through constant dialogue with the informal system.

The latter dilemma exposes our uncertainty about where to draw the boundaries between the contributions of citizens to safeguarding human welfare and those delegated to the formal service system. Important questions have been raised about whether the institutional "social safety net" can be discarded or at least loosened if citizens can do so much for themselves. Moreover, some political conservatives have welcomed the discovery of support systems, couching their goal of dismantling the welfare system in the rhetoric of citizen empowerment and the promotion of mutual aid. There is the danger that the community's informal helping networks will be exploited by policymakers seeking more cost-effective alternatives to essential government social programs and basic financial entitlements. In our zeal to promote the community's capacity to care for itself, we must be watchful not to transfer to it responsibilities that properly lie with the state. If we overtax the social network's capacity to sustain its members and deny to it a fair share of society's resources, we will inevitably suppress the ethic of mutual aid.

## SOCIAL SUPPORT AND MENTAL HEALTH PRACTICE IN THE FUTURE

Present societal trends portend a dramatic increase in the number of people whose difficulties stem, either directly or indirectly, from the loss of significant sources of support. In particular, high rates of marital disruption, divorce, and unemployment will not only take a toll on those directly affected, but will have radiating effects on their families and close associates. Former spouses experience the loss of a once confiding relationship, their friends often withdraw, the children lose a critical attachment figure or at least experience doubts and ambivalence about their relationships with one or both parents, and a geographic move must often be made by one or more family members, thus severing other community ties. In economically depressed regions of the country, wholesale population movements are occurring. As families are uprooted, so are long-standing relationships with friends, neighbors, schoolmates, family physicians, and other people around whom they anchored their lives. Moreover, job loss not only exacts a severe physical and psychological burden on the individual, but also has an adverse impact on family life. We are just beginning to learn about the child abuse, marital discord, and strained relationships with peers in the community that result from prolonged unemployment (Cunningham, 1983).

Beyond immediate questions concerning the stressful impact of these socially wrenching trends, one is led to inquire whether they will inhibit people's willingness to reinvest themselves in new social networks. When children see their parents' relationship gradually dissolve, do they unconsciously decide not to risk developing close relationships with their own peers? Do they begin to doubt the permanency of even their closest affectional bonds and begin to insulate themselves from others? Are families less inclined to invest themselves in neighborhood life when, for reasons of employment, they have relocated several times and still face job uncertainty? Increasing numbers of transient workers and single-parent families will surely force us to confront the fact that much of our work is chiefly addressed to the loss or disruption of the "personal communities" that formerly sustained people.

Faced with increasing numbers of clients who have experienced a diminished fund of social support, mental health practitioners will have to assume different roles and gain entry to new settings if they are to accomplish their work. They can collaborate with the staff of the employee assistance programs that exist in many large organizations, creating new programs that mobilize support systems on behalf of employees facing retirement, relocation, and termination. They can also act as consultants for government employment agencies and vocational training centers, helping to introduce a social support component — job clubs, employment search groups, and bartering arrangements — that meets the practical and emotional needs arising during periods of unemployment and employment preparation. There are also opportunities for germinating support groups in the religious institutions to which newcomers make their way shortly after settling in new communities. Programs for transfer students can be created in schools experiencing a large influx of transplanted families. To meet the supportive needs of families affected by divorce, mental health workers can become active in the family court system. They can organize separate groups for single parents and for their children, and, when custody and visitation disputes arise, these groups can be involved in the process of recommending new terms to the court.

In addition to their direct role in instigating support group interventions in these agencies and institutions, community mental health workers can bring resources to the informal helping networks that exist in the natural environment. They can compile directories of the self-help groups in their local catchment areas, providing details about the kinds of problems/conditions the groups address, the formats they adopt, and the procedures involved in gaining entry. They can develop stronger referral relationships with these groups, thereby also ensuring that their own work with clients does not undermine the ideology of mutual aid. They can lend technical assistance in the conduct of research about the most appropriate group candidates and the factors contributing to the group's effectiveness. Mental health workers can also recommend techniques of self-study to enrich the process of ventilation and validation, and can assist fledgling groups in creating a stable administrative structure. Finally, representatives can be invited to speak about their groups' work at professional gatherings or at staff meetings, and to participate in community health fairs.

For the mental health field, the concepts of social networks and social support thus provide both a new perspective and a broader set of options for intervention. Drawing attention to the influence of the social ecology on the help-seeking process, these concepts remind us that professional services constitute only a fraction of the pool of resources available to citizens. They also provide a new vantage point from which we can see the diversity of resources people use to cope with adversity, and where these resources need supplementing. They guide us toward interventions that capitalize on the strengths of social ties or that forge new attachments that are responsive to changing life conditions. These concepts also prompt us to add a deeper connotation to the term "community." It is more than the geographic unit in which we practice; it is a unit of social structure that brings meaning and a sense of coherence to people's lives.

# References

Adams, D. L. Correlates of satisfaction among the elderly. *Gerontologist*, 1971, *2*, 64-68.

Adams, J. Mutual-help groups: Enhancing the coping ability of oncology clients. *Cancer Nursing*, 1979, *2*, 95-98.

Adsett, C. A., & Bruhn, J. G. Short-term group psychotherapy for post-myocardial infarction patients and their wives. *Canadian Medical Association Journal*, 1968, *99*, 577-584.

Anderson, C., Hogarty, G., & Reiss, D. The psychoeducational family treatment of schizophrenia. In M. J. Goldstein (Ed.), *New developments in interventions with families of schizophrenics*. San Francisco: Jossey-Bass, 1981.

Andrews, G., Tennant, C., Hewson, D., & Vaillant, G. Life events stress, social support, coping style and risk of psychological impairment. *Journal of Nervous and Mental Disease*, 1978, *166*, 307-315.

Antonovsky, A. *Health, stress, and coping*. San Francisco: Jossey-Bass, 1979.

Arthur, G. L., Donnan, H. H., & Lair, C. V. Companionship therapy with nursing home aged. *Gerontologist*, 1973, *13*, 167-170.

Auerswald, E. Interdisciplinary vs. ecological approach. *Family Process*, 1968, *7*, 202-215.

Austin, M. J., & Kosberg, J. I. Nursing home decision makers and the social service needs of residents. *Social Work in Health Care*, 1976, *1*, 447-455.

Azrin, N. H., Flores, T., & Kaplan, S. J. Job finding club: A group assisted program for obtaining employment. *Behavior Research and Therapy*, 1975, *13*, 17-27.

Bachrach, L. *Deinstitutionalization: An analytical review and sociological perspective*. Rockville, MD: Division of Biometry and Epidemiology, National Institute of Mental Health, 1977.

Baker, L. H. *Natural support systems and the previously hospitalized psychiatric patient*. Paper presented at the meeting of the American Psychological Association, New York, 1979.

Barnes, J. Social networks. *Addison-Wesley Module in Anthropology*, 1972, *26*, 1-29.

Barrera, M., Jr. Social support in the adjustment of pregnant adolescents. In B. H. Gottlieb (Ed.), *Social networks and social support*. Beverly Hills, CA: Sage, 1981.

Barrera, M., Jr., Sandler, I. N., & Ramsay, T. B. Preliminary development of a scale of social support: Studies on college students. *American Journal of Community Psychology*, 1981, *9*, 435-447.

Barrett, C.J. Effectiveness of widows' groups in facilitating change. *Journal of Consulting and Clinical Psychology,* 1978, *46,* 20-31.

Beard, J. H. The rehabilitation services of Fountain House. In L. I. Stein & M. A. Test (Eds.), *Alternatives to mental hospital treatment.* New York: Plenum, 1978.

Beard, J. H., Malamud, T.J., & Rossman, E. Psychiatric rehabilitation and long-term rehospitalization rates: The findings of two research studies. *Schizophrenia Bulletin,* 1978, *4,* 622-635.

Bengtson, V. L., & Manuel, R. *Ethnicity and family patterns in mature adults: Effects of race, age, SES and sex.* Unpublished manuscript, Department of Sociology, University of Southern California, 1976.

Bengtson, V. L., & Treas, J. The changing family context of mental health and aging. In J. E. Birren & R. B. Sloane (Eds.), *Handbook of mental health and aging.* Englewood Cliffs, NJ: Prentice-Hall, 1980.

Bercheid, E., & Walster, E. H. *Interpersonal attraction.* Reading, MA: Addison-Wesley, 1978.

Berkman, L. F., & Syme, S.L. Social networks, host resistance, and mortality: A nine-year followup study of Alameda County residents. *American Journal of Epidemiology,* 1979, *109,* 186-204.

Berkowitz, R., Kuipers, L., Eberlein-Freif, R., & Leff, J. Lowering expressed emotion in relatives of schizophrenics. In M.J. Goldstein (Ed.), *New developments in interventions with families of schizophrenics.* San Francisco: Jossey-Bass, 1981.

Berland, D., & Poggi, R. Expressive group psychotherapy with the aging. *International Journal of Group Psychotherapy,* 1979, *29,* 87-108.

Bilodeau, C. B. & Hackett, T. P. Issues raised in a group setting by patients recovering from MI. *American Journal of Psychiatry,* 1971, *128,* 105-110.

Birkel, R., & Repucci, N. D. *Social networks, information seeking and the utilization of services.* Unpublished manuscript, Department of Psychology, University of Virginia, 1981.

Blackman, S., & Goldstein, K. *Reciprocity networks in the community and manifest psychological symptomatology.* Paper presented at the annual meeting of the Eastern Psychological Association, Baltimore, 1976.

Blake, B. F., Weigl, K., & Perloff, R. Perceptions of the ideal community. *Journal of Applied Psychology,* 1975, *60,* 612-615.

Blanchard, E. B., & Miller, S. T. Psychological treatment of cardiovascular disease. *Archives of General Psychiatry,* 1977, *34,* 1402-1413.

Blau, X. S. Structural constraints on friendships in old age. *American Sociological Review,* 1961, *26,* 429-439.

Blood, R. O., Jr., & Wolfe, D. M. *Husbands and wives: The dynamics of married living.* New York: Macmillan, 1960.

Bloom, B. L., Asher, S. J., & White, S. W. Marital disruption as a stressor: A review and analysis. *Psychological Bulletin,* 1978, *85,* 867-894.

Bloom, J. R., Ross, R. D., & Burnell, G. The effect of social support on patient adjustment after breast surgery. *Patient Counseling and Health Education,* 1978, *1,* 50-60.

Borkman, T. Experiential knowledge: A new concept for the analysis of self-help groups. *Social Service Review,* 1976, *50,* 445-455.

Braun, P., Kochansky, G., Shapiro, R., Greenberg, S., Gudeman, J. E., Johnson, S., & Shore, M. F. Overview: Deinstitutionalization of psychiatric patients, a critical review of outcome studies. *American Journal of Psychiatry,* 1981, *38,* 736-749.

Brody, E. M. "Women in the middle" and family help to older people. *Gerontologist,* 1981, *21,* 471-480.

Brody, E. M. *Strengthening personal support systems.* Unpublished manuscript, Philadelphia Geriatric Center, 1982.

Brody, S. J., Poulshock, S. W., & Masciocchi, C. F. The family caring unit: A major consideration in the long-term support system. *Gerontologist,* 1978, *18,* 556-561.

Brown, G. W. Meaning, measurement, and stress of life events. In B. S. Dohrenwend and B. P. Dohrenwend (Eds.), *Stressful life events.* New York: John Wiley, 1974.

Brown, G. W., Birley, J. L., & Wing, J. K. Influence of family life on the course of schizophrenic disorders: A replication. *British Journal of Psychiatry,* 1972, *121,* 241-258.

Browne, A. *High risk lethality factors in abusive relationships.* Paper presented at the meeting of the American Psychological Association, Washington, D. C., 1982.

Budson, R. D., Grob, M. C., & Singer, J. E. A follow-up study of Berkeley House — A psychiatric halfway house. *International Journal of Social Psychiatry,* 1977, *23,* 120-131.

Budson, R. D., & Jolley, R. E. A crucial factor in community program success: The extended psychosocial kinship system. *Schizophrenia Bulletin,* 1978, *4,* 609-62.

Bultena, G. L., & Wood, V. American retirement community: Bane or blessing? *Journal of Gerontology,* 1969, *24,* 209-217.

Burke, R. J., & Weir, T. Giving and receiving help with work and non-work related problems. *Journal of Business Administration,* 1975, *6,* 59-78.

Burke, R. J., & Weir, T. Managers' perceptions of effective, ineffective, and non-helpers. *Journal of Business Administration,* 1976, *7,* 51-65.

Burke, R. J., & Weir, T. Marital helping relationships: The moderators between stress and well-being. *Journal of Psychology,* 1977, *95,* 121-130.

Burke, R. J., & Weir, T. Organizational climate and informal helping processes in work settings. *Journal of Management,* 1978, *4,* 91-105.

Burke, R. J., Weir, T., & Duncan, G. Informal helping relationships in work organizations. *Academy of Management Journal,* 1976, *19,* 370-377.

Butler, R. Nursing home care: An impossible situation unless. *International Journal of Aging and Human Development,* 1977-1978, *8,* 291-294.

Callan, D., Garrison, J., & Zerger, F. Working with the families and social networks of drug abusers. *Journal of Psychedelic Drugs,* 1975, *7,* 19-25.

Campbell, A. *The sense of well-being in America.* New York: McGraw-Hill, 1981.

Cantor, M. H. Life space and the social support system of the inner city elderly of New York. *Gerontologist,* 1975, *15,* 23-27.

Cantor, M. H. The informal support system of New York's inner city elderly: Is ethnicity a factor? In D. E. Gelfand & A. Kutzik (Eds.), *Ethnicity and aging.* New York: Springer, 1979.

Cantor, M. *Caring for the frail elderly: Impact on family, friends, and neighbors.* Paper presented at meeting of the Gerontological Society of America, San Diego, CA, 1980.

Caplan, G. *Principles of preventive psychiatry.* New York: Basic Books, 1964.

Caplan, G. Support systems. In G. Caplan (Ed.), *Support systems and community mental health.* New York: Basic Books, 1974.

Caplan, R. Organizational stress and individual strain: A social-psychological study of risk factors in coronary heart disease among administrators, engineers, and scientists (Doctoral dissertation, University of Michigan, 1971). *Dissertation Abstracts International*, 1971/1972, *32*, 6706B-6707B. (University Microfilms No. 72-14822)

Carveth, W. B., & Gottlieb, B. H. The measurement of social support and its relation to stress. *Canadian Journal of Behavioural Science*, 1979, *11*, 179-187.

Cassel, J. Psychosocial processes and stress: Theoretical formulations. *International Journal of Health Services*, 1974, *4*, 471-482.

Cassel, J. The contribution of the social environment to host resistance. *American Journal of Epidemiology*, 1976, *104*, 107-123.

Cherniss, C. *Staff burnout*. Beverly Hills, CA: Sage, 1980.

Chilman, C. Programs for disadvantaged parents: Some major trends and related research. In B. H. Caldwell & H. N. Ricciuti (Eds.), *Review of child development research* (Vol. 3). Chicago: University of Chicago Press, 1973.

Cobb, S. Social support as a moderator of life stress. *Psychosomatic Medicine*, 1976, *38*, 300-314.

Cochrane, M., & Brassard, J. Child development and personal social networks. *Child Development*, 1979, *50*, 601-616.

Cohen, F. Coping with surgery: Information, psychological preparation, and recovery. In L. W. Poon (Ed.), *Aging in the 1980s*. Wahington, DC: American Psychological Association, 1980.

Cohen, F., & Lazarus, R. S. Coping with the stresses of illness. In. G. C. Stone, F. Cohen, & N. E. Adler (Eds.), *Health psychology – A handbook*. San Francisco: Jossey-Bass, 1979.

Cohen, M. G. Alternative to institutional care of the aged. *Social Casework*, 1973, *54*, 447-452.

Cohen, S., & Hoberman, H. Positive events and social supports as buffers of life change stress. *Journal of Applied Social Psychology*, in press.

Cohler, B. J., & Lieberman, M. A. Social relations and mental health. *Research on Aging*, 1980, *2*, 445-469.

Collins, A. H. Natural delivery systems: Accessible sources of power for mental health. *American Journal of Orthopsychiatry*, 1973, *43*, 46-52.

Collins, A. H., & Pancoast, D. L. *Natural helping networks*. Washington, DC: National Association of Social Workers, 1976.

Conner, K. A., Powers, E. A., & Bultena, G. L. Social interaction and life satisfaction: An empirical assessment of late-life patterns. *Journal of Gerontology*, 1979, *34*, 116-121.

Corder, M. P., & Anders, R. L. Death and dying — Oncology discussion group. *Journal of Psychiatric Nursing and Mental Health Services*, 1974, *12*, 10-14.

Cowen, E. L. Help is where you find it: Four informal helping groups. *American Psychologist*, 1982, *37*, 385-395.

Cowen, E. L., Gardner, E. A., & Zax, M. (Eds.). *Emergent approaches to mental health problems*. New York: Appleton-Century-Crofts, 1967.

Creech, R. H. The psychologic support of the cancer patient: A medical oncologist's viewpoint. *Seminars in Oncology*, 1975, *2*, 285-292.

Creecy, R. F., & Wright, R. Morale and informal activity with friends among black and white elderly. *Gerontologist*, 1979, *19*, 544-547.

Croog, S. H., Lipson, A., & Levine, S. Help patterns in severe illness: The roles of kin network, non-family resources and institutions. *Journal of Marriage and the Family,* 1972, *34,* 32-41.

Crowe, A., & Middleman, R. The elder program: A strategy for prevention. *Journal of Primary Prevention,* 1982, *3,* 133-139.

Cumming, E., & Henry, W. E. *Growing old: The process of disengagement.* New York: Basic Books, 1961.

Cunningham, S. Shock of layoff felt deep inside family circle. *APA Monitor,* January 1983, pp. 10-11.

D'Afflitti, J. G. & Weitz, G. W. Rehabilitating the stroke patient through patient-family groups. *International Journal of Group Psychotherapy,* 1974, *25,* 323-332.

Danish, S. J., D'Augelli, A. R., & Brock, G. W. An evaluation of helping skills training: Effects on helpers' verbal responses. *Journal of Counseling Psychology,* 1976, *23,* 259-266.

D'Augelli, A. R., Vallance, T. R., Danish, S. J., Young, C. E., & Gerdes, J. L. The community helpers project: A description of a prevention strategy for rural communities. *Journal of Prevention,* 1981, *1,* 209-224.

David, T., Moos, R., & Kahn, J. Community integration among elderly residents of sheltered care settings. *American Journal of Community Psychology,* 1981, *9,* 513-526.

Davis, M. S. Variations in patients' compliance with doctors' orders: Analysis of congruence between survey responses and results of empirical investigations. *Journal of Medical Education,* 1966, *41,* 1037-1048.

Depner, C., & Ingersoll, B. *Supportive interactions with family and friends in later life.* Unpublished manuscript, Institute for Social Research, University of Michigan — Ann Arbor, 1982.

Dichter, E., Alfaro, J., & Holmes, M. *Helping the informal support network — A new approach to serving the elderly* (Vol. 1). Unpublished manuscript, Community Research Applications, Inc., New York, 1981.

DiMatteo, R. A social-psychological analysis of physician-patient rapport: Toward a science of the art of medicine. *Journal of Social Issues,* 1979, *35,* 12-33.

DiMatteo, R., & Hays, R. Social support and serious illness. In B. H. Gottlieb (Ed.), *Social networks and social support.* Beverly Hills, CA: Sage, 1981.

Dincin, J. Psychiatric rehabilitation. *Schizophrenia Bulletin,* 1975, *1,* 131-148.

Doane, J. A. *A mental health training and consultation program for family practice attorneys.* Unpublished manuscript, University of California — Los Angeles, 1977.

Doehrman, S. R. Psycho-social aspects of recovery from coronary heart disease: A review. *Social Science and Medicine,* 1977, *11,* 199-218.

Dohrenwend, B. S., & Dohrenwend, B. P. (Eds.). *Stressful life events.* New York: John Wiley, 1974.

Dohrenwend, B. S., & Dohrenwend, B. P. Some issues in research on stressful life events. *Journal of Nervous and Mental Disease,* 1978, *166,* 7-15.

Dohrenwend, B. S., & Dohrenwend, B. P. Life stress and illness: Formulation of the issues. In B. S. Dohrenwend & B. P. Dohrenwend (Eds.), *Stressful life events and their contexts.* New York: Prodist, 1981.

Duck, S. The personal context: Intimate relationships. In P. Feldman & J. Orford (Eds.), *Psychological problems: The social context.* New York: John Wiley, 1980.

Dunkel-Schetter, C., & Wortman, C.B. Dilemmas of social support: Parallels between victimization and aging. In S.B. Kiesler, J.N. Morgan, & V.K. Oppenheimer (Eds.), *Aging: Social change*. New York: Academic, 1981.

Durlak, J.A. Comparative effectiveness of paraprofessional and professional helpers. *Psychological Bulletin*, 1979, *86*, 80-92.

Dushenko, T.W. Cystic fibrosis: A medical overview and critique of the psychological literature. *Social Science and Medicine*, 1981, *15E*, 43-56.

Eaton, W.W. Life events, social supports, and psychiatric symptoms: A re-analysis of the New Haven data. *Journal of Health and Social Behavior*, 1978, *19*, 230-234.

Eckenrode, J., & Gore, S. Stressful events and social supports: The significance of context. In B.H. Gottlieb (Ed.), *Social networks and social support*. Beverly Hills, CA: Sage, 1981.

Eddy, W., Papp, S., & Glad, D. Solving problems in living: The citizen's viewpoint. *Mental Hygiene*, 1970, *54*, 64-72.

Edmunson, E., Bedell, J.R., Archer, R.P., & Gordon, R.E. Integrating skill-building and peer support in mental health treatment: The early intervention and community network development projects. In A.M. Jeger & R.S. Slotnick (Eds.), *Community mental health: A behavioral-ecological perspective*. New York: Plenum, 1982.

Edwards, J.N., & Klemmack, D.L. Correlates of life satisfaction: A re-examination. *Journal of Gerontology*, 1973, *28*, 497-502.

Epley, S.W. Reduction of the behavioral effects of aversive stimulation by the presence of companions. *Psychological Bulletin*, 1974, *81*, 271-283.

Erickson, G.D. The concept of personal network in clinical practice. *Family Process*, 1975, *14*, 487-498.

Erickson, G.D., Rachlis, R., & Tobin, M. Combined family and service network intervention. *Social Worker*, 1973, *4*, 276-284.

Fairweather, G.W., Sanders, D.H., Maynard, H., & Cressler, D.L. *Community life for the mentally ill: An alternative to institutional care*. Chicago: Adline, 1969.

Falloon, I., Boyd, J., McGill, C., Strang, J., & Moss, H. Family management training in the community care of schizophrenia. In M.J. Goldstein (Ed.), *New developments in interventions with families of schizophrenics*. San Francisco: Jossey-Bass, 1981.

Fengler, A.P., & Goodrich, N. Wives of elderly disabled men: The hidden patients. *Gerontologist*, 1979, *19*, 175-183.

Fox, J. Effects of retirement and former work life on women's adaptation to old age. *Journal of Gerontology*, 1977, *32*, 196-202.

Freidson, E. Client control and medical practice. *American Journal of Sociology*, 1960, *65*, 374-382.

French, J.R.P., Jr. Person-role fit. In A. McLean (Ed.), *Occupational stress*. Springfield, IL: Charles C. Thomas, 1974.

Fried, M. Grieving for a lost home. In L.J. Duhl (Ed.), *The urban condition*. New York: Basic Books, 1963.

Friedman, M., & Rosenman, R. *Type A behavior and your heart*. New York: Knopf, 1974.

Froland, C., Brodsky, G., Olson, M., & Stewart, L. Social support and social adjustment: Implications for mental health professionals. *Community Mental Health Journal*, 1979, *15*, 82-93.

Froland, C. Pancoast, D., Chapman, N., & Kimboko, P. *Helping networks and human services.* Beverly Hills, CA: Sage, 1981.

Furstenberg, F. F., Jr., & Crawford, A. G. Family support: Helping teenage mothers to cope. *Family Planning Perspectives,* 1978, *10,* 322-333.

Garrison, J. Network techniques: Case studies in the screening-linking-planning conference method. *Family Process,* 1974, *13,* 337-354.

Garrison, V. Ecological anthropology in community mental health. *Division 27 Newsletter,* American Psychological Association, August 1981.

Gartner, A., & Reissman, F. *Self-help in the human services.* San Francisco: Jossey-Bass, 1977.

Gatti, F., & Colman, R. Community network therapy: An approach to aiding families with troubled children. *American Journal of Orthopsychiatry,* 1976, *46,* 608-617.

Glidewell, J. C., Tucker, S., Todt, M., & Cox, S. Professional support systems: The teaching profession. In A. Nadler, J. D. Fisher, & B. M. De Paulo (Eds.), *Applied research in help-seeking and reactions to aid.* New York: Academic, 1982.

Goldberg, P. P. *The detection of psychiatric illness by questionnaire.* Maudsley Monograph 21. London: Oxford University Press, 1972.

Goldenberg, I. I. *Build me a mountain: Youth, poverty and the creation of new settings.* Cambridge: MIT Press, 1971.

Goldstein, M. J. Editor's notes. In M. J. Goldstein (Ed.), *New developments in interventions with families of schizophrenics.* San Francisco: Jossey-Bass, 1981.

Golodetz, A., Evans, R. Heinritz, G., & Gibson, C. The care of chronic illness: The "responser" role. *Medical Care,* 1969, *7,* 385-394.

Goodman, G. *Companionship therapy: Studies in structured intimacy.* San Francisco: Jossey-Bass, 1972.

Gore, S. The effect of social support in moderating the health consequences of unemployment. *Journal of Health and Social Behavior,* 1978, *19,* 157-165.

Gore, S. Stress-buffering functions of social supports: An appraisal and clarification of research models. In B. S. Dohrenwend & B. P. Dohrenwend (Eds.), *Stressful life events and their contexts.* New York: Prodist, 1981.

Gottlieb, B. H. Lay influences on the utilization and provision of health services: A review. *Canadian Psychological Review,* 1976, *17,* 126-136.

Gottlieb, B. H. The development and application of a calssification scheme of informal helping behaviors. *Canadian Journal of Behavioral Science,* 1978, *10,* 105-115.

Gottlieb, B. H. Mutual-help groups: Members' views of their benefits and of roles for professionals. *Prevention in Human Services,* 1982, *1,* 55-67.

Gottlieb, B. H., & Carveth, W. B. *An investigation into the use of formal and informal helping resources by low income families.* Unpublished report, Department of Psychology, University of Guelph, Ontario, Canada, 1981.

Gottlieb, B. H., & Todd, D. M. Characterizing and promoting social support in natural settings. In R. F. Munoz, L. R. Snowden, & J. G. Kelly (Eds.), *Social and psychological research in community settings.* San Francisco: Jossey-Bass, 1979.

Gurin, G., Veroff, J., & Feld, S. *Americans view their mental health.* New York: Basic Books, 1960.

Gurland, B., Dean, L., Gurland, R., & Cook, D. Personal time dependency in the elderly of New York City: Findings from the U.S.-U.K. cross-national geriatric community study. In *Dependency in the elderly of New York City*. New York: Community Council of Greater New York, 1978.

Guttmann, D. Use of informal and formal supports by white ethnic aged. In D.E. Gelfand & A. Kutzik (Eds.), *Ethnicity and aging*. New York: Springer, 1979.

Hackett, T. P. The use of groups in the rehabilitation of the postcoronary patient. *Advances in Cardiology*, 1978, *24*, 127-135.

Hammer, M. Influence of small social networks as factors on mental hospital admission. *Human Organization*, 1963, *22*, 243-251.

Hammer, M. Social networks and the long term patient. In R. D. Budson & L. Barofsky (Eds.), *The chronic psychiatric patient in the community: Principles of treatment*. New York: Spectrum, 1982.

Hammer, M., Makiesky-Barrow, S., & Gutwirth, L. Social networks and schizophrenia. *Schizophrenia Bulletin*, 1978, *4*, 522-545.

Hansell, N. Casualty management method: An aspect of mental health technology in transition. *Archives of General Psychiatry*, 1968, *19*, 281-289.

Hansell, N. *The person-in-distress*. New York: Behavioral, 1976.

Harrison, R.K. *The doctor-patient relationship: The physician as a mental health resource*. Unpublished doctoral dissertation, Department of Psychology, State University of New York — Buffalo, 1979.

Heller, K. The effects of social support: Prevention and treatment implications. In A. P. Goldstein and F. H. Kanfer (Eds.), *Maximizing treatment gains: Transfer enhancement in psychotherapy*. New York: Academic, 1979.

Henderson, S. Social relationships, adversity and neurosis: An analysis of prospective observations. *British Journal of Psychiatry*, 1981, *138*, 391-398.

Henderson, S., Byrne, D. G., Duncan-Jones, P., Adcock, S., Scott, R., & Steele, G. P. Social bonds in the epidemiology of neurosis: A preliminary communication. *British Journal of Psychiatry*, 1978, *132*, 463-466.

Henderson, S., Byrne, D. G., Duncan-Jones, P., Scott, R., & Adcock, S. Social relationships, adversity, and neurosis: A study of associations in a general population sample. *British Journal of Psychiatry*, 1980, *136*, 574-583.

Henderson, S., Duncan-Jones, P., Byrne, D. G., & Scott, R. Measuring social relationships: The interview schedule for social interaction. *Psychological Medicine*, 1980, *10*, 1-12.

Henderson, S., Duncan-Jones, P., McAuley, H., & Ritchie, K. The patient's primary group. *British Journal of Psychiatry*, 1978, *132*, 74-86.

Hilberman, E., & Munson, K. Sixty battered women. *Victimology*, 1977-78, *2*, 460-470.

Hill, R., Foote, N., Aldous, J., Carlson, R., & MacDonald, R. *Family development in three generations*. Cambridge, MA: Schenkman, 1970.

Hinkle, L. E., Jr., & Wolff, H. G. Health and social environment: Experimental investigations. In A. H. Leighton, J. A. Clausen, & R. N. Wilson (Eds.), *Explorations in social psychiatry*. New York: Basic Books, 1957.

Hinkle, L. E., Jr., & Wolff, H. G. Ecologic investigations of the relations between illness, life experiences and the social environment. *Annals of Internal Medicine*, 1958, *49*, 1373-1388.

Hirsch, B.J. Natural support systems and coping with major life changes. *American Journal of Community Psychology*, 1980, *8*, 159-172.

Hochschild, A. R. *The unexpected community*. Englewood Cliffs, NJ: Prentice-Hall, 1973.

Hoffman, L., & Long, L. A systems dilemma. *Family Process*, 1969, *8*, 211-234.

Holahan, C. J., & Moos, R. H. Social support and psychological distress: A longitudinal analysis. *Journal of Abnormal Psychology*, 1981, *90*, 365-370.

Holland, J. C. Coping with cancer: A challenge to the behavioral sciences. In J. W. Cullen, B. H. Fox, & R. N. Isom (Eds.), *Cancer: The behavioral dimensions*. New York: Raven, 1976.

Holmes, T. H., & Rahe, R. H. The social readjustment rating scale. *Journal of Psychosomatic Research*, 1967, *11*, 213-218.

Holub, N., Eklund, P., & Kennan, P. Family conferences as an adjunct to total coronary care. *Heart and Lung*, 1975, *4*, 767-769.

House, J. S. *Work stress and social support*. Reading, MA: Addison-Wesley, 1981.

House, J. S., Robbins, C., & Metzner, H. The association of social relationships and activities with mortality: Prospective evidence from the Tecumseh Community Health Study. *American Journal of Epidemiology*, 1982, *116*, 123-140.

House, J. S., & Wells, J. A. Occupational stress, social support, and health. In A. McLean, G. Black, & M. Colligan (Eds.), *Reducing occupational stress: Proceedings of a conference*. NIOSH publication 78-140. Washington, DC: U. S. Department of Health and Human Services, 1978.

Howard, J., & Strauss, A. (Eds.), *Humanizing health care*. New York: John Wiley, 1975.

Hudis, I., & Buchsbaum, M. *Components of community-based group programs for family caregivers of the aging*. Paper presented at the meeting of the Gerontological Society, Dallas, 1978.

Ibrahim, M. A., Feldman, J. G., Sultz, H. A., Staimin, M. G., Young, L. J., & Dean, D. Management after myocardial infarction: A controlled trial of the effect of group psychotherapy. *International Journal of Psychiatric Medicine*, 1974, *5*, 253-268.

Jamison, K. R., Wellisch, D. K., & Pasnau, R. O. Psychosocial aspects of mastectomy: I. The woman's perspective. *American Journal of Psychiatry*, 1978, *134*, 432-436.

Janis, I. L. Psychodynamic aspects of stress tolerance. In S. Klausner (Ed.), *The quest for self-control*. New York: Macmillan, 1965.

Jaslow, P. Employment, retirement, and morale among older women. *Journal of Gerontology*, 1976, *31*, 212-218.

Jenkins, C. D. Recent evidence supporting psychologic and social risk factors for coronary disease. *New England Journal of Medicine*, 1976, *294*, 987-994; 1033-1038.

Jersilid, E. A. Group therapy for patients' spouses. *American Journal of Nursing*, 1967, *67*, 544-549.

Johnson, S. *Idle haven: Community building among the working-class retired*. Berkeley: University of California Press, 1971.

Johnson, S. B. Psychosocial factors in juvenile diabetes: A review. *Journal of Behavioral Medicine*, 1980, *3*, 95-116.

Joint Commission on Mental Illness and Health. *Action for mental health*. New York: Basic Books, 1961.

Jones, M. *Maturation of the therapeutic community: An organic approach to health and mental health*. New York: Human Sciences, 1976.

Kadushin, C. The friends and supporters of psychotherapy: On social circles in urban life. *American Sociological Review,* 1966, *31,* 781-802.

Kagan, A., Olsson, A., & Shalit, B. *Identification of needs for psychosocial support in postmastectomy (carcinoma of breast) patients.* Stockholm: Laboratory for Clinical Stress Research, Karolinska Institute, 1980.

Kagan, N. I. Teaching interpersonal relations for the practice of medicine. *Lakartitningen,* 1974, *71,* 4758-4760.

Kahn, R. L. Aging and social support. In M. W. Riley (Ed.), *Aging from birth to death: Interdisciplinary perspectives.* Boulder, CO: Westview, 1979.

Kahn, R. L., Wolfe, D. M., Quinn, R. P., Snoek, J. D., & Rosenthal, R. A. *Organizational stress: Studies in role conflict and ambiguity.* New York: John Wiley, 1964.

Kanner, A. D., Coyne, J. C., Schaefer, C., & Lazarus, R. S. Comparison of two modes of stress management: Daily hassles and uplifts versus major life events. *Journal of Behavioral Medicine,* 1981, *4,* 1-39.

Kaplan, E. M., & Cowen, E. L. The interpersonal help-giving behaviors of industrial foremen. *Journal of Applied Psychology,* 1981, *66,* 633-638.

Karlsruher, A. E. The nonprofessional as a psychotherapeutic agent: A review of the empirical evidence pertaining to his effectiveness. *American Journal of Community Psychology,* 1974, *2,* 61-77.

Kastenbaum, R., & Aisenberg, R. *The psychology of death.* New York: Springer, 1972.

Katz, D., & Kahn, R. L. *The social psychology of organizations* (2nd ed.). New York: John Wiley, 1978.

Katz, E., & Lazarsfeld, P. F. *Personal influence.* New York: Macmillan, 1955.

Kauffman, C., Grunebaum, H., Cohler, B., & Gamer, E. Superkids: Competent children of psychotic mothers. *American Journal of Psychiatry,* 1979, *136,* 1398-1402.

King, N. J. The behavioral management of asthma and asthma-related problems of children: A critical review of the literature. *Journal of Behavioral Medicine,* 1980, *3,* 169-190.

Kiritz, S., & Moos, R. H. Physiological effects of social environments. *Psychosomatic Medicine,* 1974, *36,* 96-114.

Klein, K. J. *Work and well-being in employee-owned companies.* Doctoral thesis proposal, Department of Psychology, University of Texas — Austin, 1982.

Kleiner, R. J., & Parker, S. *Network participation and psychosocial impairment in an urban environment.* Washington, DC: U. S. Department of Health, Education and Welfare, National Institute of Mental Health, 1974.

Krant, M. J., Beiser, M., Adler, G., & Johnson, L. The role of a hospital-based psychosocial unit in terminal cancer illness and bereavement. *Journal of Chronic Diseases,* 1976, *29,* 115-127.

Lamb, H. R. The new asylums in the community. *Archives of General Psychiatry,* 1979, *36,* 129-134.

Lamb, H. R., & Oliphant, E. Schizophrenia through the eyes of families. *Hospital and Community Psychiatry,* 1978, *29,* 803-806.

LaRocco, J., House, J. J., & French, J. R. P. Social support, occupational stress, and health. *Journal of Health and Social Behavior,* 1980, *21,* 202-218.

LaRocco, J. M., & Jones, A. P. Coworker and leader support as moderators of stress-strain relationships in work situations. *Journal of Applied Psychology,* 1978, *63,* 629-634.

Larson, R. Thirty years of research on the subjective well being of older Americans. *Journal of Gerontology*, 1978, *33*, 109-125.

Lawton, M. P. Community supports for the aged. *Journal of Social Issues*, 1981, *37*, 102-115.

Lazarus, R. S. Cognitive and coping processes in emotion. In B. Weiner (Ed.), *Cognitive views of human motivation*. New York: Academic, 1974.

Lazarus, R. S. The stress and coping paradigm. In C. Eisdorfer, D. Cohen, A. Kleinman, & P. Maxim (Eds.), *Theoretical bases for psychopathology*. New York: Spectrum, 1981.

Lazarus, R. S., & Launier, R. Stress-related transactions between person and environment. In L. A. Pervin & M. Lewis (Eds.), *Perspectives in interactional psychology*. New York: Plenum, 1978.

Leavitt, D. *The effects of a support group on adjustment to the changes of aging in elderly women living in a community*. Unpublished master's thesis, University of Rochester, 1978.

Lemon, B. W., Bengtson, V. L., & Peterson, J. A. An exploration of the activity theory of aging: Activity types and life satisfaction among in-movers to a retirement community. *Journal of Gerontology*, 1972, *27*, 511-523.

Lesser, R., & Watt, M. Untrained community help in the rehabilitation of stroke sufferers with language disorder. *British Medical Journal*, 1978, *2*, 1045-1048.

Levy, S. M. The adjustment of the older woman: Effects of chronic ill health and attitudes toward retirement. *International Journal of Aging and Human Development*, 1980-81, *12*, 93-110.

Lewis, M., & Feiring, C. The child's social network: Social object, social functions, and their relationship. In M. Lewis & L. A. Rosenblum (Eds.), *The child and its family*. New York: Plenum, 1979.

Liang, J., Dvorkin, L., Kahana, E., & Mazian, F. Social integration and morale: A re-examination. *Journal of Gerontology*, 1980, *35*, 746-757.

Lieberman, M., & Gourash, N. Evaluating the effects of change groups on the elderly. *International Journal of Group Psychotherapy*, 1979, *29*, 283-304.

Likert, R. *New patterns of management*. New York: McGraw-Hill, 1961.

Likert, R. *The human organization: Its management and value*. New York: McGraw-Hill, 1967.

Lin, N., Simeone, R. S., Ensel, W. M., & Kuo, W. Social support, stressful life events, and illness: A model and an empirical test. *Journal of Health and Social Behavior*, 1979, *20*, 108-119.

Lindemann, E. Symptomatology and management of acute grief. *American Journal of Psychiatry*, 1944, *101*, 141-148.

Linn, J. G., & McGranahan, D. A. Personal disruptions, social integration, subjective well-being, and predisposition toward the use of counseling services. *American Journal of Community Psychology*, 1980, *8*, 87-100.

Litwak, E. Research patterns in the health of the elderly: The community mental health center. In E. F. Borgatta & N. G. McCluskey (Eds.), *Aging and society: Current research and policy perspectives*. Beverly Hills, CA: Sage, 1980.

Litwak, E., & Meyer, H. J. A balance theory of coordination between bureaucratic organizations and community primary groups. *Administrative Science Quarterly*, 1966, *11*, 21-58.

Lowenthal, M. F., Berkman, P. L., et al. *Aging and mental disorder in San Francisco*. San Francisco: Jossey-Bass, 1967.

Lowenthal, M. F., & Haven, C. Interaction and adaptation: Intimacy as a critical variable. *American Sociological Review,* 1968, *33,* 20-30.

Lowenthal, M. F., & Robinson, B. Social networks and isolation. In R. H. Binstock & E. Shanas (Eds.), *Handbook of aging and the social sciences.* New York: Van Nostrand Reinhold, 1976.

Lowenthal, M. F., Thurnher, M., Chiriboga, D., et al. *Four stages of life: A comparative study of women and men facing transitions.* San Francisco: Jossey-Bass, 1975.

Lusky, R. A., & Ingman, S. R. The pros, cons and pitfalls of self-help rehabilitation programs. *Social Science and Medicine,* 1979, *13A,* 113-121.

Lynch, V. J., Budson, R. D., & Jolley, R. E. Meeting the needs of former residents of a halfway house. *Hospital and Community Psychiatry,* 1977, *28,* 585.

Mace, M., & Rabins, P. *The 36-hour day.* Baltimore: Johns Hopkins University Press, 1981.

Maddox, G. L. Activity and morale: A longitudinal study of selected elderly subjects. *Social Forces,* 1963, *42,* 195-204.

Markel, W. M. The American Cancer Society's program for the rehabilitation of the breast cancer patient. *Cancer,* 1971, *28,* 1676-1678.

Markides, K. S., & Martin, H. W. A causal model of life satisfaction among the elderly. *Journal of Gerontology,* 1979, *34,* 86-93.

Maslach, C. Burned-out. *Human Behavior,* 1976, *5,* 16-22.

McGann, M. Group sessions for the families of post-coronary patients. *Supervisory Nursing,* 1976, *7,* 17-19.

McGuire, J., & Gottlieb, B. H. Social support groups among new parents: An experimental study in primary prevention. *Journal of Child Clinical Psychology,* 1979, *8,* 111-116.

McKinlay, J. Some approaches and problems in the study of the use of services: An overview. *Journal of Health and Social Behavior,* 1972, *13,* 115-151.

McKinlay, J. Social networks, lay consultation and help-seeking behavior. *Social Forces,* 1973, *51,* 275-292.

Medalie, J. H., & Goldbourt, U. Angina pectoris among 10,000 men. *American Journal of Medicine,* 1976, *60,* 910-921.

Mellor, M. J., Rzetelny, H., & Hudis, I. *Self-help groups for caregivers of the aged.* Unpublished manuscript, Community Service Society of New York, 1979.

Mendoza, L. *The Servidor system: Policy implications for the elderly Hispano.* San Diego, CA: University Center on Aging, San Diego State University, 1981.

Messinger, L., Walker, K., & Freeman, S. Preparation for remarriage following divorce: The use of group techniques. *American Journal of Orthopsychiatry,* 1978, *48,* 263-272.

Meyerowtiz, B. E. Psychosocial correlates of breast cancer and its treatments. *Psychological Bulletin,* 1980, *87,* 108-131.

Minde, K., Shosenberg, N., Marton, P., Thompson, J., Ripley, J., & Burns, S. Self-help groups in a premature nursery — A controlled evaluation. *Journal of Pediatrics,* 1980, *96,* 933-940.

Mitchell, G. W., & Glicksman, A. S. Cancer patients: Knowledge and attitudes. *Cancer,* 1977, *40,* 61-66.

Mitchell, R. E., Billings, A. G., & Moos, R. H. Social support and well being: Implications for prevention programs. *Journal of Primary Prevention,* 1982, *3,* 77-98.

Mone, L. C. Short-term psychotherapy with post-cardiac patients. *International Journal of Group Psychotherapy*, 1970, *20*, 99-108.

Moore, W. E. *Man, time and society*. New York: John Wiley, 1963.

Moos, R. H. *The social climate scales: An overview*. Palo Alto, CA: Consulting Psychologists Press, 1974.

Mosher, L. R., & Menn, A. Z. Lowered barriers in the community: The Soteria model. In L. I. Stein & M. A. Test (Eds.), *Alternatives to mental hospital treatment*. New York: Plenum, 1978.

Moss, G. E. *Illness, immunity and social interaction*. New York: John Wiley, 1973.

Mueller, D. P. Social networks: A promising direction for research on the relationship of the social environment to psychiatric disorder. *Social Science and Medicine*, 1980, *14A*, 147-161.

Murray, J. Family structure in pre-retirement years. In M. Irelan (Ed.), *Almost 65: Base line data from the retirement history study*. Washington, DC: Government Printing Office, 1976.

Newman, S. J. Housing adjustments of the disabled elderly. *Gerontologist*, 1976, *16*, 312-317.

Nickoley, S. *Promoting functional level of health and perception of control in elderly women in the community through supportive group intervention*. Unpublished master's thesis, University of Rochester, 1978.

Nickoley-Colquitt, S. Preventive group interventions for elderly clients: Are they effective? *Family and Community Health*, 1981, *2*, 67-85.

Nuckolls, K. B., Cassel, J., & Kaplan, B. H. Psychosocial assets, life crisis and the prognosis of pregnancy. *American Journal of Epidemiology*, 1972, *95*, 431-441.

Parsell, S., & Tagliareni, E. M. Cancer patients help each other. *American Journal of Nursing*, 1975, *74*, 650-651.

Pattison, E. M. Social system psychotherapy. *American Journal of Psychotherapy*, 1973, *18*, 396-409.

Pattison, E. M. Psychosocial system therapy. In R. G. Hirschowtiz (Ed.), *Handbook of community mental health practice*. New York: Spectrum, 1976.

Pattison, E. M. A theoretical-empirical base for social system therapy. In E. F. Foulks, R. M. Wintrob, J. Westermeyer, & A. R. Favazzo (Eds.), *Current perspectives in cultural psychiatry*. New York: Spectrum, 1977.

Pattison, E. M., de Francisco, D., Wood, P., Frazier, H., & Crowder, J. A. A psychosocial kinship model for family therapy. *American Journal of Psychiatry*, 1975, *132*, 1246-1251.

Pattison, E. M., Llamas, R., & Hurd, G. Social network mediation of anxiety. *Psychiatric Annals*, 1979, *9*, 56-67.

Pearlin, L. I., Lieberman, M. A., Menaghan, E. G., & Mullan, J. T. The stress process. *Journal of Health and Social Behavior*, 1981, *22*, 337-356.

Peters-Golden, H. Breast cancer: Varied perceptions of social support in the illness experience. *Social Science and Medicine*, 1982, *16*, 483-491.

Petty, B. J., Moeller, T. P., & Campbell, R. Z. Support groups for elderly persons in the community. *Gerontologist*, 1976, *15*, 522-528.

Pilisuk, M., & Froland, C. Kinship, social networks, social support and health. *Social Science and Medicine*, 1978, *12B*, 273-280.

Pilisuk, M., & Minkler, M. Supportive networks: Life ties for the elderly. *Journal of Social Issues*, 1980, *36*, 95-116.

Pines, A. M., & Aronson, E. *Burnout: From tedium to personal growth.* New York: Macmillan, 1981.

Pines, A., & Maslach, C. Characteristics of staff burnout in mental health settings. *Hospital and Community Psychiatry,* 1978, *4,* 233-237.

Polak, P. Social systems intervention. *Archives of General Psychiatry,* 1971, *25,* 110-117.

Polak, P. Techniques of social system intervention. In J. H. Masserman (Ed.), *Current psychiatric therapies.* New York: Grune & Stratton, 1972.

Polak, P., Egan, D., Vandenbergh, R., & Williams, W. V. Prevention in mental health: A controlled study. *American Journal of Psychiatry,* 1975, *132,* 146-149.

Powell, D. R. Family-environment relations and early child rearing: The role of social networks and neighborhoods. *Journal of Research and Development in Education,* 1979, *13,* 1-11.

President's Commission on Mental Health. *Task panel reports* (Vols. II-IV). Washington, DC: Government Printing Office, 1978.

Presser, H. B. Sally's corner: Coping with unmarried motherhood. *Journal of Social Issues,* 1980, *36,* 107-129.

Rabkin, J. G. & Struening, E. L. Life events, stress, and illness. *Science,* 1976, *194,* 1013-1020.

Rahe, R. H., Tuffli, C. F., Suchor, R. J., & Arthur, R. J. Group therapy in the outpatient management of post-myocardial infarction patients. *Psychiatry and Medicine,* 1973, *4,* 77-88.

Rahe, R. H., Ward, H. W., & Hayes, V. Brief group therapy in myocardial infarction rehabilitation: Three-to-four-year-follow-up of a controlled trial. *Psychosomatic Medicine,* 1979, *41,* 229-242.

Rappaport, J. *Community psychology.* New York: Holt, Rinehart & Winston, 1977.

Ratcliffe, W. D., Zelhart, P. F., & Azim, H. F. *Social networks and psychopathology.* Unpublished manuscript, Department of Psychology, University of Alberta, 1975.

Rathbone-McCuan, E. Geriatric daycare: A family perspective. *Gerontologist,* 1976, *16,* 517-521.

Ray, C. Adjustment to mastectomy: The psychological impact of disfigurement. In P. C. Brand & P. A. van Keep (Eds.), *Breast cancer: Psychosocial aspects of early detection and treatment.* Baltimore: University Park Press, 1978.

Reinke, B. J., Holmes, D. S., & Denney, N. W. Influence of a "friendly visitor" program on the cognitive functioning and morale of elderly persons. *American Journal of Community Psychology,* 1981, *9,* 491-504.

Riessman, F., Cohen, J., & Pearl, A. (Eds.), *Mental health of the poor.* New York: Macmillan, 1964.

Riley, M. W., & Foner, A. *Aging and society* (Vol. 1): *An inventory of research findings.* New York: Russell Sage, 1968.

Roberts, B., & Thorsheim, H. The approach of social ecology: A partnership of support and empowerment. *Journal of Primary Prevention,* 1982, *3,* 140-143.

Robins, E. G. *Therapeutic daycare: Progress report on experiments to test the feasibility of third party reimbursement.* Paper presented at the meeting of the Gerontological Society, Portland, OR, 1974.

Rog, D. J., & Rausch, H. L. The psychiatric halfway house: How is it measuring up? *Community Mental Health Journal,* 1975, *11,* 155-162.

Rosenberg, G. S. *The worker grows old.* San Francisco: Jossey-Bass 1970.

Rosencranz, H. A., Pihlblad, C. T., & McNevin, T. E. *Social participation of older people in a small town.* Unpublished manuscript, Department of Sociology, University of Missouri — Columbia, 1968.

Rosenman, R. H. The interview method of assessment of the coronary-prone behavior pattern. In T. M. Dembroski, S. M. Weiss, J. L. Shields, S. G. Haynes, & N. Feinleib (Eds.), *Coronary-prone behavior.* New York: Springer-Verlag, 1978.

Rosenmayr, L. The family — Source of hope for the elderly of the future. In E. Shanas & M. B. Sussman (Eds.), *Older people, family and bureaucracy.* Durham, NC: Duke University Press, 1976.

Roskin, M. Coping with life changes — A preventive social work approach. *American Journal of Community Psychology,* 1982, *10,* 331-340.

Rosow, I. *Social integration of the aged.* New York: Macmillan, 1967.

Rowe, A. R. Scientists in retirement. *Journal of Gerontology,* 1973, *28,* 345-350.

Rueveni, U. Network intervention with a family in crisis. *Family Process,* 1975, *14,* 193-203.

Rueveni, U. *Networking families in crisis.* New York: Human Sciences, 1977.

Ruiz, P., & Langrod, J. The role of folk healers in community mental health services. *Community Mental Health Journal,* 1976, *12,* 392-398.

Ryan, W. *Distress in the city: Essays on the design and administration of urban mental health services.* Cleveland, OH: Case Western Reserve University Press, 1969.

Rzetelny, H., Kasch, E., Topperman, E., & Hudis, I. *Supporting the caregiving efforts of family, friends and neighbors of the elderly: A community-based multimodal approach.* Paper presented at the meeting of the American Orthopsychiatric Association, Toronto, 1980.

Rzetelny, H., & Mellor, M. J. *Support groups for caregivers of the aged: Training manual for facilitators.* Available from Natural Supports Program, Community Service Society of New York, 1982.

Sainsbury, P., & Grad de Alarcon, J. The psychiatrist and the geriatric patient: The effects of community care on the family of the geriatric patient. *Journal of Geriatric Psychiatry,* 1970, *1,* 23-41.

Sandler, I. N. Social support resources, stress and the maladjustment of poor children. *American Journal of Community Psychology,* 1980, *8,* 41-52.

Sandler, I. N., & Barrera, M., Jr. Toward a multi-method approach to assessing the effects of social support. *American Journal of Community Psychology,* in press.

Sandler, I., & Lakey, B. Locus of control as a stress moderator: The role of control perceptions and social support. *American Journal of Community Psychology,* 1982, *10,* 65-81.

Sanford, J. F. Tolerance of debility in elderly dependents by supporters at home. *British Medical Journal,* 1975, *3,* 471-473.

Sarason, S. B. *The psychological sense of community: Prospects for a community psychology.* San Francisco: Jossey-Bass, 1974.

Schachter, S. *The psychology of affiliation.* Palo Alto, CA: Stanford University Press, 1959.

Schaefer, C., Coyne, J. C., & Lazarus, R. S. The health-related functions of social support. *Journal of Behavioral Medicine,* 1981, *4,* 381-406.

Schulz, R. Effects of control and predictability on the physical and psychological well-being of the institutionalized aged. *Journal of Personality and Social Psychology,* 1976, *33,* 563-573.

Seashore, S. E. *Group cohesiveness in the industrial work group.* Ann Arbor: Survey Research Center, Institute of Social Research, University of Michigan, 1954.

Shanas, E. *The health of older people: A social survey.* Cambridge, MA: Harvard University Press, 1962.

Shanas, E. The family as a social support system in old age. *Gerontologist,* 1979, *19,* 169-174.

Shanas, E., Townsend, P., Wedderburn, D., Friis, H., Milhaj, P., & Stehouwer, J. *Old people in three industrial societies.* London: Routledge & Kegan Paul, 1968.

Shantz, C. The development of social cognition. In E. M. Hetherington (Ed.), *Review of child development research* (Vol. 5). Chicago: University of Chicago Press, 1975.

Silberfeld, M. Psychological symptoms and social supports. *Social Psychiatry,* 1978, *13,* 11-17.

Silverman, P. R. *If you will lift the load I will lift it too: A guide to developing Widow-to-Widow programs.* New York: Jewish Funeral Directors of America, 1976.

Smith, S. A. *Natural systems and the elderly: An unrecognized resource.* Unpublished manuscript, School of Social Work, Portland State University, OR, 1975.

Smyer, M. A. The differential usage of services by impaired elderly. *Journal of Gerontology,* 1980, *35,* 249-255.

Synder, K. S., & Liberman, R. P. Family assessment and intervention with schizophrenics at risk for relapse. In M. J. Goldstein (Ed.), *New developments in interventions with families of schizophrenics.* San Francisco: Jossey-Bass, 1981.

Sokolovsky, J., Cohen, C., Berger, D., & Geiger, J. Personal networks of ex-mental patients in a Manhatten SRO hotel. *Human Organization,* 1978, *37,* 5-15.

Sosa, R., Kennell, J., Klaus, M., Robertson, S., & Urrutia, J. The effect of a supportive companion on perinatal problems, length of labor, and mother-infant interaction. *New England Journal of Medicine,* 1980, *303,* 597-600.

Speck, R. V., & Attneave, C. *Family networks.* New York: Pantheon, 1973.

Speck, R. V. & Rueveni, U. Network therapy: A developing concept. *Family Process,* 1969, *8,* 182-191.

Spiegel, D., Bloom, J. R., & Yalom, I. Group support for patients with metastatic cancer: A randomized prospective outcome study. *Archives of General Psychiatry,* 1981, *38,* 527-533.

Spivack, G. Interpersonal problem-solving thought: Mental health promotion for the elderly. In F. D. Perlmutter (Ed.), *Mental health promotion and primary prevention.* San Francisco: Jossey-Bass, 1982.

Stack, C. *All our kin: Strategies for survival in a black community.* New York: Harper & Row, 1974.

Stehouwer, J. The household and family relations of old people. In. E. Shanas, P. Townsend, D. Wedderburn, H. Friis, P. Milhoj, & J. Stehouwer (Eds.), *Old people in three industrial societies.* New York: Atherton, 1968.

Stein, L. I., & Test, M. A. An alternative to mental hospital treatment. In L. I. Stein & M. A. Test (Eds.), *Alternatives to mental hospital treatment.* New York: Plenum, 1978.

Stern, M. J. The treatment of post-myocardial infarction depression. *Practical Cardiology,* 1978, *23,* 35-46.

Stern, M. J., Pascale, L., & McLoone, J. B. Psychosocial adaptation following an acute myocardial infarction. *Journal of Chronic Diseases,* 1976, *29,* 513-526.

Sussman, M. B. The family life of old people. In R. H. Binstock & E. Shanas (Eds.), *Handbook of aging and the social sciences.* New York: Van Nostrand Reinhold, 1976.

Syme, S. L. Behavioral factors associated with the etiology of physical disease: A social epidemiological approach. *American Journal of Public Health*, 1974, *64*, 1043-1045.

Tannenbaum, A. S. Employee-owned companies. In B. M. Cummings & J. Staw (Eds.), *Research in organizational behavior* (Vol. 5). Greenwich, CT: JAI, 1982.

Thomas, S. G. Breast cancer: The psychosocial issues. *Cancer Nursing*, 1978, *36*, 53-60.

Thralow, J., & Watson, C. Remotivation for geriatric patients utilizing elementary school students. *American Journal of Occupational Therapy*, 1974, *28*, 469-473.

Tobin, S. S., & Kulys, R. The family in the institutionalization of the elderly. *Journal of Social Issues*, 1981, *37*, 145-157.

Todd, D. M. *Social networks, psychosocial adaptation, and preventive/developmental interventions: The support development workshop.* Paper presented at the meeting of the American Psychological Association, Montreal, September 1980.

Tolsdorf, C. C. Social networks, support, and coping: An exploratory study. *Family Process*, 1976, *15*, 407-418.

Tracy, G. S., & Gussow, Z. Self-help health groups: A grass-roots response to a need for services. *Journal of Applied Behavioral Science*, 1976, *12*, 381-396.

Treas, J. Family support systems for the aged: Some social and demographic considerations. *Gerontologist*, 1977, *17*, 486-490.

Turner, R. J. Social support as a contingency in psychological well-being. *Journal of Health and Social Behavior*, 1981, *22*, 357-367.

U. S. Department of Health, Education and Welfare, Public Health Service. *Home care for persons 55 and over, United States: July 1966-June 1968.* (Vital and Health Statistics, Ser. 10, No. 73) Washington, DC: Government Printing Office, 1972.

Vachon, M. I., & Lyall, W. A. Applying psychiatric techniques to patients with cancer. *Hospital and Community Psychiatry*, 1976, *27*, 582-584.

Vachon, M., Lyall, W., Rogers, J., Freedman-Letofsky, K., & Freeman, S. A controlled study of a self-help intervention for widows. *American Journal of Psychiatry*, 1980, *137*, 1380-1384.

Valle, R., & Vega, W. (Eds.). *Hispanic natural support systems.* Sacramento: State of California Department of Mental Health, 1980.

Vaughn, C. E., & Leff, L. P. The influence of family and social factors on the course of psychiatric illness: A comparison of schizophrenic and depressed neurotic patients. *British Journal of Psychiatry*, 1976, *129*, 125-137.

Vaughn, C. E., & Leff, J. P. The measurement of expressed emotion in the families of psychiatric patients. *British Journal of Social and Clinical Psychology*, 1976, *15*, 157-165. (b)

Vaughn, C. E., & Leff, J. P. Patterns of emotional response in relatives of schizophrenic patients. *Schizophrenia Bulletin*, 1981, *7*, 43-44.

Wagenfeld, M. O., & Wagenfeld, J. K. Values, culture, and delivery of mental health services. In M. O. Wagenfeld (Ed.), *New directions for mental health services: Perspectives on rural mental health, no. 9.* San Francisco: Jossey-Bass, 1981.

Wallach, H., Kelley, F., & Abrahams, J. Psychosocial rehabilitation for chronic geriatric patients: An intergenerational approach. *Gerontologist*, 1979, *19*, 464-470.

Warheit, G. J. Life events, coping, stress and depressive symptomatology. *American Journal of Psychiatry*, 1979, *136*, 502-507.

Weinman, B., & Kleiner, R. J. The impact of community living and community member intervention on the adjustment of the chronic psychotic patient. In L. I.

Stein & M. A. Test (Eds.), *Alternatives to mental hospital treatment*. New York: Plenum, 1978.

Weisenfeld, A. R., & Weis, H. M. A mental health consultation program for beauticians. *Profesional Psychology,* 1979, *10,* 786-792.

Weiss, R. S. The provisions of social relationships. In Z. Rubin (Ed.), *Doing unto others*. Englewood Cliffs, NJ: Prentice-Hall, 1974.

Wellman, B. Applying network analysis to the study of support. In B. H. Gottlieb (Ed.), *Social networks and social support*. Beverly Hills, CA: Sage, 1981.

Wells, J. A. Objective job conditions, social support, and perceived stress among blue collar workers. *Journal of Occupational Behavior,* 1982, *3,* 79-94.

Wentowski, G. J. Reciprocity and the coping strategies of older people: Cultural dimensions of network building. *Gerontologist,* 1981, *21,* 600-609.

Wilcox, B. L. Social support in adjusting to marital disruption: A network analysis. In B. H. Gottlieb (Ed.), *Social networks and social support*. Beverly Hills, CA: Sage, 1981. (a)

Wilcox, B. L. Social support, life stress and psychological adjustment: A test of the buffering hypothesis. *American Journal of Community Psychology,* 1981, *9,* 371-386. (b)

Williams, A. W., Ware, J. W., Jr., & Donald, C. A. A model of mental health, life events, and social supports applicable to general populations. *Journal of Health and Social Behavior,* 1981, *22,* 324-336.

Winick, L., & Robbins, G. F. Physical and psychologic readjustment after mastectomy: An evaluation of Memorial Hospital's PMRG program. *Cancer,* 1977, *2,* 478-486.

Wood, V., & Robertson, J. F. Friendship and kinship interaction: Differential effect on the morale of the elderly. *Journal of Marriage and the Family,* 1978, *40,* 367-375.

Wortman, C. B., & Dunkel-Schetter, C. Interpersonal relationships and cancer: A theoretical analysis. *Journal of Social Issues,* 1979, *35,* 120-155.

Youmans, E. G. *Leisure-time activity of older persons in selected rural and urban areas of Kentucky* (Progress report 115). Lexington: Kentucky Argricultural Experiment Station, 1962.

Zavit, S. H., Reever, K. E., & Bach-Peterson, J. Relatives of the impaired elderly: Correlates of feelings of burden. *Gerontologist,* 1980, *20,* 649-655.

Zimmer, A., & Sainer, J. *Strengthening the family as an informal support for the aged: Implications for social policy and planning*. Paper presented at the meeting of the Gerontological Society, Dallas, 1978.

# About The Author

BENJAMIN H. GOTTLIEB is Associate Professor of Psychology at the University of Guelph, Ontario, Canada. He is a graduate of the University of Michigan's Joint Doctoral Program in Social Work and Psychology (Community). He edited the fourth volume in this series, *Social Networks and Social Support,* which was published in 1981.